7

Torah Lights
Bereshit: Confronting Life, Love & Family

MAGGID

Rabbi Shlomo Riskin

TORAH LIGHTS

BERESHIT: CONFRONTING LIFE, LOVE & FAMILY

Maggid Books

Bereshit: Confronting Life, Love & Family

Second Edition 2009

Maggid Books
An Imprint of Koren Publishers Jerusalem Ltd.

POB 8531, New Milford, CT 06676-8531, USA
& POB 2455, London W1A 5WY, England
& POB 4044, Jerusalem 91040, Israel
www.korenpub.com

ISBN 978 1 59264 272 4, *hardcover*

A CIP catalogue record for this title is
available from the British Library.

Typeset by KPS

Printed and bound in the United States

Contents

vii

Foreword

During the most formative period of my life, between the ages of ten and sixteen, I spent every Friday evening dinner with my maternal grandmother, Haya Bayla bat Rav Shlomo HaKohen and Mindel. She was a remarkable woman, steeped in Jewish knowledge and commitment, who came to Brooklyn, New York, from the shtetl of Lubien, Poland, in 1922 and died in 1960, without ever having learned to speak a proper English sentence. Her world remained the world of Yiddish and Hebrew, the world of the Siddur, the Bible and the *Morgen Journal*, and her closest friends were all from the same shtetl in which she grew up. Her synagogue was called Etz Haim Anshei Lubien, a congregation founded by the *landsmen* (townspeople) of the same European shtetl. The congregants sat in the very rows in which they had sat in the synagogue in Lubien, and their burial plots (in the Lubien section of the Washington Cemetery in Bensonhurst, Brooklyn) were parceled out accordingly, one's ultimate resting place alongside those with whom one spent divine time on the sabbaths and festivals in this world.

Despite her language limitations, Grandma was fiercely patriotic to America. She had miraculously managed to become a *tzititzen* and – in the midst of the open and often political discussions around her kitchen table – refused to have anyone speak unkindly about one of her contemporary heroes, to her mind a genuine representative of the 'righteous gentiles' and a savior of the Jewish people, President Franklin Delano Rosenfeld. She enjoyed the Yiddish theater, and was an especial devotee of cantorial music, above all, the pieces of Yossele Rosenblatt. She had read Goethe and Heine in her youth, at the instigation of her husband, my Grandfather Haim, who had been well educated. Nevertheless, her greatest passion, after her children and grandchildren, was the study of Torah. Her father, Rabbi Shlomo HaKohen Kowalsky (after whom I was named) had been the *dayan* (Judge) of Lubien, and since his first three children were daughters, and she was the eldest, he had taught her not only Ḥumash and Rashi, but also Mishna and even Gemara. Family tradition records that he lived to be 115 years old and outlived three consecutive wives, but he continued to teach his brilliant Baltcha (diminutive for Bayla) until she was married.

Not unlike most of her contemporaries, each of her seven children retained strong ethnic ties and nostalgic bonds to Jewish tradition, although their desire for American acculturation proved to be far stronger than the divine commands of shabbat and kashrut. As I was the eldest child of her youngest daughter, and having been sent to yeshiva only because it had better academic standing than the local public school in a racially mixed and rapidly changing neighborhood, I was her last hope. She supplied my mother with kosher meat, supervised my Jewish education through weekly visits with the day school principal, and invited me to spend Friday evenings with her (Grandpa Haim had suffered a stroke and was in a convalescent home).

Those unforgettable evenings began with her *licht bentschen* (lighting of candles). She would stand before the seven-tiered candelabrum, which she had lovingly held in her hands all through the steerage class boat journey from Lubien, for at least twenty minutes, speaking to God as to an old and trusted friend, enumerating each child and grandchild with an appropriate request or thanksgiving. We would then pray together word for word. How I would smile when in the prayer *Lekha Dodi*, grandma, with her Polish accent, would say *Iri iri* (Arise, arise), and would then try to correct herself and make her prayer more in consonance with her yeshiva boy grandson's Lithuanian pronunciation of *Uri uri*. The food was delectable. Between courses we sang *zmirot* (Shabbat songs), just as great grandpa Shlomo sang in Lubien, and we studied together the portion of the week with Yiddish *teitsch*.

Grandma had a marvelous way of making the biblical person-alities live. She skipped nothing, and I learned the facts of life from the various biblical passages and prohibitions I studied with her. Most importantly, her God was truly a father in heaven, a kind of exalted Great-Grandpa Shlomo, who loved and protected from above. She never spoke of divine punishment for sin: only of divine disappointment. (And to this day I am not so much afraid that God will punish me as I am ashamed of possible divine disappointment with my actions or lack thereof.)

She especially loved to describe the courtships of our patriarchs and matriarchs and specifically the love affair between Jacob and Rachel. That's how it was with your grandfather and me, she said. And I heard many times how Great-Grandpa Shlomo refused to accept money for Torah learning and rulings. He owned a hay and oats store, and had a group of young men work with him half a day and then get their renumeration by studying with him during the other half. They would awaken at midnight for *tikkun ḥatzot*, study until just before dawn, go the mikveh, pray, work for the bulk of the morning and much of the afternoon, and then study some more. The young men would obviously take their *tefillin* with them in the middle of the night, lay them down carefully on a mattress on the grass, and put them on after returning from the mikveh at sunrise.

My grandmother did not like this disrespect to the *tefillin*. She would get up at the same time as the student workers, and when they had begun studying and she thought they did not notice, she would hang the *tefillin* bags up on the clothesline. She would then return them to the mat-tress to be ready for the young men upon their return from the mikveh.

My grandfather was a grandson of the brother of the son-in-law of the *Sefat Emet* and a Gerer Hassid in his own right. He came from the larger nearby city of Wrozlawek, where he had been betrothed to a young woman he had only seen once. He noticed my grandmother's special care for the *tefillin*; he apparently noticed something else besides, and fell deeply in love. He prevailed upon his father to sever the other relationship, and Haim married Baltcha. The young couple lived in Rabbi Shlomo Kowalsky's home in Lubien.

And so my Grandma and I would spend each Friday night with delicious food, delightful stories, interesting Torah and stimulating songs. I felt I was being transported to an almost magical shtetl, Lubien. I felt I really knew the streets, the smells, the people, even better than the Bedford Stuyvesant area where I lived.

Grandma died in 1960 at age ninety.

*   *   *

In 1993 I was invited to participate in the March of the Living. To visit Poland, to return to Poland and the opportunity to visit my hometown of Lubien. I accepted with alacrity.

But where was Lubien? The atlas listed three possibilities: Lubien near Wrozlaw, very close to the German Border; Lubien near Teczycay on the road to Lodz; and Lubien Kujawski some 29 km from Wrozlawek. Grandpa Haim knew German well, but I was certain that Grandma had spoken of Wrozlawek and not Wrozlaw. Moreover, a very detailed road map delineated a lake at the entrance to Lubien Kujawski, and Grandma had spoken of the lake where she had gone swimming in the summer and ice skating in the winter, until her brother drowned in it the week of her *sheva brakhot*. Lubien Kujawski must be my Lubien.

At 5:00 A.M. Monday morning the 28th day of Nisan 5753 (1993) I set out from the Forum Hotel in Warsaw, with a specially recommended driver named Greg (short for Gregor, a Polish physicist who spoke a perfect English), for my home shtetl of Lubien. I was excitedly expectant although my wise wife had warned me that I would not find Great-Grandpa Shlomo waiting for me with an open Gemara in his hand, and a Gerer *niggun* (tune) on his lips.

As we left the city of Warsaw and began to approach the smaller towns, there seemed something vaguely familiar about the green expanses, the wooded forests, the small hut homes, the horses and buggies. Here I thought I saw Tevye the dairyman teaching his son a portion of Ḥumash on the way to a delivery, and there I was sure I noticed a hassid returning home after having spent the Pesaḥ holidays with his

Rebbe. Unfortunately I was all too aware of the fact that Poland had become virtually *Judenrein*. My heart gave a lurch when we came to the sign Lubien Kujawski, and sure enough, there were the farmlands abutting on the lake, the Christian cemetery, the large church, everything Grandma had described, seemingly with hardly a change.

My Polish driver was more than a little surprised at how the town I had lovingly described from my imagination appeared in reality before our eyes. 'Are you sure you were never here before?' he asked. 'Yes, I was here. I was actually born here,' I replied, which I understand must have confused him thoroughly. There was however one discrepancy. Grandma had described the Jewish cemetery as being opposite the Christian cemetery, on the other side of the lake at the entrance to Lubien. I had hoped to find Great-Grandpa Shlomo's grave, and move it to Israel, even to Efrat. But there was no Jewish cemetery on the other side of the lake; there was merely a parking lot.

We entered the small town, consisting of some three hundred families. There were the open-air market stalls, unpaved streets, horses and bicycles, old wooden houses, an impressive church. Greg left me in the car to guard my luggage and went in search of someone who might remember the Kowalsky family. One Polish resident led him to another, until the daughter of a ninety-one-year-old woman, who had always lived among the Jews, felt certain that if we returned in an hour, her mother would be awake and be able to help. In the interim, we managed to explore Lubien and even before 9:00 A.M., an elderly woman with a cheery face and smiling eyes was anxiously awaiting us at her doorstep. 'Pan Kowalsky, Pan Kowalsky,' she greeted me, half bowing as she spoke, happily prattling in Polish, and ushering me into her modest home. The table was prepared for us with many types of cakes and cookies, and Greg translated her Polish words which came forth in a friendly torrent:

'Of course I remember your family. Your great-grandfather was the Rabbiner of the Rabbiner [he was the *dayan*, or judge, of the town]. Of course he was a very old man when I was a young girl, everyone said that the angel of death forgot about him. My father was the mayor of Lubien, and so the rabbi, Rabbi Petrofsky, and for the more important issues, your great-grandfather, would always visit our home. I see you're not eating my cakes. I'll give you what my mother used to give your great-grandfather, tea in a glass, with a cube of sugar on the side. That, you too can drink.

'This was a beautiful Jewish community when your family lived here. There were one hundred and fifty Jewish families and one hundred and fifty Polish families. Burack was the one who circumcised the eight-day-old boys. His daughter was Rabbi Petrofsky's wife. Zhilitowsky was the 'Knocker', or the *veker* (waker-upper). All the Jewish men went to the prayer service early in the morning. Brystgowsky was the baker; all the Jews brought their meat to his ovens on Friday afternoon, to be collected and eaten on Saturday. I think they called it *cholent*. No Jew lit a fire on the sabbath. Your great-grandfather was a very wise man, a great judge; but he insisted on working for his salary, and until he died he sold hay and oats to the neighboring farmers. His oldest daughter married one of his students, a learned gentleman from Wlozlawek. He went off to America and until he called for her and her children, she ran an inn and restaurant in the extension of her father's house. It was there, right across the street, on the side of the church.

'The synagogue was a beautiful building. In 1939, when the Nazis came in, every Jew, men, women and children, went in to pray. The Nazis set the building on fire and refused to allow our fire department to put the fire out. Not only the synagogue but the entire block went up in smoke, they were all wooden buildings. Your great-grandfather's house survived the fire, it was on the other side I told you, on the side of the church. It burnt down after the war, in an electrical fire. But it was rebuilt, right across the street.

'The Jews, they were all taken away and killed. The last Kowalskys were tailors. Maybe a few survived – most were killed. The Jewish cemetery? It used to be on the other side of the lake, opposite the Christian cemetery. The Nazis razed it to the ground. They took the gravestones, and used them to pave the paths of their concentration camps.'

I thanked the kind woman, Helene Michalak. I was stunned and entranced by her memory and the confirmation she provided of the stories which had nourished my childhood and forged my life's passion. She even let me use her camera, sold me some film, and, still in a trance-like state, I took pictures of Lubien. At every corner I felt ghosts from my past (and gurus of my future). The only time I broke down in tears was when I stood on the even ground at the entrance to the lake opposite the Christian cemetery. I chanted *El Male Raḥamim* for my great-grandfather, and left quickly.

I returned home to Israel sad and bitter at what was lost, but grateful for the memory. I had traveled to Poland to find Lubien, to recapture my childhood, to discover my roots. But where is Lubien? I understand now that Lubien is not near Wrozlaw, it is not even near Wrozlawek. In fact, Lubien is not in Poland anymore. Lubien is with me, and with my Israeli grandchildren, here in Efrat…Israel, and hopefully Lubien is in these words, attempting to provide some added insight into our eternal Torah.

Tribute

I want to thank my revered teachers, Rabbi Joseph B. Halevi Soloveitchik, z'l, Prof. Nehama Leibowitz, z'l, and Rabbi Moshe Besdin, z'l, for their many insights into the words and commentaries of the Torah. Much of what is written here is based upon lectures and discussions I was privileged to have had with them – as well as with many great Torah scholars from whom I have learned throughout the years. Although I have attempted to give proper attribution so as to help bring redemption to the world, I am certain that there are insights I may have derived from others which I have come to think of as my own; suffice it to say that whatever may be worthy in this volume was derived from my teachers, but I assume complete responsibility for whatever may not be deemed worthy.

I am most appreciative to Sheldon Gewirtz, who originally urged me to begin writing a weekly commentary on the Torah portion, and to Jacob Lampert, who helped in the writing of the columns during the early years of this activity. The congregations I have been privileged to serve as rabbi and preacher, Lincoln Square Synagogue in Manhattan and the many synagogues of the city of Efrat, Israel, as well as my students at the Ohr Torah Stone Institutions served as the original sounding boards for these commentaries, which were then written and distributed in weekly columns for *The Jerusalem Post* and additionally in some thirty Anglo-Jewish newspapers worldwide. Hopefully each additional rendering helped improve my formulation and understanding.

My beloved family and extended family – and especially my cherished wife and life-partner, Vicky – have not only heard these ideas around the Sabbath table, but have also questioned them, argued with them and certainly refined them.

Most of all, I must give tribute to the Almighty, who has enabled me to labor in the vineyard of Torah during these last forty years as rabbi and educator, a calling which has made the five books of the Torah my constant guide and companion.

כִּי אִם בְּתוֹרַת ה׳ חֶפְצוֹ וּבְתוֹרָתוֹ יֶהְגֶּה יוֹמָם וָלַיְלָה

Introduction

The world of biblical commentary reveals many secrets. First and foremost, the Bible – which contains the wisdom of the divine – may be likened to a magnificent diamond, glistening with many brilliant colors all at the same time. And although the different hues often appear to be contradictory, when you view the totality of the light emanating from the diamond, you begin to appreciate how complementary they really are. Thus the sages of the Talmud understood that there are many possible truths contained in each biblical statement, each adding its unique melody to the magnificent symphony of the whole, synthesizing not in conflicting dissonance but in holy dialectic:

> The school of R. Ishmael taught: 'As a hammer shatters a rock' (Jer. 23:29) – just as a hammer subdivides into many different sparks, so does the biblical verse extend into many different interpretations.
>
> *Sanhedrin* 34a

Hence the code word for biblical commentary, which encompasses different approaches to the same verse, is *PaRDeS* (literally – 'orchard'), comprising *P'shat* (the plain meaning of the text), *Remez* (symbolic meaning of the text), *D'rash* (rabbinic explication of the text), and *Sod* (the secret, mystical meaning of the text). The sum total of these add up to the 'seventy faces' of the Torah, symbolizing the seventy nations of the world, the seventy distinctive approaches to life, reflecting the myriad possibilities and entrance-ways to the meaning of the Bible and to an understanding (however imperfect and incomplete) of the divine.

And so the Bible has the glorious and uncanny ability to speak to us with many voices – and all at the same time! And perhaps most remarkable of all: not only does one hear through the words of the Bible the commanding voice of God still impressing upon us His will of four thousand years ago at Sinai; not only do we experience the insights of the rabbinic sages of the Talmud, who informed the text with their unique insights and traditions; but I find that each week the Torah appears to be speaking directly to me, to my individual and communal concerns and commitments, in a manner that is always relevant and inspiring. The Talmud calls the Bible *mikra*, and this is usually interpreted as coming from the verb *kra* – to read, since the Written Law is publicly read on Mondays, Thursdays, Sabbaths and festivals. But Yisrael Eldad* masterfully suggests that indeed the term comes from the same root *kra*, but is to be interpreted as meaning 'to call.' The Bible calls out to us, sometimes comforting and sometimes chiding, sometimes as appearing from the distant past and sometimes as if from the immediate present, but always with the imperative that we change our ways and reach for a higher level of morality and sanctity. This indeed is the meaning of the public blessings the individual called to the Torah is commanded to recite: 'Blessed art Thou, O Lord our God, King of the universe, who has chosen us from all other nations and has given us the Torah [past tense]. Blessed art Thou, the One who gives the Torah [in the present tense].'

And it is precisely because the Torah is at one and the same time the oldest recorded document still directing human lives as well as most relevant and contemporary, that teaching and studying the Bible is such an important stepping-stone into the glories of our tradition. A multi-

---

* Yisrael Eldad, *Hegyonot BaMikra* (*Reflections of the Bible*), Tel Aviv, 2001, in the Introduction.

plicity of possibilities constantly expands and contemporizes the significance of the various commandments, the relevance of the various stories,
enabling each individual of every generation to discover a subjectively
significant spiritual/ethical motif in the specific accounts and rituals of
our tradition. Each will discover his *p'shuto shel mikra* – his 'plain meaning' of the text which, after all, takes on 'renewed significance each day.'*

As I study the pages of the Torah and its commentators, I often
hum the words of the Psalmist: 'Were the Torah not my delight, I would
have perished in my affliction.' The Five Books of Moses in particular
have been a constant source of comfort and inspiration. When I was
planning *aliya*, the importance of living in Israel screamed out at me
from virtually every page; during the Gulf War and the various Palestinian wars, the verses about God's hardening the heart of Pharaoh took on
renewed meaning; as I experienced the very human tensions between
parents and children, the book of Genesis provided comfort as well as
insights and direction. My struggle with many Torah texts reflects my
struggle with life itself. The ability of the Torah to speak to every generation and every individual at the same time is the greatest testimony to its
divinity. I consider it a great privilege to share with others the manifold
truths I glean from Torah every day. And if my words be found wanting,
it is only because of the smallness of my perceptions when compared
to the infinite wisdom of the giver of Torah....

---

* See Rosen's *Introduction to the Commentary of the Rashbam*, and his citation of
  Rashi's letter to his grandson.

Bereshit

What is Torah?

> *In the beginning God created the heavens and the earth.*
>
> GENESIS 1:1

Why does the Torah, the word of God given to Moses as His legacy to the Jewish people, begin with an account of creation, going off into gardens of Eden and towers of Babel? It could, and perhaps should, have begun at the point when the Jews are given their first commandment as a nation after departing from Egypt: 'This month shall be unto you the beginning of months' [Ex. 12:2], referring to the month of Nissan, when Pesaḥ, the uniquely Jewish festival commemorating our emergence as a nation, is celebrated. After all, is not the Bible primarily a book of commandments? So asks Rashi at the beginning of his commentary on *Bereshit*.

I would like to suggest three classical responses to this question, each of which makes a stunning contribution to our opening query, What is Torah? Rashi's answer to this question is the Zionist credo. We begin with an account of creation because, if the nations of the world point

7

their fingers at us, claiming we are thieves who have stolen this land from the Canaanites and its other indigenous inhabitants, our answer is that the entire world belongs to God; since He created it, He can give it to whomever is worthy in His eyes. From this perspective, Rashi has masterfully taken a most universal verse and given it a nationalistic spin. He has placed our right to the land of Israel as an implication of the very first verse of the Torah!

It is also possible to give Rashi's words an added dimension. He concludes this particular interpretation, 'and He (God) can give (the land) to whomever is worthy in his eyes.' These words can be taken to mean to whomever He wishes, i.e., to Israel, because he so arbitrarily chooses, or they can mean to whomever is morally worthy of the land, which implies that only if our actions deem us worthy, will we have the right to Israel. Jewish history bears out the second explanation, given the fact that we have suffered two exiles – the second of which lasting close to two thousand years. If this is indeed the proper explanation, Rashi's words provide a warning as well as a promise.

Nahmanides also grapples with this question. For him, it is clear that God's creation of the world is at the center of our theology, and so it was crucial to begin with this opening verse.

After all, the Torah is a complete philosophy of life. The first seven words of the Bible most significantly tell us that there is a Creator of this universe, that our world is not an accident, 'a tale told by an idiot, full of sound and fury, signifying nothing,' a haphazard convergence of chemicals and exploding gases. It is a world with a beginning, and a beginning implies an end, a purpose, a reason for being. Moreover, without the creation of heaven and earth, could we survive even for an instant? Our very existence depends on the Creator; and in return for creating us, He has the right to ask us to live in a certain way and follow His laws. The first verse in the Torah sets the foundation for all that follows.

First of all, there is a beginning. Second, there is a Creator who created heaven and earth. Third, everything in heaven and on earth owes its existence to the Creator; and fourth, in owing one's existence to the Creator, there could very well be deeds the Creator wants and expects from His creation. According to Nahmanides, the opening verse of the Torah is the one upon which our entire metaphysical structure rests!

After all, the Creator has rights of ownership: He owns us, our very beings. He deserves to have us live our lives in accord with His will and not merely in accord with our own subjective, and even selfish desires. He deserves our blessings before we partake of any bounty of the universe and our commitment to the lifestyle He commands us to lead.

In addition, Nahmanides further suggests that the entire story of the Garden of Eden teaches us that the punishment for disobeying God's laws will be alienation and exile, just as Adam and Eve were exiled from the garden of Eden after eating the forbidden fruit. This process is experienced by Israel during our difficult exile. This too is a crucial element in Jewish theology.

The Midrash [Gen. Raba 12] offers yet a third explanation. Implied in our opening biblical verse is a principle as to how we ought to live our lives. 'In the beginning God created heaven and earth.' In this sentence, 'created' is the verb; the world reveals to us the creative function of the divine. And since one of the guiding principles in the Torah is that we walk in His ways, our first meeting with God tells us that, just as He created, so must we create, just as He stood at the abyss of darkness and made light, so must we – created in His image – remove all pockets of darkness, chaos and void, bringing light, order and significance. In effect, the first verse of Genesis is also the first commandment, a command ordained by God to all human beings created in His image: the human task in this world is to create, or rather to re-create a world, to make it a more perfect world, by virtue of the 'image of God' within each of us.

The Midrash sees the human being in general, and the Jew in particular, as a creative force. Our creative energies – religious, ethical, scientific and artistic – must work in harmony with the Almighty to perfect a not yet perfect world, to bring us back to the peace and harmony of Eden.

All too often, Bible critics make two fatal errors. They divest the Torah of context and subtext, losing sight of what the Torah really wants to say. They take apart the grammatical mechanics of the words, disregarding the majesty and the fire, the vision and the message.

What we must remember is that essentially the Bible is not merely a book of laws, no matter how important they may be, and is certainly not written by man in his feeble attempt to understand creation and

God; it is rather the Book of Books emanating from God, which gives instruction and life direction.* It reveals not only what humanity is, but what we must strive to become; it teaches us that we must not merely engage the world, but attempt to perfect it in the majesty of the divine.

---

* The root *yrh* of the Hebrew, Torah, means to instruct or direct.

The Copernican Revolution and
the Place of the Human Being

*And God saw everything that He had made and
behold it was very good.*

A sensitive reading of the biblical description of the creation of the world forces the reader to come to some understanding of the relationship between Judaism and scientific discovery. Contrary to popular opinion, Judaism does not balk at modernity, especially if it furthers God's honor. For example, the invention of the printing press more than 500 years ago changed the nature of reading and literary transmission. The rabbinic leadership at the time welcomed it as a way to make sacred texts available to everyone. Now we're living in the midst of another communications revolution, and many Jews are involved in the development of the computer and Internet, allowing almost instantaneous call-up of a specific passage in the Talmud or a difficult area of medical ethics in our Responsa literature. The challenge is not to reject inventions but to refine them, not to censor modernity, but to sanctify it.

Commenting on the opening verse of Genesis, 'In the beginning God created the heavens and the earth,' the Seforno demonstrates how to place Torah insights into the context of scientific developments. He points out that the word *shamayim*, (usually translated as 'heavens') is the plural of the Hebrew *sham*, meaning 'there' or 'two theres,' and writes: 'therefore the word *ha-shamayim* indicates a distant object in relation to us, the distance being equal from each side, which cannot be unless it is situated in a wheel that is revolving in a completely circular fashion.' Thus every point on the planet is equidistant from the heavens (*ha-shamayim*) and for this phenomenon to be true, the world must be moving in a spherical pattern. Two 'far-aways' that are the same distance can only exist if the planet is a revolving sphere.

Interestingly, Seforno lived approximately at the same time as Copernicus (1473–1543), the famed astronomer who spent considerable time in Italy pursuing his studies before returning to his native Poland. Before Copernicus, the center of the universe was the earth; his new scientific theory, suggesting that the earth revolves around the sun, clearly demotes the earth from its formerly exalted position as the center of divine concern.

It stands to reason that a rabbi of Seforno's stature, who was also a doctor by profession and a respected intellectual of his day, had heard of Copernicus' theories and had apparently accepted his vision of an earth revolving around the sun. But especially noteworthy for us is how Seforno interprets the ramifications of a scientific theory rejected as blasphemous by most Christian theologians of the period. Not only does Seforno accept the Copernican position, which we now know to be scientifically accurate; he deduces a crucial moral lesson from an earth constantly revolving on its own axis, as it revolves around the sun. This lesson is that the human being is placed squarely at the center of the earth, equidistant from the two 'theres' or 'far-aways' of the heavens, which can only happen if the earth is constantly revolving.

The medieval sages speak of four levels of creation: the inanimate level of earth and rock, the vegetative level of plants and trees, the locomotive level of roaming animals and beasts, and finally the communicative level of humans who speak. Each level receives its sustenance from the previous level: vegetation depends on earth and water, animals receive sustenance from the vegetation, and humans gather food, drink, garments and tent-skins from the animals. If the human being communicates both horizontally and vertically with the world and with God, he has the capacity to uplift and ennoble the world, to redeem the earth; if he short-circuits his relationship to the divine, if he poisons rather than perfects the physical environment all around him, the entire earth will fall and fail with him.

With this in mind, the human being stands at the center of the universe. Only the human being has the gift of free choice. Our planet earth depends on proper human exercise of his free choice if it is to be redeemed and not destroyed. This is what I believe Seforno meant to extract from a constantly revolving earth. Interestingly enough, Rashi deduces a similar lesson from a later verse. At the end of our portion of *Bereshit*, after human conduct disappointed the Divine Creator, the Bible states:

> And God saw that the wickedness of man was great in the earth …. And God said, I will blot out the human being whom I have created … both human and beast, and creeping thing, and fowl of the air …
>
> Gen. 6:5–7

The obvious question asked is, why blot out the innocent animals and the silent beasts if the sin belongs to human beings? Rashi explains:

> Everything was created for the human being, and if he is to be destroyed, what need is there for the rest?!
>
> Rashi on Gen. 6:7

A central biblical dictum proclaims that 'human beings must walk in God's ways.' Yet, how do we determine God's ways? When Moses requested of God: 'Now therefore I pray Thee, if I have found grace in Your eyes, show me now Your ways, that I may know You …' [Ex. 33:13], God's answer is that Moses cannot hope to see Him completely, but can receive a partial glimpse into the divine – His back, as it were: 'And God passed by before him, and proclaimed: The Lord, the Lord, God, merciful and gracious, long-suffering and abundant in goodness and truth' [Ex. 34:6]. Maimonides insists that God is not merely informing us of a description of His conceivable essence, but He is presenting us with a divine injunction as to how we humans ought to live:

> Just as He is gracious, so ought you to be gracious; just as He is compassionate, so ought you to be compassionate; just as He is called holy, so ought you to be called holy.
>
> Laws of Knowledge 1:6

This divine description, as it were, is not as significant for its theology as it is for its anthropology; it is less a definition of God and more a guide for human morality. Once again, humanity is the central concern even of a definition of the divine!

After each creation, there is a biblical value judgment, 'And God saw that it was good.' There is but one exception: the creation of the human being, after which the Bible does not give its usual afterword, 'And God saw that it was good.' Seforno explains the reason: the human being is not functional but moral. Whether or not his creation will turn out to have been good depends on his free choice. This is the sense in which the human being stands smack at the center of the earth. Will he sanctify and redeem it, or plunder and destroy it? Will he realize his potential to act in God's image, placing God's attributes as the measure of all things and thereby perfect the world, or will he idealize his own frailty and ultimately drown in his weakness, bringing the entire world down with him? The jury has not yet come in with the final verdict. Until that time, the human being remains at center stage, to a great extent holding the whole world in his hands and in the grip of his free will.

Why Do Bad Things Happen to Good People?

> *And these are the generations of the heavens
> and of the earth when they were created, in the
> day that the Lord God made the earth and the
> heavens.*
>
> GENESIS 2:4

I

Undoubtedly, Judaism believes in one absolutely invisible deity who cannot be grasped by the imperfect human intellect. Nevertheless, God does reveal different aspects of his ineffable being to his human creations – and these must be understood and even acted upon. These practical, but important facets of the divine essence are expressed in terms of the different names by which the Almighty is referred to within the biblical narrative. Rashi was very much aware of this descriptive function of the various appellations of the deity, and comments upon it – Julius Wellhausen not withstanding – in his opening commentary on this first verse of the Bible.

Rashi writes:

> It does not state Lord [YHWH, *Hashem*, the four-letter name] because at first God (*Elohim*, Judge) intended to create [the world] under the attribute of strict justice. However, the Almighty realized that the world could not endure in such a mode, and therefore gave precedence to divine mercy (*rahamim*), uniting it with divine justice, and that is why we find one chapter later: 'And these are the generations of the heaven and of the earth when they were created, in the day that the Lord God [*Hashem Elokim*] made the earth and the heavens [Gen. 2:4].'
>
> Rashi on **Gen. 1:1**

What does Rashi mean? Why could the world not endure under the rule of divine justice?

A world run in accordance with divine justice would mean that as soon as someone does wrong, punishment is immediately meted out. We would never have the question of why bad things happen to good people because an evil act would be stopped in its tracks; after all, any innocent person's suffering would violate the principle of divine justice. The Nazi's hand would wither in the process of his even lifting the knife to hurt a hair on the head of a Jewish baby. The individual's voice would be silenced before he even was able to articulate the slander he had planned to spread. What kind of world would this be? If evil could not exist because of the all embracing powers of divine justice, how would a human being differ from a rat in a laboratory experiment that is conditioned to move down a certain tunnel, jolts of electricity guiding its choices?

Simply stated, the human being, a creature who makes choices and either learns from his mistakes or is 'doomed to repeat them,' either succumbs or does not succumb to temptation, could not exist as anything more than a pawn if divine justice ruled the world. There would be no room for the wavering personality torn between two equally compelling choices. In a world where a human being could not possibly make an immoral choice, he/she would be no different from an animal ruled by instinct, albeit in a positive way.

For the world to exist with human beings granted the choice to wield either a murderer's knife or a physician's scalpel, with human beings not as impotent puppets but rather as potential partners with the divine, God must hold back from immediate punishment. Compassion must be joined with justice so that the Almighty will grant the possibility of the wicked to return, the opportunity to those who have fallen to rise once again, and offer the challenge to a fallible humanity to perfect an imperfect world.

> Rabbi Joshua ben Levi said: Why were they called the 'Men of the Great Assembly'? Because they restored the crown to its place of glory. Moses came and said, 'the great, powerful and awesome God.' Jeremiah came and said, 'Gentiles [the Babylonians] are uprooting His Temple, where is His awesomeness?' He did not say 'awesome' [in his praise to God in the Amida]. Daniel came and said, 'Gentiles are subjugating His children, where is his power?' He did not say 'powerful.' The [Men of the Great Assembly] came and said, 'The opposite is true! This is His powerfulness, that He conquers His will [to immediately destroy the wicked before they can perpetuate evil against God] and He grants a tolerant, long-suffering reprieve to the wicked [to enable them eventually to repent]'; and this is His awesomeness, that were it not for God's awesomeness, how could the one [powerless] nation Israel have survived among the nations of the world?
>
> *Yoma* 69b

The price we must pay for this divine compassion and human freedom of choice is the phenomenon of the innocent who suffer. Indeed, God's only guarantee or promise is that the Jews will continually survive and ultimately redeem this world. A major school in Rabbinic theology even reinforces the position that 'there is no reward for the righteous in this world' [*Kiddushin* 39b], apparently leaving divine reward (and punishment) for the next dimension of existence, for the life after life, where our divine soul continues to live even after our physical bodies are united with the earth. In effect, argues this school of Jewish theology, divine compassion allowing for free will and ultimate repentance must enable individuals to do even what God, in a perfect world, would not allow them to do!

II

In accordance with this theology, a Hassidic teaching provides an alternative way of reading the first three words in the Torah, '*Bereshit bara Elohim*,' usually translated, 'In the beginning God created...' Since there is the *etnachta* ('stop' sign; semicolon) cantillation underneath the third word in the phrase, the words can also be taken to mean, 'Beginnings did God create.' This reading provides hope and optimistic faith even in a world devoid of the reward of the commandments. Anyone who has experienced significant lifestyle changes, 'born again' Jews, reformed alcoholics, or even second or third marriages between widowed and/ or divorced people, understands the significance of the challenge and opportunity of 'another chance.' Free will, the concept of making your own choices, implies that sometimes mistakes will be made and tragedies will occur. But instead of divine justice descending as a bolt of lightning, divine mercy emerges to absorb the lethal voltage. Holding off divine justice is saying we always have another chance to better ourselves, to redeem the tragedy, to try again. And isn't this what 'beginnings' are all about!

True repentance means carving out a new beginning for oneself. Beginnings, therefore, go hand in hand with divine mercy, and divine faith in the human personality to re-create him/herself and to forge a new destiny. To make a new beginning!

In fact, if we forget for a moment the account of Adam and Eve as an esoteric tale of a primordial world of gardens and snakes and trees of good and evil, but instead concentrate on the basic outline of the events, we find that we are in the middle of a domestic tragedy. A man and a woman had two sons: to their growing horror, one son turned out to be a murderer, and the other son was his victim.

What happens to such parents? How do they go on with their lives after this double tragedy? Clearly, they could be in mourning for the rest of their lives, brooding about what went wrong, the sheer waste of it all. But instead these two first parents have a third son, Seth. In effect, they created the opportunity of a new beginning.

This idea also fits well with that reason we previously offered as to why the Torah begins with the creation of the world rather than the first commandment given to Israel. We suggested that the opening of the Torah also reflects the most fundamental commandment in the Torah, the commandment to emulate the divine: 'And you shall walk in His ways' [Deut. 28:9]. Just as God created, so are we commanded to create. And what is it that He created? First and foremost He created a beginning, a starting again, a possibility of redeeming oneself from failure and tragedy and making another effort. The sinner isn't shut out forever; he is always given another opportunity through repentance, another possibility of re-creating himself and his immediate environment, a new beginning. Perhaps this is what our sages meant when they suggested that the Almighty had previously created and destroyed worlds before He created our world. This is why the history of humanity begins with Adam's and Eve's fall – and their subsequent rise. And this is God's message to Cain and all future generations: 'Sin may crouch at your door, but you can conquer it' [Gen. 4:7].

Thus it turns out that in the Torah's opening word, *Bereshit* (beginning), we find not only the theme of the Torah, but of the entirety of existence: God created an imperfect and sometimes unjust world to allow the possibility of change and growth. If change weren't possible, if human behavior were as fixed as that of all other mammals, then there would be no need for, and no uniqueness within, human beings. The glory of God and humanity is to be found in the opening phrase of the Bible: 'God created beginnings' – new opportunities, manifold re-awakenings.

The First Marriage:
Overcoming Loneliness and 'Aloneness'

... It is not good for man to be alone; I will make a help-opposite for him.

GENESIS 2:18

The Torah opens on the grandest scale possible, the creation of the world: heavens and earth, firmament, sun, moon, stars and the planet itself. Each day we climb the ladder of creation until the sixth day, when the human being appears. But even after his appearance, the epoch described still seems remote, carved out of a meta-historic consciousness dealing with such realities as the Garden of Eden and the Tree of Knowledge of Good and Evil. Our imagination only goes so far in understanding that age, and without relying on symbol and metaphor most of us would be lost.

But directly after the prohibition of tasting the forbidden fruit, we read in the Bible the first verse which has an immediate and relevant bearing on the modern human condition: 'God said, It is not good for the human being to be alone. I will make a 'help-opposite'* for him' [Gen. 2:18]. Adam may be in the Garden of Eden, but who doesn't understand what it means to be alone? With this verse we recognize his flesh-and-blood reality. His dilemma is our dilemma, and the next paragraph – which should be read closely – deals with the major existential issues of humanity, then and now: how the Torah views the fundamental human predicament, the human need which only marriage can fulfill, and the ideal relationship between husband and wife, and the significance of the sexual act between them.

The first problem in the biblical text is the strange Hebrew term, *ezer k'negdo*, the phrase God uses to describe the creature He will provide for Adam to overcome his being alone. The literal translation is 'help-opposite.' Other translations are 'help-mate' or 'a help to match him' or 'compatible helper', terms which do not fully reflect the inner tension expressed by the biblical Hebrew form.

Rashi, in explaining the phrase, writes: 'If the man is worthy, then his wife will be an *ezer*, a helper, and if he is unworthy then she will be *k'negdo*, against him, an opposite force.' This interpretation does take into account the oxymoron, or antithetical nature of the phrase – indeed one of my college professors once introduced his wife to the class as 'Mrs. K'negdo' – but neglects to explain how two such different concepts can come together.

Thus, despite Rashi's commentary, a 'help-opposite' still remains a difficult construction. If it's not good for Adam to be alone, why doesn't God simply create a 'helper' for him? Why an 'opposite'?

Second, if God is so worried about Adam being alone, then why, in the midst of the segment dealing with the creation of Eve, does the text digress and turn to something entirely different – Adam's naming of the animals? 'The Lord God had created from the earth all the beasts of the field, and all the fowl of the heavens, and he brought them to the human to see what he ought to call them. And whatever name the human gave to any of these creatures, that was its name. So the human called names to all of the animals and the fowl of the heavens and all of

* In Hebrew, *Ezer k'negdo*.

the beasts of the field. But Adam did not find a help-opposite who was compatible for him' [Gen. 2:19–20].

This question is compounded by the fact that the Torah seems to be weighing the possibility that Adam's help-opposite might be found among the donkeys, camels or other four-legged creatures – a preposterous idea, to say the least.

I believe that the key to understanding the difficult term 'help-opposite' lies in the introductory verse: 'It is not good for the human being to be *levado* – alone.' Rabbi Joseph B. Soloveitchik discusses the tragedy of aloneness most poignantly in his classical novella, *The Lonely Man of Faith*. Aloneness has two aspects: First there is social loneliness, the lack of someone with whom to share one's innermost thoughts and emotions. Several verses back we read 'the Lord God formed the human being of the dust of the ground, and breathed into his nostrils the breath of life; and the human being became a living soul' [Gen. 2:7]. The Targum (original Aramaic translation of the Bible) translates 'living soul' as *ru-ah memalela* – a spirit that speaks. It would seem axiomatic that a human being is a creature that speaks – must speak – in order to feel alive. Aristotle even defines the human being as a social animal. Clearly, the act of communication is built into the very psyche of our being. Indeed, one of the worst punishments imaginable is that of solitary confinement.

The second type of aloneness cuts close to the very bone of life and death. We could call it existential aloneness, a concept already alluded to in the Torah with the odd form of the verb *heyot* in our key verse, which connotes existence, literally: 'it is not good...existing (*heyot*)...human alone' [Gen. 2:8]. In this form the word *heyot* suggests the existential condition of one's being, not only our being socially lonely, but specifically relating to an aloneness that penetrates to the depths of one's very existence. We generally live each day as though we will continue to live for eternity, but at the back of our minds we are aware of the painful truth that the day will arrive when we must, each of us, embark upon a journey that we must take alone. The bleak, black specter of non-existence at the end of the road, is the angst which echoes God's declaration that 'it is not good for man to be alone.'

The Torah is telling us, therefore, that what a human being desperately needs is a relationship that will help assuage both social loneliness as well as existential aloneness; one's complement/companion must serve as share- and soul-mate, as well as a link to eternity.

How does the *ezer k'negdo* help overcome social loneliness? Only if there is a willingness to limit oneself and allow the other person not to necessarily agree, sometimes to stand opposite and think opposite. A marriage partner is not a geisha girl or boy, an automatic amen-sayer, constantly regaling his/her spouse with compliments and praises, a trophy accessory who serves drinks, sets the table or provides money in the bank. A genuine life partner must be able to say 'no' if that is what is necessary – the *k'negdo* part – because if you marry a yes-sayer, you aren't really confronting or being confronted by an 'other'; you are not sharing your life with a truly significant 'other.'

Moreover, if the partner is always expected to agree, the lips may be moving 'yes,' but the heart may be saying 'no' silently until the heart breaks from the weight of 'noes.' In the end, a help-opposite on both sides creates its own synthesis, and only with this formula can a new oneness emerge. The couple must drink together, but not always from the same cup, so that one can correct the other, complement the other, cheer and comfort the other, help and be helped by the other. Only then is the one not alone; only then is there a partner each can respect, thereby creating a relationship in which the whole is greater than the sum of its parts – a unit in which one plus one equals three. Hence, the greatest help is provided specifically by a loving partner who at times stands in opposition for the good of the other as well as for the good of the relationship.

From this perspective we can answer the second textual question which queries why God, *in media res creatio*, turns to the creatures of the world to line up and be named by man. The Midrash makes the daring suggestion that Adam cohabited with all of the animal creatures, but was totally unsatisfied; 'He did not find in them a help-opposite.' The reason for Adam's failure in attaining satisfaction is suggested by the fact that the Almighty asks him to name the animals. When we name something, we define it, and when we define it, we control it.

However, a relationship of control is not a relationship of complement; it is one-sided and not mutual, taking and not giving. Indeed, humanity is commanded to control the physical, animal world ('and you shall subdue them ...' [Gen. 1:28]), but one spouse is not to control the other. For if one does, he/she has lost out on discovering the *ezer k'negdo* and overcoming social loneliness. (Indeed, when the Bible declares 'And he shall rule over you' [Gen. 3:6], it is only as a result of the sin of the forbidden fruit, and not a description of the ideal relationship. The goal of humanity is both to overcome sin, and to overcome the attempt to control one's spouse as well!)

From this perspective, we can appreciate one of the most profound verses of the Bible: 'Therefore shall a human being leave his father and his mother, cleave unto his spouse, and they shall be one flesh' [Gen. 2:24]. The biblical Hebrew word for 'cleave' – *davok* – generally connotes a compatibilty of values and ideals, sensitivities and goals, a unity of mind and spirit. The Bible is telling us that such a real 'togetherness' of personalities might logically and happily lead to a oneness of body in the sexual union – a union which may very well result in a permanent relationship, but provides a literal oneness only temporarily – a union which hopefully renders each filled and fulfilled as a part of the other, but still retains each individual apart and distinct in his/her own right.

Thus, clearly, the individual is enabled to reach his/her greatest potential precisely because he/she is not isolated and lonely, but is also a part of another and a complement within a family whose wholeness is greater than the sum of its parts.

The author of Ecclesiastes puts it very well: 'Two are better than one ... woe to one who is alone when he falls, for there is no one to lift him! If two sleep together they keep warm, but how can one keep warm alone? ... A three-ply cord is not easily severed' [Ecc. 4:9–12]. If the text is praising the importance of two together, how do we come to a three-ply cord? The answer is, that in a caring and mutual marital relationship, the added strength of the two together creates the new third entity which is the marital relationship itself; one plus one equaling not two, but three!

But what of existential aloneness? The result of a man-woman relationship of mutuality is the birth of a child, the creation of a family with intra-generational concern and cultural continuity, our entry into the future beyond our individual life span, our gateway to eternity.

Children and grandchildren who are a reflection of ourselves not only genetically, but also culturally and ideologically help assuage our fear of death by providing the individual with a sense of continuity. Since this is impossible with an 'animal' relationship, Adam must be provided with another partner compatible with the possibility of birth, a partner who can provide a child who will naturally project parents into the future.

Hence Rashi interprets the verse, 'You shall be one flesh' not as referring to the sexual union of the couple, but rather to the one flesh which emerges from husband and wife. Afterward, in our child, part of us lives on even after we die. Hence, our help-opposite provides both companionship and continuity, helping to assuage both aloneness and loneliness.

We have seen how the initial creation of humanity deals with the existential tragedy of loneliness and aloneness, the human need for communication and companionship, for self-transcendence and generational continuity. Hence the Almighty declares, 'I will make a help-opposite for him,' an alter ego, a genuine soul mate. But how do we succeed in establishing such a relationship? Does the Bible actually spell it out for us? And what is the relationship, if any, between sex and love?

Remember that when the first human fails to find his help-opposite from among the animals, a deep sleep falls over Adam. 'And He (God) took one of his sides, and closed up the flesh in its place; and from the side, which the Lord God had taken from the man, He made a woman, and brought her to the man' [Gen. 2:21–22].

Why is the 'birth' of Eve seemingly surrounded with a mythical quality? Why is she created from Adam rather than as a separate creature in her own right? In the question lies the answer. Eve's unique 'birth' marks her unique role, as an inextricable part of her male counterpart, as a being with whom he must share, and not a creature he must control. After all, if she is part of him, then he is part of her!

In an earlier verse we read: 'God created the human being in His image, in the image of God created He him, male and female created He them' [Gen. 1:27]. Rashi cited the later reference to Eve's 'birth' from Adam's rib, quoting a midrashic interpretation that God originally created the human with two 'faces,' Siamese twins as it were, an androgynous male-female human being. Hence when God puts Adam into a deep sleep, it's not to remove a rib, but to separate the female side from the male side.

According to this midrashic interpretation, God's original human being was both male and female. While Adam sleeps, God divides the creature into two so that each half will seek completion in the other. So that the one will understand his dependency upon, and ultimate wholeness through, the other. Indeed, in every relationship of mutuality, there are times when one must play a more passive role, enter into a deep sleep as it were, in order to enable the other to fully emerge!

Awakening, Adam says of Eve 'This time, bone of my bone, and flesh of my flesh' [Gen. 2:23]. His search is over. And what's true for Adam is true for humankind. The human personality will be in anguish until he/she finds completion by means of a true life partner. Thus in the next verse, God announces the second basic principle in life, 'Therefore shall a human being leave his father and mother, and shall cleave unto his spouse, and they shall be one flesh' [Gen. 2:24]. 'Leave' does not mean reject; it does mean, however, a certain degree of emotional and economic separation; one must be mature and independent in order to enter into a relationship of mutuality with one's mate. After all, how many divorces can be traced to crippling parent-child relationships which extend into, and seriously impede, the husband-wife relationship?

Moreover, since the goal of a human being is to become united with another human being, this, the truest of partnerships, can be achieved only with someone who is really part of yourself, only with someone to whom you cleave intellectually and emotionally. If a relationship suffers from a lack of concern and commitment, sexuality suffers as well; the oneness of two bodies becomes a false act of deceit, suggesting a unity which is in fact a lie. The Torah wants us to know that for humans, sex is not merely a function of procreative needs, not merely a biological release, but is rather an expression of mutuality on a profound level, a coupling in the deepest sense. For the human being, the sexual relationship must be an expression of concern and commitment for each other, and not merely a means towards procreation, or a biological release of physical pressure. It is a merging of bodies which reflects a unity of minds, souls and destinies. It is for this reason the Midrash suggests that only human beings – and not animals – face each other during the sexual act.

Without the fullness of a relationship, the sexual act of union descends to harlotry or masturbation, and ultimately leaves each participant unsatisfied and unfulfilled. In many ways, it is worse than no relationship at all, because there was the promise of a relationship which then resulted in severe disappointment. The bitter price paid by 'married singles' is that in addition to their loneliness they must suffer the mockery and hypocrisy of their physical setup. Benjamin, the major character of the award winning movie of the sixties, *The Graduate*, ends his 'affair' with his classmate's mother because he only knows her as 'Mrs. Robinson'; they do not even call each other by their first names. In effect, he is saying: If I don't know you, how can I care about you; and if I don't care about you, how can I sleep with you (shades of Joseph's rejection of 'Mrs. Potiphar'!)?

Moreover, Nahmanides, ad loc, maintains that only human beings – and not animals – have constant sexual needs rather than periods of heat, and maintain sexual capacity long after menopause sets in. This is because for human beings – unlike animals – the sexual relationship is not merely a means of procreating the species, but is an expression of relationship, communication and concern. Such a sexual act truly enables us to transcend ourselves and merge into the other. Nahmanides speaks of one flesh in allegoric and even mystical terms: through a transcendent sexual act conceived in marriage, the two become one, which is the ultimate realization of the state in which they had initially been created.

The entire biblical sequence ends with the startling statement, 'And they were both naked, the man and his wife, and they were not ashamed' [Gen. 2:25]. Given the Torah's strict standards of modesty and sexuality, how are we to understand a description which seems to contradict traditional Jewish values?

Perhaps we are dealing with a more symbolic interpretation: Nakedness without shame means that two people must have the ability to face each other and reveal the nakedness of their souls without external pretense. Usually we play games, pretending to be what we're not, putting on a front. The Hebrew word *beged* (garment) comes from the same root as the word *bagod*, to betray. Similarly, the word *me'il*, cloak, comes from the same root as the word *m'al*, to deceive. With garments I can betray, wearing my 'public' mask and playing out my public role while I hide and mask over my true inner self. If there is any truth at all to the advertising hyperbole, 'clothes **make** the man,' there is an even greater truth to my advertisement, 'clothes **fake** the man.'

I remember, soon after my *aliya*, I suddenly returned to wearing the ties and jackets which I had thankfully put into storage as soon as I assumed Israeli citizenship. Upon analyzing my reversion to my 'former life' sartorial style, I realized that it was a psychological function of fear and self-doubt that I wouldn't 'make it' professionally in my new surroundings and Israeli identity. After a few setbacks, I turned to the external garb which I identified with my former Manhattan success.

The Torah wants husband and wife to remove garments which conceal truth, to be free to express fears and frustrations, not to be afraid to cry and scream in each other's presence without feeling the 'shame of nakedness.' This is the ideal *ezer k'negdo*, flesh of one flesh, bone of one bone.

In marital counseling, I am never put off when one partner screams at the other; as one wife said to her husband who complained that she often yelled at him: 'With whom then can I let out my frustrations, the stranger next door?' Of course, I'm not advocating shouting, but a far more serious danger sign is silence – non-communication – between the couple.

The result of all of this is that individuals must spend a lifetime working on themselves and working on their relationship with their spouses. Most important of all, we must be honest with ourselves and honest with our spouses, loving our spouses as we love ourselves and giving to our spouses no less – especially in respect and concern – than we wish to receive from them. Then our sexual relationship will be an expression of our mutual love and commitment, and we will be married soul mates rather than married singles.

Why the Forbidden Fruit was Forbidden

*...from all the trees in the garden you may freely
eat, but of the Tree of Knowledge of Good and
Evil you may not eat...*

GENESIS 2:16–17

From Michelangelo to Milton, one of the most popular biblical moments to capture the imagination of great artists and writers is Adam and Eve eating the forbidden fruit from the Tree of Knowledge of Good and Evil. The instructions were clear: '...from all the trees in the garden you may freely eat, but of the Tree of Knowledge of Good and Evil you may not eat...' [Gen. 2:16–17]. So why, after the initial prologue introducing the basic characters in the drama of the creation, is the Torah's first concern a tale of commandment and disobedience? What is the significance of the term 'Tree of Knowledge of Good and Evil'? Did the forbidden fruit inject an aspect into the human personality which had not been there initially?

Different commentators have their own view. Nahmanides suggests that before Adam and Eve ate from the Tree of Knowledge of Good and Evil, they didn't have the power to make decisions. Created like the sun and the moon and the stars, Adam and Eve were functionaries, a movement in a landscape with a predetermined direction. However, the Tree of Knowledge of Good and Evil gave them the power to cease being functional creatures. Now they could become moral beings, or immoral ones – should they choose evil.

Rashi writes that the fruit of the Tree of Knowledge of Good and Evil introduced the 'evil instinct', the idea of an erotic character as part of the sexual act which until then had been natural and innocent. Rashi anticipates the Freudians who regard the serpent as a male sexual symbol of seduction [Gen. 2:25, Rashi ad loc].

Maimonides, in the very beginning of his *Guide to the Perplexed*, suggests that Adam and Eve always had the ability to make choices, but that the Tree of Knowledge now enabled them to make choices based not only on the objective criteria of truth and falsehood (e.g. if the stones are wet, rubbing them together won't create fire) but on the more subjective plane of good vs. evil (e.g., what appears to me to be good is good, and what appears to me to be evil is evil).

Rabbi Samson Raphael Hirsch adds a striking interpretation that emerges from Maimonides. He insists that the fruit did not add anything to the human personality that had not been there previously. When we look at the biblical forbidden fruit, it's described in purely positive terms: '*tov le-ma'akhal*' – good as food, suggesting it was low in cholesterol, calories and fat content; and it was '*ta'avah le-ainayim*' – lustful for the eyes – apparently beautifully packaged, an aesthetic delight, worthy of a gourmet's table, and '*neḥmad le-haskil*' – sweet for the mind, probably protein-rich to strengthen brain cells. So if this fruit had so many positive attributes, why couldn't Adam and Eve eat it? The answer is simple: because God said no! 'Of the Tree of Knowledge of Good and Evil you shall not eat…'. My appreciation of Rabbi Hirsch's view resonates strongly with a number of seminal experiences in my youth.

I grew up in Bed-Stuy, an old Jewish neighborhood in Brooklyn, in the days before kosher Chinese restaurants. When I was about seven or eight, an exotic Chinese eatery opened down the block, advertising itself as 'kosher-style'. I asked my grandmother if I could eat there. I adored my grandmother, a deeply religious woman whose influence on my life was most profound. She said no, explaining that if I wanted to grow up big and strong, I should not eat non-kosher food, and that 'kosher-style' was not kosher enough. Naturally, growing up big and strong was more important to me than an egg roll – especially since I was small for my age.

Years later, while I attended Yeshiva University, I was on the varsity debating team. The first debate of the term was against West Point Military Academy. Sundays were special at West Point: football, a steak dinner, and afterwards a college function. That particular Sunday, the function was our debate. As guests of the military academy, we spent the entire day on campus. Dinner was the thickest T-bone steak I had ever seen, surrounded by french fries. The three Yeshiva debaters dug into our kosher plates of cottage cheese and tomatoes. Then came the debate, and debating courtesy dictates that the home team approaches the visitors to shake hands. Compared to the West Pointers, the three-man YU team was short and scrawny. Looking up at my debating adversary, I had to crane my head and my eyes were barely parallel with his navel! He reached out his hand to shake mine, and I felt his grip nearly crush the bones in my hand. As I remembered that he had eaten the non-kosher steak while I had to be satisfied with a tomato, I whispered to an invisible presence, 'Grandma, I think you lied to me.'

Hirsch is telling us that, in effect, the first commandment in the Torah is a kashrut commandment, a command concerning a forbidden food. And from a biblical perspective, kashrut has nothing to do with physical prowess; indeed later on in the text [Lev. 11:45], the Torah itself will link kashrut to human sanctity. In the opening verses of the Torah, we are being taught that sanctity is linked to obedience to the divine. Our obligation is to do what the Almighty tells us we ought do, and not what we subjectively might think is best for us to do.

The struggle between the characters in the Garden is the very essence of the human struggle in every generation: do I accept a higher religio-legal authority, or do I claim to be my own highest authority, acting as I see fit, deciding morality solely on my own? The Torah insists that the division between good and evil or right and wrong cannot be left to the whim of an individual. Good is what God says is good, evil is what God says is evil. Rabbi Hirsch is teaching us that the fruit, despite its appearances, was evil only because God determined it so.

The serpent's seductive message is the very antithesis of this concept. 'The moment you eat of the tree you will be become like God' [Gen. 3:5]. Once you disobey God's instructions, you have dethroned God and made yourselves the sole arbiters of what is good and what is evil.

The struggle between a divine or heteronomous order of morality as opposed to a man-made subjective order of morality never leaves the pages of history. From the Garden of Eden to the terrorist 'freedom fighter', the pieces in the drama are virtually the same. Left to his own devices, every human is a genius in the art of self-justification, says the immortal Sigmund Freud. Stalin could kill millions and call it justice, suicide-bombers can wreak havoc, murdering innocent women and children 'for the sake of Allah'; your neighbor can sleep with his best friend's distressed wife and call it an act of mercy. The human mind can always rationalize and justify what the human body wishes to do.

The story of Adam and Eve in the Garden of Eden is mythic in its reverberations. It did not happen only once in historical time, but in fact happens again and again. And our biblical story concludes that, especially in our postmodern world of free choice, we must nevertheless remember that every human being is a genius at self-justification and rationalization. There must be a higher religio-legal-moral structure above the individual which provides a solid infrastructure, an anchor of stability and direction, in a world filled with conflicting possibilities and constant temptation. From a biblical perspective, the source for this structure is a God-given system of ultimate morality, which has not only a vote, but also a veto regarding the ethical choices of the individual.

The Human Being: More Like God or More Like Beast?

> *And the Lord said to Cain, why are you angry*
> *and why are you crestfallen? If you do well, shall*
> *you not be accepted? And if you do not do well,*
> *sin crouches at your doorstep.*
>
> GENESIS 4:4–5

Adam and Eve sin against God – and perhaps against themselves. Cain sins against – even slays – his brother, and so begins the very checkered and frustrating history of humanity. But before Cain commits this act of murder, the Almighty gives him a lesson in human nature, a lesson which can greatly benefit us today, and which links this first portion of the Bible with the calendrical period of sin and atonement which precedes its reading, the Days of Repentance, forgiveness and joy.

Cain has brought a sacrifice – in effect, given a gift – to God, merely 'from the fruit of the land'. His brother Abel, on the other hand, gives to God from the choicest of his flock, 'from the first-born of his sheep and from their fat'. As a consequence, the Almighty looks with favor upon Abel and his offering, but not so upon Cain and his offering. Cain, obviously smitten with jealousy, becomes angry, his face crestfallen. The divine response, a crucial commentary on both human weakness and potential strength, comprises one of the most difficult as well as one of the most important verses in the Bible. Rabbi Meir Lubush, in his commentary, the Malbim, translates it as follows:

> Whether you give a good gift [*S'et* as a noun, from *maset*, an offering] or you do not give a good [gift, it is of no real consequence]; sin crouches at your doorstep, against you is its desire, but you can overcome it.
>
> Malbim on Gen. 4:7

The Malbim understands God's response to Cain as a fundamental belittlement of sacrifices or indulgences; forget about the divine acceptance (or lack thereof) of the offerings, and concentrate upon proper actions. In the final analysis, it is your deeds to your fellow humans – and not your gifts to God – which will define your relationship to the divine.

Rashi, Onkelos and Ibn Ezra have another interpretation, in which God's words in this context do not relate to sacrificial gifts at all. For them, the Hebrew *s'et* is a verb which either means 'you will be forgiven' or 'your face will be lifted' – but emphasizes the fundamental compassion and willingness to forgive which is the major characteristic of the divine. From the perspective of these commentaries, God is telling Cain that, despite the fact that he sinned by bringing an inadequate offering, if he will do well from now on, he will be forgiven (and/or, his face will be lifted). If, however, he does not repent and do well, then sin will crouch at his doorstep, and desire his ensnarement. Nevertheless, and no matter what, 'you can overcome [sin]'. The human being has the power to redeem himself and consequently the Almighty loves him/her and is always ready to forgive.

This divine message of human choice and divine love certainly became internalized by subsequent Jewish history, and is indeed the major emphasis of the High Holy Day season – Rosh Hashanah as the days of judgement and repentance (highlighting the Malbim's concern for proper human actions) and Yom Kippur as the day of forgiveness (highlighting Rashi's concentration on divine compassion). Whether the emphasis is placed on human weakness and divine grace or human potential and divine support depends on the specific outlook of any given text. Indeed, the Mishna teaches as follows:

> On Rosh Hashanah all of humanity passes before Him like children of Maron (*Bnai Maron*).
>
> *Rosh Hashanah* 18a

The Talmudic text goes on to give us three interpretations for the word Maron, the first rabbi suggesting 'Like a flock of sheep (*kibnai marna*)'; Resh Lakish saying: 'As in the ascent of Maron' and Rav Judah maintaining in the name of Shmuel, 'Like the troops of the house of David.' The first interpretation apparently stresses the sheeplike, animalistic drive of human beings; after all, it is characteristic of sheep that they lack independence, each animal following the tail of the sheep ahead of it. The second interpretation emphasizes the precarious position of humanity, citing a specific location – Bnai Maron – the steps of whose entrance were like a narrow precipice, from which even a well-intentioned but careless climber could easily fall into an abyss on either side. This is reminiscent of the famous teaching of Rabbi Nahman of Bratzlav:

> The entire world is a very narrow bridge; but the essence is not to be afraid.

Both of these views emphasize divine readiness to forgive. The third interpretation insists upon the exalted and protecting quality of humans, who are literally disciples, soldiers, partners-in-victory of the master (Maron), infantrymen of King David, forerunner of the messianic redeemer of the world. This view sees humanity as God's respected partners, whose actions are crucial for ultimate salvation.

Which is correct? What truly constitutes the essence of a human being? The truth is, all three. We read in Genesis, 'Let us make the human being in our image and after our likeness...' [Gen. 1:26]. Most of the commentaries are perplexed by the divine's usage of the plural form 'Let us'. Rashi suggests that the Almighty took counsel with the angels and Rabbeinu Saadia Gaon calls this the 'majestic plural' of kings. But Nahmanides maintains that the Almighty is addressing the physical creation which He has already made, the animals and the beasts who are limited in time and strength, those physical creatures who are born, develop, wither and die, and who require nutrition, rest, secretion, excretion, and sexual reproduction. 'Let us make the human being in our image,' says God to these creatures. The human being will be subject to the same limitations and drives as you are, but at the same time – since he/she will also be created in My image – he/she will have the capacity to love, to create, to choose and even to transcend his/her very human weaknesses. However, let no mistake be made. The human being is also part beast, and developing the 'image of God' is no mean feat. God commands: '...and let them have dominion over the fish of the sea, and over the fowl of the air, and over the cattle...'. The word used for 'have dominion' is *v'yirdu*, which can mean to rule (*rdh*), but can also mean to descend (*yrd*). The human being, part God part beast, can go either way: he can soar to supernal heights of spirituality or sink to bestial depths of depravity. And when the human being falls, it is to levels of cruelty far below the brute beasts.

This idea is given poignant meaning in Zvi Kolitz's masterpiece *Yosel Rakover's Appeal to God*, a fictionalized account of notes found in the ruins of the Warsaw Ghetto Uprising. Rakover writes, 'The beasts of the field in their freedom and gentleness seem to be so lovable and dear that I feel a deep pain whenever I hear the evil fiends that lord it over Europe referred to as beasts. It is untrue that the tyrant who rules over Europe now has something of the beast in him. He is a typical child of modern man; mankind as a whole spawned him and reared him. He is merely the frankest expression of its innermost, most deeply buried instincts.' Kolitz is saying that when we call the Nazis beasts, we insult the animals. After all, animals only kill if they need to eat, but the Nazis turned killing into an enterprise, an industry, and sometimes even a sport. They became the efficiency experts of the world in the game of mass murder. Like all human beings, they were created in the 'image of God,' but since they used their unique status to kill as many people as possible and invent the implements of genocide, they descended to levels of cruelty far lower than the capability of beasts. Indeed, 'At the doorstep, evil crouches, and against you is its desire.'

Having said all this, we must nevertheless stress that the most fundamental essence – and distinction – of the human being is the divine image within him. Traditional Jewish thought never accepted Rousseau's 'noble savage' or Sartre's 'no exit' as the last word on human nature. Hence, in the *Ne'ila* prayer at the conclusion of Yom Kippur, the liturgy begins 'The difference between human being and beast is of no account, for everything is a breath' (*hevel*, Abel, a life which can so easily be snuffed out by one's sibling). But then the prayer goes on to say 'But You (God) have chosen and distinguished the human being from the very beginning… and Your right hand is outstretched to draw the penitent near.' Throughout the High Holy Day period we reiterate: 'Lord, Lord, God of compassion and forgiveness…,' with our Sages explaining the two names Lord to mean 'the God of love before you sin and the God of love after you sin.' The human being can sink to deeper levels than the beast, but he/she can also rise to levels higher than the angels.

This is precisely what the Almighty is telling Cain. Even though your offering was brought with the wrong intention – a sin compounded by the jealousy you feel toward your brother – nonetheless you may still be forgiven. God loves you even after you've sinned. It's not too late. All you have to do is repent, begin to do good deeds, and then your down-. cast face will become uplifted, and you will be purified. Undoubtedly, repentance is difficult. After all, 'Sin lies crouching at your doorstep.' But the God who desires human purification and perfection bears testimony at the very dawn of human history: 'You can conquer it, humanity can overcome!'

The Laurels and Limits of Science

*And Lemekh said unto his wives: "Adah and
Tzillah – hear my voice; wives of Lemekh –
hearken unto my speech; for I have slain a man
by wounding and a child by bruising; If Cain
shall be avenged sevenfold then Lemekh seventy
and sevenfold."*

GENESIS 4:23–24

How should the Torah observant community approach
the explosion of scientific discoveries including the experiments in
cloning, fertilization, and genetic engineering? Do we rely on inductive
reasoning and logical deduction as the basis of our supreme and absolute truth? Or do we adopt a much more circumscribed outlook, insisting that 'the heavens belong to God, the earth was given to humanity'
[Ps. 115:16] – and that there are many areas which human beings dare
not touch but must leave to God? Are there limits to the extent of our
scientific inquiry and discovery?

There is a difficult and almost mysterious biblical account lodged between the murder of Abel and the birth of Seth, the third son of Adam and Eve, that reveals an interesting approach to my opening question. After Cain kills his brother, the Torah records that Cain's punishment is that he will be a perennial rover and roamer, a *'na' ve-nad.'* The next few verses list Cain's descendants, and except for names, no details are given about the five generations of Cain's progeny until we arrive at Lemekh, the sixth generation.

Lemekh has two wives, Adah and Tzilla. Adah gives birth to two sons: Yaval the 'father of such as abide in tents, and graze herds' and Yuval, '...the father of such as handle the harp and pipes.' Tzilla also gives birth, to Tuval-Cain, 'forger of every sharp implement in brass and iron...' and to a girl Na'ama, who is named but not described. (The Midrash identifies her as Noah's wife.) So far, the genealogy is clear, but what follows is a strange, cryptic monologue:

> And Lemekh said unto his wives: 'Adah and Tzilla – hear my voice; wives of Lemekh – hearken unto my speech; for I have slain a man by wounding [him] and a child by bruising [him]; If Cain shall be avenged sevenfold [or, "in the seventh generation"] then Lemekh seventy and sevenfold [or, "in the seventy-seventh generation"].'
>
> Gen. 4:23–24

What exactly is Lemekh talking about, and what is the context of his declaration? Why is the verse speaking of Tuval-Cain forging brass and iron next to the verse about Lemekh's murders?

This question also bothered Rashi and he provided some answers. According to a midrash he cites, Lemekh was blind, and he would go out hunting with his son Tuval-Cain. On one occasion, upon hearing noise behind a bush which they assumed to be a wild animal, Tuval-Cain told his father to release the bow. Afterwards they discovered – to their horror – that the 'animal' was none other than their ancestor Cain. In anguish, the blind Lemekh chafed his two hands together, squashed his young son's head between his powerful palms and killed him. Lemekh's wives were understandably distraught, and refused to have intimate relations with their husband. Rashi comments:

He endeavored to appease them. 'Hear my voice' – that is, obey me and return to me; for the man Cain I slew – was he slain by my wounding? Did I then kill him or the young lad by premeditation?... And if Cain was punished for the premeditated murder of Abel only in the seventh generation, I will certainly be reprieved until the seventy-seventh generation!'

Rashi on Gen. 4:23–24

Conveniently, Rashi closes a circle. Abel's murder is finally avenged with Cain's death – albeit seven generations later. But Rashi's interpretation does not provide any reasoning for the explicit inclusion of the professions of Lemekh's sons in the verses immediately prior to his confession. Nahmanides illuminates:

> ... Lemekh was a very wise man in every craft. He taught his eldest son Yaval the business of pasturing according to the nature of the cattle, and his second son Yuval the art of music. He taught the third one (Tuval-Cain) to forge metals and make swords, spears, javelins and all instruments of war. His wives were then afraid that he might be punished because he brought the sword and murder into the world, thus continuing the evil deed of his ancestor [Cain].
>
> Nahmanides on Gen. 4:24

This observation brings us back to the opening questions of this chapter. Throughout the book of Genesis, fierce sibling rivalry emanates from the tension between civilization and culture, science and humanity, technology and ethics. Abel was a shepherd, sensitively watching over his flock with much time for study, prayer and contemplation. Cain was a tiller of the fields, the father of agricultural technology and deeply connected to the earth. Perhaps it was the tension between these two contrasting lifestyles and philosophies that brought about humanity's first murder. As the generations progressed, the aggressive and wily hunter Esau is contrasted with the more studious and naive shepherd tent-dweller Jacob. Joseph, the dreamer and master of Egyptian farming techniques is contrasted with Judah, the traditional Israelite shepherd.

Joseph proves himself to be a master of Egyptian civilization, adept at politics and economics, whereas Judah – at least according to our Sages – founds the first Torah academy in Goshen.

*　*　*

In returning to Lemekh's sons, we find Yaval the shepherd tent-dweller (shades of Jacob) and Yuval the musician representing culture *par excellence*, while in stark contrast stands Tuval-Cain, 'the forger of every sharp implement in brass and iron.' Brass and iron can be used to make tools for the trade of agriculture or weaponry for destructive warfare; in either case, Tuval-Cain represents civilization rather than culture, technology rather than ethics. Rashi suggests that the Hebrew 'Tuval' comes from 'tavlin', meaning 'spice'. Just as spices refine and improve the taste of food, Tuval-Cain – our spiced-up Cain – 'refined and improved the works of Cain by providing weapons for murderers.' Now we understand that the wives of Lemekh refused to consort with him because he had brought weapons of destruction into the world. His response that he did not strike a premeditated blow, but rather used the available technology, can easily be transposed to the more modern arguments of Oppenheimer and Einstein: yes, atomic energy may very well be used to produce bombs of mass destruction, but it can also serve to cure cancer! Ultimately, it was atomic weaponry that enabled the free world to triumph over the Nazi threat!

Interestingly, the names Yaval and Yuval resonate with a noble concept derived from the same root: *yovel*, the fiftieth Jubilee year that offers freedom from slavery, a remission of debts, and a return to one's ancestral lands – in short, the 'yovel' offers redemption. However, the Jubilee can only announce freedom, peace and redemption when we learn to emphasize the spiritual values of Yaval and Yuval over the material values of Tuval-Cain. It's clear that the Torah does not want to eliminate one set of values; rather the challenge for the brothers is to live and work together in order to complement, rather than kill each other. It is only when those who represent Tuval-Cain understand that their technology must be refined and ennobled by architects of the spirit that humanity will be free to soar upwards.

Noaḥ

Outreach or Inreach, Family vs. World

> *Noah was a righteous man, whole-hearted in his generations; Noah walked with God.*
>
> GENESIS 6:9

Was Noah truly righteous? And what does true righteousness entail? At first blush, this shouldn't even be a question. Surely, the opening verse of the portion suggests that it's an open and shut case. After all, does any other figure in the Torah receive three adulatory statements in one verse, or even come close to such seemingly boundless praise? Not even Moses is called a *tzadik* (righteous man).

Before the testimonials for Noah are approved and sealed, Rashi reminds us that although certain Sages look upon Noah favorably, others were meager with their praise. The text states, 'righteous ... wholehearted in his generations.' The Talmud (*Sanhedrin* 108a) suggests that there are two ways to interpret this qualifying phrase: on the one hand, if he is so worthy of praise in a generation so completely evil, how much more praiseworthy would he have been in the generation of Abraham when he would have had righteous company. On the other hand, perhaps the qualifying phrase suggests that Noah is only praiseworthy in comparison with his generation of scoundrels. Had he lived in the generation of Abraham, he would not even be worthy of mention.

But the question remains: Why even suggest the possibility that Noah is second-rate when the plain meaning of the text is so adulatory? Let us compare and contrast Noah and Abraham in similar circumstances. When Abraham is told that the wicked cities of Sodom and Gomorrah are about to be destroyed, he argues with the Almighty as though he were bargaining in the marketplace of Jerusalem's Mahane Yehudah:

> Will the Almighty destroy the righteous with the wicked, will not the Judge of the entire earth do justice? If there are fifty righteous men, forty righteous men…even ten righteous men, will the cities not be saved?
>
> Gen. 18:24–33

In stark contrast, when Noah is informed of the impending destruction of the world, he obediently goes about constructing a private ark to rescue himself, his family, and a requisite number of earthly creatures. While Abraham emerges as the missionary who breaks walls as well as idols, as one who opens doors to his tent in every direction to welcome and influence as many people as possible, Noah would rather cut himself off from all adverse influences in order to erect an enclosure to protect his high-level communication with his God.

Whether one identifies with the Abraham camp or the Noah camp reflects one's outlook on Judaism and its relationship to the modern world. Hassidism, which began as a distinctive Jewish outreach movement, usually sided with Abraham in its biblical interpretations. Rabbi Jacob Joseph of Polnoy, the famous disciple of the Ba'al Shem Tov in the eighteenth century, writes in his *Toledot Yakov Yosef* that when the Torah describes Noah as 'walking with God,' it is a pejorative description. Noah walked only and exclusively with God, tragically neglecting the wayward individuals all around him. Noah missed the opportunity of bringing God to humanity.

On the other hand, the Ketav Sofer, probably reacting to the Jewish Enlightenment (*Haskala*) and the Reform movement which threatened the Orthodox community during his lifetime (Pressburg, Hungary, late eighteenth and early nineteenth century), utilizes his biblical commentary to justify turning inwards. He argues that Noah was absolutely correct in maintaining the wall between himself and the world. After all, Noah had good reason to fear that if he went outside to battle the prevailing winds, his own children might be tossed to the edges – and even cast beyond the pale – by their strong impact. The risk just wasn't worth it.

Interestingly, the Ketav Sofer was projecting the view of his father, the Hatam Sofer (1762–1839), one of the major leaders of Ashkenazi Jewry who vehemently fought against the breaches into traditional Judaism during his lifetime. He insisted that *hadash** is forbidden by the Torah. The Ketav Sofer argued that the behavior of the prophet Samuel's wayward children [I Sam. 7:15–8:3] was a direct consequence of the fact that their father preached all over Israel and returned home for only one visit each year (*tekufat ha-shana*). If you go out to save the world, you might lose your own children!

Clearly, there is no singular view in the biblical and rabbinic sources. However, it is the outgoing Abraham, and not the in-reaching Noah, who is declared the first Jew. We are unequivocally commanded to teach our fellow co-religionists who are straying from the path [Lev. 19:17]. Maimonides goes so far as to define the commandment to love God as directing us to ensure that God is beloved and known throughout the world, and insists that God instructed Moses to teach Israel the 613 commandments and the rest of the world the seven laws of morality [Laws of Kings 8:10]. Further, our prophets instruct us to be a 'light unto the nations,' the Torah defines our mission as a kingdom of priest-teachers, and the *Aleinu* prayer sets forth the vision of perfecting the world under the kingdom of ethical monotheism.

Faced with the contemporary challenges of assimilation and alienation of many Jews from traditional Judaism, can one mediate a balanced position between the Abrahams and the Noahs, between the advocates of in-reach and practitioners of out-reach?

---

* Anything new – a play on the biblical-halakhic term for wheat harvested before the sixteenth day of Nissan.

I believe that the correct balance is suggested by Rabbi Yitzhak Arama in his commentary *Akedat Yitzhak*, in his remarks on the mishna in the *Ethics of our Fathers*:

> Raban Shimon ben Gamliel says: 'The world endures on three things: justice, truth and peace....'
>
> *Avot* 1:18

Justice, he explains, is the relationship between the Jew and his society, our obligation to the world at large. Peace, on the other hand, is *shalom bayit*, the relationship between the Jew and his home, our obligation to family. And truth is the balanced combination of both.

As a source for his interpretation, R. Arama turns to the lesson taught by Jethro, the Midianite priest, to Moses, his son-in-law. Jethro is considered an important biblical hero because the advice he gave Moses radically reformed the entire judicial structure in the desert. (Consequently, the biblical portion containing the Decalogue bears his name.) And Moses listened to Jethro:

> And Moses chose able men out of all Israel, and made them heads over the people, rulers of thousands, rulers of hundreds, rulers of fifties, and rulers of tens.
>
> Ex. 18:25

But is this all that Jethro taught Moses? If we look at the opening of the encounter between Jethro and Moses, we find another, more subtle, layer of purpose behind Jethro's confrontation:

> Jethro, Moses' father-in-law, took Tziporah, Moses' wife, after he [Moses] had sent her away, and her two sons... And Jethro, Moses' father-in-law, came with [Moses] sons and with his wife unto Moses ... and he said unto Moses, 'I thy father-in-law Jethro am coming unto you, and here are your wife, and her two sons with her...'
>
> Ex. 18:1–6

The repetition of the word *hoten* (father-in-law), and the continuous mentioning of Moses' wife and his two sons, are there for a purpose. When he went on his mission to Pharaoh, Moses had apparently left his family behind. In effect, Moses gave up his family in order to minister to the Jewish nation. And, according to *Akedat Yitzhak*, Jethro is teaching Moses that he has acted incorrectly; he must first discharge his obligation to his family, and only then does he have the right to dedicate himself to his nation and the problems of the society at large.

This idea may very well be the key to balancing the tension between Noah's tight ship and Abraham's open tent. The first responsibility a person must have is to his own family. But he cannot rest on his laurels, on his own Garden of Eden in the suburbs of New York (or Jerusalem for that matter). The time must arrive in every Jew's life when he must turn the closed ship into an open tent, the Noahide perspective into an Abrahamic ideal. And when one attempts to do both simultaneously, it is crucially important that one's own family does not get left behind.

Words Make Worlds: Outreach or Inreach (continued)

> *These are the generations of Noah...*
>
> GENESIS 6:9

The story of Noah is framed by two major disasters. The *parasha* starts with notice of the impending Flood that will destroy the world's population, except for those saved in Noah's ark. It ends with the building of the Tower of Babel, an act that destroys the world's single language. Although the link between these two destructions may not be obvious at first, I think that if we examine Noah's ark on a symbolic level, we can establish the intimate connection between these two milestones of human history.

God commands Noah to build an ark (*tevah*), yet the *Zohar* points out that the Hebrew word *tevah* is primarily to be translated as 'word'. Consider the verse, 'And the earth was corrupt before God, and the earth was filled with violence' [Gen. 6:11]. Very often acts of violence are preceded by words of violence. The methods of the silent sniper –

those distant, aloof characters poised on top of high towers – are the exception and not the norm. Incarceration for violence – even between husband and wife – can be traced back to verbal insults and verbal abuse. Had the violent language been nipped in the bud, everything may have been different. Therefore, it might be reasonable to assume that if we change our vocabulary and treat language with respect, then we will have a far greater chance of creating a peaceful world around us. This helps us to appreciate how the biblical usage of the term *'tevah'* for 'ark-word' offers another perspective on protecting ourselves from violence.

In a world where even the animals had violated their innate natures by cohabiting with other species, Noah escapes into an 'ark-word' where God's directions prevail. Noah's Word is a very select place where pure animals are taken in groups of seven males with seven females and impure animals can only arrive in pairs. According to the Talmud [*Pesahim* 3a], the Torah doesn't refer to the latter as *'tamei'* (impure), but rather describes them as *'einena tehora'* (not pure) [Gen. 7:8], in order to impress upon the reader the importance of purity of speech.

The Ba'al Shem Tov, the founder of Hassidism, complements the literary theme of Noah's Word by examining its measurements: it was 300 cubits long, 50 cubits wide and 30 cubits high [Gen. 6:15]. He demonstrates how the actual physical dimensions of the ark reflect the essence of language as the letters representing the numeric value of each of these dimensions are *shin* (300), *nun* (50), *lamed* (30), which spells the word *l-sh-n* (or *lashon*), meaning 'language.'

Taking this symbolism one step further, we can connect the beginning and ending of Noah. When Aristotle called the human being a 'social animal' he was echoing an idea introduced by Targum Onkelos, who translated the final two words of 'Then the Lord God formed the human of the dust of the ground, and breathed into his nostrils the breath of life and he/she became a living soul (*nefesh haya*)' [Gen. 2:7] as *'ruah memalelah'* – a speaking spirit. The term 'social animal' reminds us that if not for the ability of speech, the human being would be an animal on two legs. The ability to communicate, to socialize and to share language with other creatures, defines our humanity. If we were to be deprived of language or the ability to communicate, we would be reduced to the level of animals.

This explains why solitary confinement is such a powerful instrument of torture. One of the great strengths of Natan Sharansky was his ability to survive, and even thrive, through the long years of solitary confinement imposed upon him by the Soviet prison system. Gifted with a power to concentrate, he was able to create an inner world through books, chess games, inner dialogues, and his tiny book of Psalms. His body may have been in solitary confinement, but his inner world of words and ideas allowed him to maintain his dignity as a human being. In a sense, Sharansky is a modern-day Noah, the survivor of the Deluge that ultimately brought Soviet Russia to its knees.

Toward the end of *Parashat Noah*, we confront another aspect of language where '...the whole earth was of one language and of one speech' [Gen. 11:1] resulting in the building of the Tower of Babel. The Midrash tells us that in their zeal to build the tower, if a brick would fall from the top of the tower, everyone would mourn, but if a human being would fall, the event would pass unnoticed. Their unity was deceptive for it didn't enable human communication and didn't allow for individual opinions or individual personalities. The process of building the Tower of Babel left no room for the diversity of ideology or discrepancy of thought. A word (*tevah*) requires at least two letters or two separate characters communing together; the 'single language' of the Tower of Babel precluded discussion or communication between two respected people with differing but respected views who were sharing their individualized uniqueness with each other – the real purpose of communication.

And so God punished them 'measure for measure' with multiple languages where they really could not understand each other or conduct even the most minimal conversation. They were destroyed by the very words that they had used – not as a means of sensitive communication but rather as an instrument of materialistic violence.

So far, we have only considered how Noah's *tevah*-ark-word was a positive development. However, some commentators feel that Noah and his *tevah* were incomplete expressions of true religiosity. After all, the *tevah* only saved Noah and his family. The goal should be to produce not only a *tevah*-word, but rather a Torah-book, in order to save all of humanity! Noah only understood the importance of God's word to save himself and his family from violence and corruption. He did not see beyond his own immediate responsibilities.

The *Zohar* goes on to maintain that Moses was a repair (*tikkun*), a necessary and therapeutic improvement, upon Noah. There are at least two interesting similarities between these two personalities: while Noah saves himself in the *tevah*, Moses is also saved by the *tevah* (an ark of bulrushes made by his mother and sister) that floats down the Nile; while Moses lived to be 120 years old, Noah, according to the Midrash, spent 120 years building his *tevah*, enduring sarcastic remarks from cynical onlookers. But there is one major difference between the two: when God declares His plan to destroy the world and to save only Noah, Noah silently acquiesces to God's plan and constructs the *tevah*. But after the Israelites worship the golden calf, and the Almighty is ready to destroy the nation and start anew with Moses alone, the prophet of Egypt cries out: 'Erase me from your book … [but save the nation]!' [Ex. 32:32]. The letters of the word 'erase me' (*mem, het, nun, yud*), the *Zohar* tells us, can be rearranged to spell out 'the waters of Noah' (*mei Noah*). In effect, Moses is telling God that he is not like Noah. He cannot countenance his safe journey when humanity is drowning. 'Destroy me, please' said Moses 'but save the people!'

Noah constructs a *tevah* – a word; Moses transmits a Torah – a book. It is a book which spells out the name of God, a book which will ultimately bring peace and redemption – sensitive communication and concord – to the entire human civilization. Moses is a *tikkun* for Noah; and the *Sefer* (book of) Torah is a *tikkun* for the *tevah* (word). As the prophets declare, our ultimate vision is for the Book of Torah to emanate from Jerusalem, teaching that 'nation shall not lift sword against nation and humanity shall not learn war anymore' [Is. 2:4].

Vegetarians and the Bible

> *Every creeping thing that lives shall be for you as food like the vegetation of the herbs have I given you everything.*
>
> GENESIS 9:3

What is the Jewish attitude toward vegetarianism? Despite the penchant for meat meals on Sabbaths and festivals, could it possibly be spiritually preferable for us to be eating rice and beans, cauliflower and carrots?

With the creation of Adam, the Almighty enjoins humanity as well as animals to eat only fruits and vegetables. It is only after the flood and the rescue of Noah that God, after blessing him to be fruitful, multiply and replenish the earth, declares that from now on, he is permitted to eat every creeping thing that lives.

I would argue that this permission is actually a concession. It comes in the wake of God's realization 'that the formation (*yetzer*) of the heart of the human being is evil from his youth,' God's inescapable conclusion as a result of the perversion and violence that were rampant prior to the flood.*

This concession to Noah is immediately followed by the command not to eat the limb or drink the blood of a living animal, not to commit suicide and not take human life. In effect, God recognizes that since the urge and ability to destroy has proven itself to be such a basic element of the human personality, let it be expressed in the taking of animal life and not in the destruction of humans.

When viewed from this perspective, our laws of kashrut serve as a limitation to our meat consumption and as a reminder of the basic moral ambiguity involved in eating meat altogether. Many animals, fowl, and fish are completely forbidden, and those that are permitted must be slaughtered in a particular and far more spiritual and humane fashion than the manner in which animals are generally killed throughout the world.

Indeed, the laws of kashrut as expressed within the Bible are certainly related to heightening our sensitivity toward the animal world. It is mostly the carnivorous animals and the birds of prey which are forbidden. Moreover, blood consumption is forbidden. Even the permissible meat must be salted and soaked in order to remove as much blood as possible, for 'blood is life.' Finally meat and milk cannot be eaten together, with the Polish Ashkenazi custom enjoining as much as a six-hour wait between eating meat (even fowl) and dairy, since 'thou shalt not boil a kid in its mother's milk' [Ex. 34:26] is apparently a plea for compassion and sensitivity extending to the animal world.

The first chief rabbi of Israel, Rabbi Abraham Isaac Hakohen Kook, even sees the Torah as issuing a hidden rebuke to the meat eater. He first explains (in accordance with the interpretation of Nahmanides) that when the Jews were still in the desert, and the Sanctuary (site of the sacrifices) was literally in the midst of the people, the only meat allowed to be eaten was the meat of the sacrifices. Obviously this limited meat intake. It was only after they left the desert, with many Israelites

---

* Rabbi Joseph B. Soloveitchik would often say that the Torah not only records the human understanding of the divine, but it also documents God's understanding of and even disappointment with human weakness and corruption.

living far from the Sanctuary, that they would be allowed to eat non-sacrificial meat, but then only in accordance with the limitation of the laws of kashrut.*

Rabbi Kook further explains that within the very words of the Bible lies a hidden admonition:

> When the Lord your God will expand your borders...and you shall say 'I will eat meat' because your soul lusts to eat meat...

It is only because of the 'lust' for meat – not a very complimentary description – that God allowed the Israelites to eat meat. Ultimately, Rabbi Kook argues, in the future period of the Third Temple, we shall return to the original vegetarian ideal and then the only Temple sacrifice will be the vegetarian grain *minha* offering.

In explaining animal sacrifices in general, Rabbi Kook maintains that the animal world receives its *tikkun* (perfection) by being brought to God's altar since, being devoid of reason, the animals cannot be uplifted except through an act done to them. In the future, however, when 'knowledge of the Lord will fill the world as the waters cover the seas' [Is. 11:9), an abundance of knowledge will spread and extend even to animal life. And since our prophets teach us that during the messianic age there will be 'no evil or destruction in all of My holy mountain' [Ibid.], it is inconceivable that animal life will be destroyed to serve the divine. At that time, God will 'find the meal offering and vegetable offerings of Judah and Jerusalem sweet' [Malakhi 3:34].

A similar notion is to be found in the writings of Rabbi Haim David Halevi. He maintains – and cites Rabbi Kook as his proof text – that it will only be the first stage of the messianic era that will include animal sacrifices in the Third Temple, since in the first messianic stage the world will be operating as it is now, including sinfulness and the need to atone; however, once the messianic era reaches its spiritual climax of universal repentance, then animal sacrifices will be a mere memory of

---

* Cf. Rabbi Kook's commentary on the sacrificial prayers of each morning, in *Olat Re'iyah* (Jerusalem 1985).

an earlier and more primitive period. After all, he writes, if there is no sin, what need will there be of animal sacrifice for atonement?

Rabbi Halevi concludes that in the Third Temple period the divine Presence will be revealed in all of its splendor and glory, and there will be no sacrifices other than the non-animal *minha* offering comprised of meal and oil.

There is a beautiful custom to cover the challah knife while reciting the Grace after Meals in order to highlight our revulsion for an implement that could be used to kill and destroy. May the time soon arrive when our swords will turn into ploughshares and our spears into pruning forks, when there will be no evil or destruction throughout the world, and the only use of knives will be for slicing the challah to be eaten with milk and honey – not meat – in honor of Sabbath and festivals.

Two Agnostics, but Only One is Righteous

And Haran died before his father, in the land of his birth, in Ur Kasdim.

GENESIS 11:28

What is so significant about Haran, the brother of Abraham, that the Bible must provide a specific detail about his untimely death? And if it is important in order to give us the background of Abram's adoption of his orphaned nephew Lot, why must we be informed as to the precise place that Haran died, in Ur Kasdim? The Midrash fills in the missing information, and expands on Haran's life as well as providing the reason for his premature death. Our sages also contrast the personality of Haran with that of Noah. It is precisely this analysis which provides us with an important response to the agnostic.

When it comes to questions of belief, the agnostic is the loneliest of all. On one side of the fence stands the atheist, confident in his rejection of God and often dedicated to the debunking of religion, which he considers to be 'the opiate of the masses'. On the other side stands the believer, who glories in his faith that the universe is the handiwork of

God. The agnostic stands in the middle, not knowing (*a-gnost*) whether or not God exists, usually despairing of the possibility of acquiring certitude about anything transcending observable material phenomena.

Noah is described as being righteous 'in his generation' [Gen. 11:28]. As previously discussed, some Talmudic rabbis see the qualification as great praise, while others find it to be somewhat of a slur: only in his generation could Noah be considered perfect; had he been born in the age of Abraham, he would not have been considered as worthy [*Sanhedrin* 109a; Rashi ad loc.].

Rashi seems to base the negative view toward Noah on a subsequent verse. Noah, along with his sons, his wife, and sons' wives, went into the ark 'because of the waters of the flood.' Rashi draws from this verse that 'Noah had little faith; he believed and he didn't believe that the flood would arrive.' He didn't enter the ark until the water literally pushed him in. The flood had to start before Noah actually made his move into the ark.

Rashi's phrase, 'he believed and he didn't believe,' is really another way of describing an agnostic who remains in the state of his uncertainty; he believes and doesn't believe.

Noah is therefore described by Rashi as the first agnostic, and herein lies his fatal flaw in comparison to Abraham, the founder of ethical monotheism. The second biblical agnostic appears in the guise of Haran – 'These are the generations of Terah. Terah begat Abram, Nahor, and Haran' – at least as he is understood by the Midrash.

Lot, the son of Haran, is a significant figure in the Bible in his own right, and is brought up by Haran's brother, Abraham, when Haran dies. Why does the text specify, 'and Haran died before his father in the land of his birth, in Ur Kasdim'? What is the importance of citing the exact place of Haran's death?

Rashi explains by citing a fascinating midrashic tradition, and at the same time extracts Haran from relative anonymity and sets him up as a counterfoil agnostic to Noah. This particular midrash details how Terah, the father of the clan and a famous idol manufacturer, brings charges in the court of King Nimrod against his own son. He accuses Abram of being an iconoclast who destroyed his father's idols while preaching heretical monotheism. As punishment, Abram is to be cast into the fiery furnace. Haran is present at the trial and takes the position of having no position. He remains on the sidelines thinking that if Nimrod's furnace will prove hotter than Abram's flesh, he will side with the king; but if Abram survives the fire, then it would be clear that Abram's God is more powerful than Nimrod's gods, and he will throw in his lot with his brother.

Only after Abram emerges unscathed, is Haran ready to rally behind his brother. He confidently enters the fiery furnace (literally: *Ur Kasdim*), but no miracles await Haran. Haran burns to death.

Is it not strange that the fate of the two agnostics should be so different? We read how Noah was a man of little faith, and yet not only does he survive the Flood, but he turns into one of the central figures of human history. He is even termed righteous in the Bible. In contrast, Haran, father of Lot, brother to Abraham, hovers on the edge of obscurity, and is even punished with death for his lack of faith.

Why is Haran's agnosticism considered so much worse than Noah's?

Rabbi Moshe Besdin once explained that while Noah and Haran shared uncertainty about God, there is a vast difference between them. Noah, despite his doubts, did nevertheless build the ark, pounding away for 120 years, even suffering abuse from a world ridiculing his eccentric persistence. Noah may not have entered the ark until the rains began – but he did not wait for the Flood before obeying the divine command to build an ark! Noah may think like an agnostic, but he acts like a believer. Haran, on the other hand, dies because he waits for someone else to test the fires. In refusing to act for God during Abram's trial, he acted against God. In effect, his indecision is very much a decision. He is an agnostic who acts like an atheist.

We must understand that indecision is also a decision. A person who is indecisive about marrying a certain potential partner ultimately takes a negative decision by not 'popping the question'; an individual who is indecisive about protesting an evil action or a malicious statement is aiding and abetting the malevolence by his very indecisive silence. After all, our sages teach that 'silence is akin to assent' (*sh'tika k'hoda'a damya*).

Noah reached his spiritual level because he acted, not so much out of faith, but despite his lack of it. Our Sages understood very well the difficulty of faith and the phenomenon of agnosticism. What they attempt to teach the agnostic is: If you are unsure, why do you act as if you are an atheist? Would it not be wiser to act as if you were a believer?

We learn from Noah's life and Haran's death that perfect faith is not necessary in order to conduct one's life like a Jew. Belief is never as important as action. In the heaven of the Jews, there is room for all kinds of agnostics. It depends primarily on how they acted on earth.

Israel and the Nations

> *The entire earth had one language and uniform words.*
>
> GENESIS 11:1

The Torah commences with the majestic pronouncement, 'In the beginning God created the heavens and the earth.' By doing so, our Bible wishes to explain at the outset that the God of Israel is the Lord of the entire universe, and that His ultimate concern is for the well-being and eventual perfection of all of its creatures. Indeed, Rabbi Joseph B. Soloveitchik often commented that the Almighty attempted to give His divine charge to all of humanity, first to Adam with the command to refrain from eating the fruit of the Tree of Knowledge, and then to Noah – the second Adam, after the flood – with the fundamental laws against bloodshed and immorality.

Unfortunately, both Adam and Noah proved disappointing – and it was not until the advent of the remarkable Abraham twenty generations after the Creation that God entered into a covenant with an individual and his descendants, the nation of Israel. Even then, however, the

Almighty did not give up on the universal vision of human perfection. At the very beginning of his election, God presents His mission to Abraham: 'All the families of the earth shall be blessed through you' [Gen. 12:3].

Indeed, these earlier biblical portions dealing with 'every-men' Adam and Noah foreshadow key events in the life of Abraham, emphasizing the parallelism between these three divinely chosen leaders, as pointed out by Rabbi Professor Mordecai Breuer in his commentary *Pirkei Breishit*.* Adam and Noah each have three sons from whom humanity emerges, just as the nation Israel develops from three patriarchs, Abraham, Isaac and Jacob. There were seventy Noahide heads-of-families from whom the world emerged after the flood, paralleling the seventy Jacobite souls who went down to Egypt from whom the nation of Israel emerged. And the fundamental blessings bestowed by God upon Adam, Noah and each of the patriarchs all feature fruitfulness and filling the land, albeit the entire land in the case of Adam and Noah, and the land of Israel in the case of the patriarchs. Israel serves as a microcosm for the world, having been chosen by God as the instrument through which the message of ethical monotheism will ultimately be accepted by the world. Israel and the world share interlocking destinies.

This parallelism between Israel and the world finds a remarkable literary allusion in the story of the Tower of Babel. Noah has died and Abraham has not yet been born; the extent to which humanity will succeed in redeeming itself from the devastation of the Flood brought about by human violence has not yet been determined. Indeed, humanity seems to be progressing. 'The entire earth had one language and uniform words' ('*Safah AHAT, devarim AHADim*') resonates with our prophetic vision which anticipates a time when 'The Lord will be King over the entire earth, and on that day the Lord will be one and His Name will be one' [Zach. 14:9]. The one fear of this united humanity, gathered together in the valley of Shinar (Sumer, identified with ancient Babylon), was that their unity would be torn asunder, that they would be exiled into different places, scattered throughout the world. In order to prevent this, 'they said, "Come, let us build ourselves a city and a tower,

* Cf. M. Breuer, *Pirkei Breishit* (Alon Shevut 1998), Vol. I.

whose tops shall reach the heavens'". This is certainly reminiscent of our Jewish dream of the holy city Jerusalem with its 'tower' (i.e., Sanctuary) reaching up to the heavens in order to ensure Israel's eternity and express Israel's mission', It even brings to mind Jacob's dream at Bet-El (lit. 'House of God'), where he saw a ladder rooted on earth but whose top reached heavenwards.

However, one major flaw in Shinar turns the entire Tower of Babel into a transgression of hubris: their purpose in construction was to 'make for *ourselves* a name,' rather than to build for the Name of God and for the sake of a just and compassionate humanity. The Midrash expresses Babel's materialistic callousness with the frightening description:

> If a stone fell to the ground and shattered, everyone groaned; if a human being fell to the ground and died, no one took notice.

Hence, the Almighty decides to 'confuse their speech, so that one person will not understand (*shma*) the language of the other.' Such a punishment perfectly fits the crime; after all, a totalitarian state united in order to establish a collective name has neither the energy nor the motivation to empathetically hear or sensitively internalize the individual needs of anyone else. God merely made the ethos which Babel created more externally obvious. And such an inhuman and godless society must be stopped in its tracks before it does even greater damage. Hence, 'from this place, God scattered them over the face of the entire earth and they stopped building the city.' This is strongly reminiscent of the punishment in store for an errant Israel, forsaking God and humanity by their great sin of causeless hatred, which led the Almighty to destroy our Holy Temple, take away our national sovereignty in the city of Jerusalem and scatter us throughout the world. 'And the Lord will scatter you among all the nations, from one end of the earth to the other.' The parallelism between the world and Israel is painfully clear.

However, unlike the peoples of the Tower of Babel, the Israelites will remain united as one nation with one sacred language and universal ideal despite their far-flung Diaspora; indeed, from the midst of their exile, and within each of their diverse host nations, they shall return to God and his ethical teachings:

> You shall seek from there the Lord your God and you shall find Him. Even if you are scattered from the ends of the heavens, from there will the Lord your God gather you and from there will He take you up. And He will bring you to the land which your fathers have inherited, and you shall inherit it.
>
> Deut. 4:29; 30:4,5

And, much more to the point, the Israelites will right the wrong of the Tower of Babel. When we return to Israel at the end of the day and rebuild our 'tower' (i.e., Sanctuary), it will be for the sake of God and not for the sake of materialistic self aggrandizement. It will serve as a meeting place for all nations in humanistic unity and not totalitarian uniformity,

> ... when nation will not lift up sword against nation and humanity will not learn war anymore, and when all the nations will walk, each in the name of his god, and we will walk in the name of the Lord our God forever.
>
> Micah 4:3, 5

Indeed, the unity of speech will be for the sake of a more sensitive and caring humanity:

> The remnant of Israel will not act callously, and the language of deception will not be found in their mouths. For then I will change the nations towards speech of purity for everyone to call on the name of God and to serve him shoulder to shoulder.
>
> Zephania 3:13

The Flood and the Tower of Babel

> *Let us build ourselves a city and a tower whose*
> *top shall reach the heavens…*
>
> GENESIS 11:1

Parashat Noaḥ opens with the flood and symmetrically concludes with the Tower of Babel* – two world disasters which bear striking resemblance to the major catastrophes which have blighted our civilization throughout the twentieth century and keep haunting us today. After the advent of Adam, the first human being, 'who was created in the image of God,' there were ten generations until the birth of Noah.

During this period we are told that:

> the multitudes of humanity acted in a secular and profane manner ['*he'hel*' from *hullin*]…and the sons of the powerful men [or of the demigods] seized whichever women they chose…. The giants

---

* The Hebrew word for flood is *mabul*, while the Tower of Babel is a translation of *Migdal Babel* – two Hebrew words which may be contracted into *MaBel*.

[*nefilim*] roamed the earth at that time, and God saw that the evil of humanity was great on earth, and that the creation of the thoughts of their hearts was only evil all day. And God regretted that he had made the human being on earth … and God said, 'I shall wipe out the humans I have created from off the face of the earth…'

Gen. 6:2–7

And a few verses into the opening portion of *Noaḥ*, the text continues along the same theme: 'And the earth was corrupt before God, and the earth was filled with violence [*hamas*].'

The picture which emerges is that of godlessness ('corrupt before God') which leads to lawlessness ('violence'), and anarchy which breeds giants, children of 'the lords' or the 'demi-gods,' who seize whatever goods or good-looking people they wish, a situation of 'whoever is more powerful, triumphs' (*Kol d'alim gevar*), a society of 'might makes right.' The giants and demi-gods are reminiscent of the Aryan Ubermenschen, the Nazi 'supermen' who believed it was their right to rule the world. The ancient society evoked by the biblical text is remarkably similar to the society of Nazi Germany which – as a fascist, totalitarian state – enslaved and murdered those non-Aryans they considered inferior, especially the Jews. Fortunately, Nazi Fascism was swept away by the *mabul* – i.e., the flood of World War II.

The Torah portion of *Bereshit* concludes, 'And Noah found favor in the eyes of the Lord.' The hope appears to be that Noah will establish a new post-flood society. Tragically, however, the following ten generations are characterized by a further degeneration, descending to its nadir with the Tower of Babel – but this time a different form of depravity than we have seen previously.

'And the entire earth was of one language and of one word' – with the Midrash Raba explaining the Hebrew phrase '*d'varim a'ḥadim*' to mean 'they spoke sharp words'* [*Gen. Raba* 38:6]. They insisted upon one language and one system of worship; whoever differed even to the slightest extent would be dealt with sharply, even killed!

I would submit that such a totalitarian uniformity is in direct

---

* The word *eḥad* means one, while the word *ḥad* means sharp.

contradiction to the biblical faith of Israel. The very watchword of faith, 'Hear O Israel, the Lord our God(s) the Lord is One' is a ringing declaration in favor of religious pluralism. YHWH is the unique, Jewish concept of One God, and *Elohim* is a plural noun standing for the sum total of all the different names by which the One God is called. The prophet Micah expresses his vision of the end of the days, when all the nations will rush to the Holy Temple 'to learn [from Jacob's] ways and walk [in Jacob's] paths … to beat their swords into ploughshares, their spears into pruning hooks, nation will not lift up sword against nation and humanity will not learn war anymore; all the nations will walk, each individual in the name of his god [*Elohav*], and we will walk in the name of the Lord our God forever' [Micah 4:1–5].

Micah is saying that while the Jewish mission is to teach ethical monotheism to the world – God as a God of justice, compassion and peace – it is not necessary for everyone to accept the 613 commands of the Torah. Such a commitment is for Israel alone. The other nations must only accept the seven Noahide laws of morality, the absolute prohibition against murder, sexual immorality, theft and the cruel and licentious activities associated with idolatry. Once they accept these fundamental ethical teachings, it does not matter by what name they call their god or which particular rituals they may choose to perform. As long as the gentile is moral, any name he refers to for God is a manifestation of the one true and absolute Lord of the Universe. 'Hear, O Israel, the Lord our God(s) the Lord is One.'

In contrast, the depraved generation of Babel speaks out against such an open-minded religious position:

> And they said, Let us build for ourselves a city and a tower with its top in the heavens, so that we can make for ourselves a name, lest we be scattered over the face of the entire earth.
>
> Gen. 11:4

The *Midrash Raba* teaches that these adherents of the temple ziggurat idolatrous religion insisted that everyone accept their gods:

> Who rules in the heavenly spheres is not up for individual choice.
>
> Gen. Raba 38:6

Their religious leadership insisted that only they who are down below can establish the only acceptable god, whose rule will extend from heaven to earth, and who will bestow his exclusive name upon the centralized totalitarian regime which will enforce not only unity but also uniformity of fanatical religious observance over world citizenry.

This is a striking parallel to Islamic fundamentalism, which has turned Allah into Satan and seeks to enforce the Moslem religion over the entire world through the sword of Jihad. The symbol of this philosophy is a ziggurat tower, a grandiose building; as the Midrash emphasizes, human life meant nothing, the bricks and mortars meant everything. These fanatics have no compunction about sending out their youth as suicidal homicide bombers targeting innocent women and children as long as it is for the greater glory of Allah-Satan.

In what appears to be a remarkable prophecy, the Torah commands – right between the flood and the tower, the scourge of fascist secularism and the threat of Islamic fundamentalism – the prohibition against murder: 'One who sheds human blood will have his blood shed by humans, since in the image of God did He make the human being' [Gen. 9:10]. And the sign (or criterion) by which God will preserve the world is the rainbow: seven magnificent and variegated colors which are all refractions of white, perhaps symbolizing the different names and rituals which are all expressions of the one Lord. This is the most fundamental teaching of Judaism:

> God created the human being as a single Adam to teach that he who destroys a single life destroys an entire world … and it is a testimony to the greatness of God that when a human king mints many coins from one model, all the coins are identical, whereas the Holy One Blessed be He minted many people from one Adam and not one of them is similar to his counterpart.
>
> Mishna *Sanhedrin* 4:13

Our Torah is the very antithesis of Islamic fundamentalism, preaching peace and unity rather than war and uniformity.

Lekh Lekha

Nationalism vs. Universalism:
The Struggle Within Abraham

> *... and in you, all the families of the earth shall be blessed.*
>
> GENESIS 12:3

Our biblical tradition seems to live in a paradox between the universal and the particular; our obligations to the world at large and our obligations to our own nation and family.

This tension is evident from the opening sentence of the Torah: 'In the beginning God created the heavens and the earth.' While it seems these words are a clear proclamation of universality, Rashi's opening comment turns the verse on its head. He argues that the fact that the Torah begins with Creation has nothing to do with a grand universal vision, but rather everything to do with establishing Jewish rights to the land of Israel. He cites a midrash that says since God created the world, He can parcel out specific areas to 'whomever is righteous in His eyes.'

This tension between the particular and the universal also

permeates the High Holy Day festival period. The universal dominates Rosh Hashanah when we crown God as the King of the entire universe, and Yom Kippur when we declare,

> ...for My house (the Holy Temple) shall be called a house of prayer for all people.
>
> Is. 56:7

Further, the seventy sacrifices offered over the course of the festival of Sukkot symbolize our commitment to the welfare of all seventy nations. But in stark contrast, Shemini Atzeret signifies a more intimate and particularistic rendezvous between God and Israel, when the Almighty sends all the other nations home, wishing to enjoy a celebration with Israel alone. Simhat Torah, the added celebration of our having completed the yearly reading of the Pentateuch during this festival, merely emphasizes the unique and separatist significance of this holiday.

The tension is apparent in God's dealings with Abraham. At first God instructs Abraham,

> Go out of your land, and from your kindred birthplace and your father's house, unto the land that I will show you.
>
> Gen. 12:1

There are no introductions or apologies. It's straight to the point: Abraham is to found a new family-nation in the specific location of the land of Israel. However, in the next verse, this ethnocentric fervor of going up to one's own land is somewhat muted by the more universalistic message of God's next mandate: '...And through you shall all families of the earth be blessed.'

From this moment onwards, both of these elements – a covenantal nation with a unique relationship to God and the universal vision of world peace and redemption – will vie for center stage in the soul of Abraham's descendants.

In the case of Abraham himself, it is the universalistic aspect of his spirit which seems the most dominant. He quickly emerges in the historic arena as a war hero who rescues the five regional nations – including Sodom – from the stranglehold of four terrorizing kings. Even after Abraham's nephew and adopted son, Lot, rejects Abraham's teachings, he still wants to continue his relationship with Lot, and even bargains with God to save the wicked cities of Sodom and Gomorrah. According to the Midrash, the ten righteous people for whom Abraham wishes to save these evil cities are none other than Lot and his family – even though Lot rejected Abraham (and presumably the Abrahamic way of life) for the greener and more permissive pastures of Sodom and Gomorrah. Abraham also initially opposed the banishment of Hagar and Ishmael – Hagar his Egyptian mistress whom Sarah gave her husband for the sake of enabling him to bear a child and who treated Sarah with derision, and Ishmael, who was the perennially mocking hedonist, interested only in immediate gratification (the *metzaḥek*) – apparently because this universalistic patriarch would have preferred a place for everyone under the Abrahamic umbrella.

The Midrash magnificently captures Abraham's concern with the world and world opinion in a trenchant elucidation of the opening verse in the portion of *Vayera*, where the Torah records the moment of God's appearance to Abraham after the patriarch's circumcision in the fields of the oak trees of Mamre. Why stress this particular location, including the owner of the parcel of trees, Mamre? The Midrash explains that when God commanded Abraham to circumcise himself, he went to seek the advice of his three allies – Aner, Eshkol, and Mamre.

> Now Aner said to him, 'You mean to say that you are one hundred years old and you want to maim yourself in such a way?' Eshkol said to him, 'How can you do this? You will be making yourself unique and identifiable, different from the other nations of the world.' Mamre, however, said to Abraham, 'How can you refuse to do what God asks you? After all, God saved all of your two hundred and forty-eight limbs when you were in the fiery furnace of Nimrod. If God asks you to sacrifice a small portion of only one of your limbs, how can you refuse?!' Because Mamre was the only person who gave him positive advice, God chose to appear to Abraham by the oaks of Mamre.
>
> *Gen. Raba* 42:14

What I believe is truly remarkable about this midrash is that it pictures Abraham as 'checking out' the advisability of circumcision with his three gentile friends and allies, in order to discover just how upset they would be by the introduction of this unique and nationalistic sign upon his flesh.

The tension between the universal and the particular poses a serious threat to Abraham's relationship with his wife, Sarah. It would seem that theirs is a union of love and genuine cooperation. After all, the very first time that the Bible mentions a husband choosing a wife is in the case of Abraham:

> And Abram and Nahor took for themselves wives; the name of the wife of Abram was Sarai...
>
> Gen. 11:29

Until that time, the women are generally anonymous, with all the 'begetting' seeming to take place because of the men alone [Gen. 5]! Hence when the Bible records:

> And Abram took his wife Sarai... and all their substance that they had gathered and the souls that they had gathered in Haran....
>
> Gen. 12:5

Rashi hastens to explain based on the Midrash, that to 'gather souls' meant that 'Abraham converted the men, and Sarah converted the women.' At least our Sages believed that they truly worked together as consecrated partners to accomplish the work of the Lord.

Indeed, Abraham is deeply committed to Sarah, and also seems to be aware of her higher gift of prophecy. When she, tragically barren after many years of marriage, suggests to her husband that he father a child with her maid-servant Hagar, the text records 'And Abraham hearkened to the voice of Sarah' [Gen. 15:2] – suggesting that Abraham's role in this matter was entirely subject to the will of Sarah. And if Sarah's suggestion seems rather jarring and out-of-wifely-character to the modern ear, it is important to note that this was precisely the method of adoption practiced by the ancient Near Eastern world. The secondary wife would literally give birth 'on the knees' of the primary wife, causing the baby to be adopted by the primary wife 'as if she had borne him.'

Moreover, Abraham assumes a purely passive role in the second marriage: 'And Sarai the wife of Abram took Hagar her Egyptian maidservant and she gave her to Abram her husband for a wife' [Gen. 16:3]. This description belies the usual biblical formula for marriage: 'When a man takes a woman....' Yet despite Abraham's total devotion to Sarah – all we have to do is consider the effort and expense he invests in the purchase of her permanent burial place in Hebron – they differ strongly in one area. Hagar may have been brought into the picture by Sarah, but when Sarah realizes that the behavior of Hagar's son Ishmael constitutes a serious threat to her family, she is not willing to compromise: Hagar and her son must be banished.

Since Abraham's vision wants to embrace all of humanity, how do we understand his willingness to cast his own flesh and blood to the desert? The Tosefta on Masekhet *Sotah*, commenting on the verse spoken by Sarah in *Lekh Lekha*: '...I was derided in her [Hagar's] eyes. Let God judge between me and you,' expands this theme and demonstrates how Abraham and Sarah held two very different world-views. The Sages in the Tosefta fill in the following dialogue between Sarah and Abraham:

> 'I see Ishmael building an altar, capturing grasshoppers, and sacrificing them to idols. If he teaches this idolatry to my son Isaac, the name of heaven will be desecrated,' says Sarah to Abraham.
>
> 'After I gave her [Hagar] such advantages, how can I demote her? Now that we have made her a mistress [of our house], how can we send her away? What will the other people say about us?,' replies Abraham.
>
> Tosefta *Sotah* 5:12

Sarah's position is crystal clear. She is more than willing to work together with Abraham to save the world – but not at the expense of her own son and family. She teaches us that our identity as a unique people must be forged and secure before we can engage in dialogue and redemption of the nations. God teaches Abraham that Sarah is right:

> Whatever Sarah says to you, listen to her voice, for through Isaac shall your seed be called.
>
> Gen. 21:12

Indeed, one of the tragedies of life is that we often fail to appreciate what we have until we lose it – or almost lose it. It may well be argued that the subsequent trial of the binding of Isaac comes in no small measure to teach Abraham to properly appreciate – and be truly committed to – his only son and heir Isaac, who, in the final analysis, will carry on his traditions and life's mission. And at the end of the day, nothing remained for Israel from 'all of those souls whom they [Abraham and Sarah] made in Haran.' The legacy of Abraham was carried on by one individual and he was Isaac!

Abraham – Path Breaker or Path Follower

> *Now the Lord said unto Abram, get out of your*
> *country, and from your kindred place, and from*
> *your fathers house, unto the land that I will show*
> *you. And I will make of you a great nation, and*
> *I will bless you, and make your name great; and*
> *you shall be a blessing.*
>
> GENESIS 12:1–2

In these words we have the first of Abraham's ten tests – the difficult divine demand that the first Jew leave hearth and home and follow God into a strange and unknown land. In return, there is the divine promise of ultimate national greatness and international leadership. But why does God single out Abraham?

At this fateful moment, the Torah seemingly takes Abraham's faith and religious quest for granted without providing a clue as to how, where and why this particular nomad is worthy of divine trust and blessing. In the closing verses of *Noaḥ*, we read about his genealogy, the names of his father, brother, nephew and spouse. We are provided with dry facts, travelogue locations on a map, ages at time of death. But there is nothing substantive telling us how the initiator and prophet of ethical monotheism arrived at the point where he even had a relationship with God. Is this the first time God speaks to him? And if it is, what makes the Divine believe that Abraham would heed His call?

What seems to be absent from the text is made up for in a charming and famous midrash which identifies Abraham's father, Terah, not only as an idolator, but also as a wealthy businessman who actually trafficked in idols. His son Abram discovered the God of the universe by his own faculties of reason at a very young age.* When Terah had to go on a business trip, he left his young son Abram in charge of the idols store. The proprietor returned to find all of his idols but one smashed to smithereens. Abram explained that a woman had brought food for her favorite idol, whereupon all of the other idols fought over the sumptuous dish. The strongest one was the victor, having vanquished all the others. When Terah expressed skepticism, Abram mocked his father's belief by proving to him that even he was aware of the limitations of the works of his hands.

Terah's shop was not some fly-by-night affair rented in temporary quarters near the busiest section in town to get the crowd before the holidays. It was rather a thriving center for the idol arts – more like the luminescent chambers in any large museum with spotlights and acres of space to dramatize the repose of the idols and to explain the philosophy of idolatry. Abraham's action was not a mere childish prank. It was a revolutionary stroke which changed the way humanity perceived its own reality and the reality of the universe for all subsequent generations.

In this midrash, Terah is seen as a primitive representative of an outmoded religion, whose iconoclast, revolutionary son broke with his father to create a new faith commitment which would ultimately redeem the world. 'Get out of your father's house,' says God to the 'born again' Abraham.

But what if there is another way of looking at Terah more in accord with the biblical text itself? What if Terah had discovered God

---

* See Maimonides, *Mishneh Torah*, Laws of Idolatry, 1, 1.

first – and so Abram was not so much a path breaker as he was a path follower? Perhaps Abraham was not so much a rebellious son as he was a respectful son, who continued and built upon the road laid out for him by his father?

After all, there is every reason to believe that when God tells Abraham to go forth from his country, his birthplace, to a land that God will reveal, God is communicating to a man who was already in an advanced state of God consciousness, a mind-set that was most probably based on a religious awareness first glimpsed at home. Terah himself may at one time have been a believer in idol power but may slowly have turned to the One God while Abraham was yet a very young lad, or even before Abraham was born. I suspect that a subtle clue testifying to the correctness of this position is to be found in an otherwise completely superfluous verse, especially when we remember that the Torah is not in the practice of providing insignificant travelogues.

> Terah took his son Abram, his grandson Lot the son of Haran and his daughter-in-law Sarai, the wife of his son Abram, and they set out together from Ur of the Chaldeans for the land of Canaan; but when they had come as far as Haran, they settled there. The days of Terah came to 205 years; and Terah died in Haran.
>
> Gen. 14:18–20

Why is it that Terah sets out for Canaan, the very place where Abraham himself ends up at the relatively advanced age of seventy-five at the behest of a call from God? Could Abraham have been completing the journey his father had begun decades earlier? And what was special about Canaan? Why would Terah have wished to journey there and why does the Torah believe the journey significant enough to be recorded even though Terah never made it to Canaan?

Further on in this *parasha*, Abram wages a successful war against four despotic kings in order to save his nephew Lot, who had been taken captive by them. The text then cites three enigmatic verses, which record that Malkizedek, the King of Shalem, a priest of God on High, greets Abram with bread and wine, and blesses him:

> Blessed be Abram to God on High, possessor of heaven and earth, and blessed be God on High, who delivered your enemies into your hand.
>
> Gen. 14:19–20

Abram then gives Malkizedek a tribute of one tenth of his spoils. Now the city of Shalem, JeruSalem, was the capital city of Canaan – and this is the first time it is mentioned in the Bible. Malkizedek literally means the King of Righteousness, and Jerusalem is biblically known as the City of Righteousness [Isaiah 1:26]. From whence did this Malkizedek, apparently older than Abram, hear of God on High (*El Elyon*)? Nahmanides maintains that from the very beginning of the world, the monotheistic traditions of Adam and Noah were preserved in one place in the world – Jeru-Salem, Canaan. Indeed, the flood never damaged Canaan. Their king, Shem son of Noah, also known as Malkizedek, was a priest to God-on-High, teaches Nahmanides. If this is the case, it seems logical to suggest that Terah was someone who had come to believe in this One God even in the spiritual wilds of Ur of the Chaldeans – and therefore set out for Canaan, the land of monotheism, where he wished to raise his family. He may even have had personal contact with Malkizedek, who greets the son of his friend with religious words of encouragement to the victor of a religious battle in which right triumphed over might, a victory of the God of ethical monotheism. Like so many contemporary Jews who set out for Israel, Terah had to stop half way and didn't quite make it. But all along God was waiting for Terah's son to embrace the opportunity to continue where his father had left off.

The common view of Terah has Abraham defy his father's way of life as he creates his own way, becoming in effect a model for many modern day penitents who radically break away from non-believing parents, rejecting everything from their past. In the alternate view that I propose, Abraham follows in his father's footsteps, builds on his father's foundation, redefines his father's way of life and for the first time in history paves the way for himself as well as others to move up the spiritual ladder by not only continuing but also advancing. Abraham is the model for those spiritual idealists who – upon embarking on a journey of religious hope – look at their pasts with an eye for reinvesting what is salvageable, attempting to improve rather than reject. Whose path survives, thrives and becomes a link to the next generation? The revolutionaries, the evolutionaries, or a combination of both? It depends probably on who and what your parents happened to have been.

To Take Advantage of is to Enslave

> *Now I know that you are a beautiful woman, and*
> *when the Egyptians will see you, they will say this*
> *is his wife and they will kill me, and you they will*
> *keep alive. Please say you are my sister, that they*
> *will be good to me for your sake and that my soul*
> *may live because of you.*
>
> GENESIS 12:11–12

Twice repeated tales in the Torah always alert our interpretive, intellectual faculties.

Famine in the Promised Land forces Abraham and Sarah to head for Egypt. Abraham suddenly understands that Sarah's beauty spells danger. Abraham's fears prove correct. Sarah is taken to the royal household and her brother receives gifts of cattle and slaves. Before she joins the harem, a plague strikes Pharaoh's court, arousing suspicion that this woman must be Abraham's wife, not his sister. Realizing how close he has come to violating another man's wife, Pharaoh sends Abraham away, flocks and all.

The similarity between the experiences of Abraham and those of his son in *Parashat Toledot*, when Isaac and Rebecca head for Gerar because of famine, illustrates the Torah's exegetical principle that *maasei avot siman lebanim* (what happens to the parents is a sign of what will happen to the children). However, this principle is not meant for one or two generations alone; the seminal occurrences of the patriarchs are to reverberate in the experiences of their descendants throughout Jewish history.

This is a major principle in the various biblical interpretations of Nahmanides, who sees continuous allusions to the events of subsequent Jewish history in all of the stories of the Bible.

In the case of Abram and Sarai in Egypt, Nahmanides maintains that in leaving the land of Israel, even because of famine, 'the first Hebrew couple committed a sin, albeit inadvertently.' Continues Nahmanides, it is because of this sin that their descendants will be enslaved in Egypt. I would suggest that a careful reading of the Bible itself will reveal an even deeper connection between the earlier experience of Abraham and Sarah in Egypt and the later Jewish enslavement by the Egyptians with major lessons to be learned by us today. Let us review the parallelism.

Both Abraham and his descendant Jacob leave Israel for Egypt because of a famine. With Abraham, this departure leads to Sarah's enslavement in Pharaoh's harem. With Jacob, this departure eventually leads to the enslavement of the Jews.

Abraham fears that Pharaoh will kill him and allow Sarah to live in order to take her as his wife. When Jacob's descendants multiply in Egypt, Pharaoh decrees that all male Jewish babies be cast into the Nile to drown while the female babies will be allowed to live.

Abraham finds a way out of danger through his 'sister,' Sarah. Moses is saved by his sister Miriam, when she hides him among the reeds and the bulrushes. It is not an exaggeration to say that the redemption of the Jewish people began with a sister.

Pharaoh takes Sarah into his household, his harem, where he intends to enslave her. Pharaoh takes the Jewish people into his home, Egypt, where he enslaves them.

To conclude Sarah's enslavement before she is seriously violated, God sends plagues (*negaim gedolim*) on the Egyptians. When God wants to put an end to the Israelite enslavement, he casts ten plagues upon Egypt.

Pharaoh sends Abraham away with gifts and material wealth, and when Pharaoh finally lets the Israelites out of Egypt the former slaves carry off vessels of gold and silver.

From a literary perspective, Abraham in Egypt certainly fore-shadows the slavery of the Jews. If we are to find an ethical teaching in Abraham's Egyptian sojourn, a certain flaw in Abraham's conduct (as Nahmanides maintains), then the Egyptian enslavement must provide not only 'measure for measure' punishment, but also a moral message for all subsequent generations.

We have already seen that Nahmanides views Abraham's leaving the land of Israel, even for reasons of famine, as an inadvertent transgres-sion. In light of the events which took place in Egypt, it is clear that no matter how tantalizing life in exile may appear to be from an economic point of view, a child of Abraham and Sarah must never leave God's holy and promised land of Israel. If it is seemingly difficult to survive in our own land, it will be much more difficult to make it in a land in which we are strangers! This is a leitmotif which repeats itself throughout the Bible.

As far as Abraham's actions vis-a-vis Sarah are concerned, we may justify Abraham by saying that had he said nothing, he would have been killed and Sarah would have ended up in Pharaoh's harem in any case. However, we cannot possibly justify Abraham's inelegant language, in which he suggests that Sarah claim to be his sister 'so that they may be good to me for your sake.'

Apparently, in addition to saving his life, Abraham anticipates that Pharaoh will also give him gifts once the beautiful Sarah is harem-bound. Even if the profit he reaps was only a post facto dividend, his choice of words conveys the notion that Sarah is being used to further Abraham's ends.

I believe the Bible is teaching us that here, too, Abraham sinned inadvertently.

Our relationships, even between husband and wife, must be devoid of any of the subtle ways used in taking advantage of one another, even if it is not done intentionally. Often we tend to take advantage of people, or at least to take them for granted – especially those who are closest to us. We tend to forget that each person must be seen as his or her own ultimate reality, an end unto himself. Using someone else as a means to our own ends, merely in order to fulfill our goals, is a subtle form of slavery. This includes one's spouse. The broadest meaning of slavery is to use another person for one's own purposes as a means to further one's own end. This can be done even while speaking softly and in a gentleman-like way. In Martin Buber's terms, people must be seen as subjects, not as objects. Our relationships must be 'I-thou' rather than 'I-it.'

From this perspective, the parallelism in language between this first Egyptian experience of Abraham and Sarah and the seminal Egyptian experience of their descendants in the book of Exodus conveys two crucial lessons. First of all, the children of Abraham and Sarah must learn that no foreign country will ever provide a political and cultural homeland for the nation of the covenant. Joseph's family settled in Egypt with great expectations of security and respectability, only to be enlisted in Pharaoh's slave-based systematic design which ultimately robbed them of their elementary rights to freedom and life itself. Second of all, the children of Abraham and Sarah must have seared into their consciousness the fundamental evil which is slavery in any and all of its forms. 'You must love the stranger, for you were strangers in the land of Egypt.' Faithfulness to our homeland and respect for every human being as an end in and of him/herself are the principles upon which our nation was formed. Have we learned these lessons?

The Miracle of Believing

> *And the King of Sodom came out to meet him after he returned from routing Kedarleomer and the kings who were with him.... And the King of Sodom said to Abraham, "Give me the captives, and the bounty of the wealth you may take for yourself."*
>
> GENESIS 14:17, 21

Many people will tell you that if only they would experience a miracle, they would certainly believe in God. Consequently, they easily justify their agnosticism because this mystical, magical and miraculous event they are waiting for hasn't happened yet.

Yet interestingly, the daily *Amida* prayer (which is the cornerstone of our thrice daily prayer service), composed by the Men of the Great Assembly more than two thousand years ago, suggests that miracles surround us:

> We give thanks to You, who are the Lord our God and the God of our fathers forever... for Your miracles which are with us every

day and for Your wondrous acts and for Your goodnesses which happen constantly, evening, morning and afternoon.

So, are miracles a rare phenomenon, or are miracles a constant companion? And if miracles are truly such a usual occurrence, then why are there so many agnostics?

The answer is simple: an individual must be a believer in order to recognize the miracle. In the final analysis, a miracle – similar to beauty – is in the eyes of the beholder. Hence, just as it may be said that for the believer there are no questions and for the heretic there are no answers, so may it be said that for the skeptic there are no miracles and for the religious personality every 'natural' phenomenon is a miracle. Indeed, one of the most meaningful blessings the observant Jew recites is the one that he invokes several times each day after washing his hands after going to the bathroom:

> The source of blessings are You O God, Sovereign of the Universe, who has formed the human being with wisdom, having created him/her with apertures and openings that – if one which should be open is closed or if one which should be closed is open – it would be impossible to exist and stand before You. The source of all blessings are You, the healer of all flesh, who performs wondrous acts.

Observant Jews have this religious response for a natural bodily function, because they recognize it is a veritable miracle!

A textual irregularity in this portion of *Lekh Lekha* reaffirms the idea that a miracle is in the eyes of the beholder. Chapter 14 recounts the four terrorist monarchs who maintained a stranglehold of fear over the five other nations inhabiting the 'fertile crescent.' The despotic marauders made the tragic mistake of forcing innocent residents of Sodom into captivity – including Lot, Abraham's orphaned nephew and adopted son. The patriarch springs into military action – and wins a decisive victory over the terrorist nations.

> And the King of Sodom came out to meet [Abraham] after he returned from smiting Kedarleomer and the kings who were

with him ... And the King of Sodom said to Abraham, 'Give me the captives [you freed], and the bounty of the wealth you may take for yourself'.

Gen. 14:17, 21.

But Abraham takes nothing, explaining to the King of Sodom that he will not take even a thread or a shoelace, for he never wants it said that the king made Abraham rich!

While the two verses I cited describing the encounter between Abraham and the King of Sodom seem to follow each other in logical sequence, you will notice that they are in fact, verses 17 and 21, separated by three verses which interrupt the natural flow of the King of Sodom's meeting with Abraham.

In verse 18, instead of continuing to describe the encounter between these two leaders, we are introduced to an entirely new personality whom we have not met before and will not meet again.

And Malkizedek the King of Salem took out bread and wine, and he is a *Kohen*-Priest to the Lord on High. And he blessed [Abraham], and he said, 'Blessed is the Lord on High who owns the heavens and the earth. And blessed is the Lord on High who has given over your enemies into your hands.' And he [Abraham] gave him [Malkizedek] a tithe of everything.

Gen. 14:18–20

And then we pick up our story in verse 21, 'And the King of Sodom said to Abram ...'

What is Malkizedek doing in the midst of a meeting between Abraham and the King of Sodom? And who is Malkizedek? While his name literally means King of Righteousness, he is described as the King of Salem. Salem is Jerusalem (literally, City of Peace), and Jerusalem is known by our prophets as the City of Righteousness [Isaiah 1:26]. Malkizedek is identified by the Midrash as Shem, the son of Noah. Nahmanides suggests that Jerusalem, the capital of Israel from time immemorial, was the one place in the world which never forgot the message of ethical monotheism, the lesson of an inviolate humanity created in the divine image which God taught Adam and Eve, and Noah and his descendants.

Rabbi Moshe Besdin suggests that the Bible is demonstrating how two different individuals can view the very same historical phenomenon – and give it two totally different interpretations. Abraham has saved innocent captives, as well as the entire fertile crescent, from four terrorist, despotic nations. For the King of Sodom, it's business as usual: you take the booty, I'll take the freed captives. For Malkizedek, the King of Salem it's a miraculous act of God, who is to be praised for enabling this wondrous victory.

A Hassidic Postscript

Further on in this *parasha*, after the Almighty promises Abraham progeny:

> He takes him outside, saying 'look please at the heavens and count the stars, if you can count them,' and He said to him [Abraham] 'So shall be your seed.'
>
> Gen. 15:5

Most commentaries maintain that this prophecy guarantees that Abraham's descendants will be as innumerable as the stars. But we all know that, at least up to this point, we certainly can be counted; we are hardly as numerous as the other major religions. The *Sefat Emet* has another interpretation. Just as counting the stars is a mission impossible, securing the future history of Israel is a mission impossible. After all, historically, sociologically and anthropologically, we should have ceased to exist as a nation shortly after the destruction of the Holy Temple. Our continuing presence as a people and a nation can only be explained as a miracle – to this very day!

A Modern Israeli Postscript

Immediately after the Six Day War, Jews from all over Israel headed for Jerusalem, making their way to the Kotel (Western Wall), where passions ran high in joyous celebration. In the midst of it all, there was a man who was totally bent over, a gnarled hunchback who merely attracted a few prolonged stares. No one anticipated that in the midst of all the revered generals, politicians, chief rabbis and diplomats, he would stand out as the central figure. He slowly approached the stones and kissed them tenderly. Suddenly he stood up straight, as if the kiss had bestowed upon him the gift of a cured spine. Clearly, it was a miracle!!

Witnessed by the crowd, including tough-minded reporters and no-nonsense photographers, people were sure that what had transpired at the Western Wall was the advent of a Jewish Lourdes.

But alas, it turned out not to have been a miracle at all. The elderly Jews recounted how as a seventh-generation Jerusalemite, this old man was forced to evacuate the Old City in 1948. Upon leaving, he took a vow that as long as he could not return to the Holy City of his people, he would never stand up straight. Thus, he went about his daily business always gazing downwards, developing the gait of a hunchback. But now that the city had been liberated, he was returning to his former home and had walked up to kiss and touch the holy stones of the Western Wall. After he mouthed the blessing, 'Blessed Art Thou, O Lord, our God, King of the Universe, who causes the bowed down to stand straight and tall,' he was able to look up again for the first time in nineteen years.

Was this a miracle? Indeed it was! The miracle of Israel's return to Jerusalem after close to 2,000 years in exile; the miracle of Israeli Independence Day; the miracle of Jerusalem Day!

A Contract or a Covenant?

> *I am the Lord who took you out of Ur Kasdim to*
> *give you this land as an inheritance.*
>
> GENESIS 15:7

A careful analysis of the *berit bein ha-betarim* (literally, 'Covenant between the Pieces') will help us understand how it is the cornerstone of Jewish theology and gives meaning to all of Jewish history. After the difficult battle between the four kings and the five kings, Abraham emerges victorious. For the first time he appears as a major historical figure and international leader. The Almighty then appears to Abraham in a vision and assures him that his reward shall be very great. But Abraham is worried that he will have no offspring. Our forefather longed for a child who would be his heir. As the founder of a new faith, he had received a prophetic vision that he wanted to hand on to the next and all subsequent generations. Abraham acutely feels the tragedy of seeing his life's work and his dream perishing with him. The Almighty responds with a promise that Abraham will indeed be a father and that his seed will be as numerous as the stars of heaven. At the time of this divine promise,

Abraham and his wife, Sarah, were already well past the age of physical vigor. But Abraham believed in God's word, and he emerges from this encounter as a man of faith.

In the next verse, the Almighty extends His promise: 'I am the Lord who took you out of Ur Kasdim to give you this land as an inheritance.' Suddenly Abraham becomes a skeptic: 'How will I know that I shall inherit it?' The Almighty then commands Abraham to take a number of animals and cut them in half, and in another vision Abraham and the mysterious Presence of God pass together between the pieces, thus concluding a covenant in the manner customary among the people of Abraham's time. At the conclusion of the vision, God makes another promise to Abraham in which He informs him that his descendants will be slaves in a strange land but that they will eventually be set free, with great wealth.

The biblical commentators are perplexed at how the same Abraham who so readily accepted the promised miracle of Sarah having a child, though she was past the age of childbearing, suddenly cannot believe that his descendants will inherit the land of Israel. Why did Abraham, the man of faith, turn into Abraham the doubter? Nahmanides' response to this question illuminates one of the fundamental concepts of Jewish theology. Before the *berit bein ha-betarim*, Abraham felt that he had a special relationship with God, which he regarded as akin to a contract. In every contractual relationship there are two mutually obligated parties. If one party does not fulfill its obligations, the other is free from doing its part. When Abraham was assured a child, he was full of confidence in the 'contract', for he knew he could live up to his part of the agreement, namely – to be a loyal and righteous servant of the Almighty. But when it came to the promise that his descendants would inherit the land, Abraham was no longer so confident. 'How do I know that I will inherit it?' he asks, meaning, 'How do I know that my descendants will be worthy of the inheritance?' Abraham understood that if his children were not worthy, God would not be obligated to carry out His part of the agreement.

Responding to Abraham's anxiety, God explains that His relationship to the Jewish people is not contractual but rather covenantal – it involves a *berit*. A contract can remain in force for as long as the parties abide by it or it can be revoked entirely. In contrast, a covenant, by definition, is irrevocable, and a covenant with the Almighty is both irrevocable and eternal. God stood as the guarantor that there would always be a faithful remnant, and that although there might be times of separation, there would be an ultimate reunion between the people and the land. God became the eternal guarantor of the eternal covenant. The Jewish people is the *am ha-berit*, the people of the covenant, and all of Jewish history is the practical expression of this eternal divine–human encounter.

In his farewell speech to his people, Moses recalls the stipulations of the covenant as he warns the children of Israel not to turn away from the Almighty. Moses understood that in His displeasure with their wicked ways, God will turn away from them. Persecution and pogrom will hound them at every step, but in the end, He will not fail them because the Jews themselves will never completely abandon the Lord; 'He will not forget the covenant which He made under oath [with your fathers]' [Deut. 4:25–31]. While near-total assimilation might occur in the Diaspora, the Jews will never completely assimilate. Their bond to God will ultimately prevail. This almost miraculous force is evident in our very day.

Consider the case of Leonid Riegerman, whose communist parents made their 'aliya' from the Bronx, New York to the Soviet Union in 1930. His story is but one of the many inspiring tales of courageous Russian refuseniks who stood up to be counted as Jews. Born in Moscow, Riegerman was raised as a communist and an atheist. He had never entered a synagogue. One day he chanced upon an English translation of the Bible in a library. Thumbing through its pages he read the passage about Joseph's encounter with a mysterious stranger. 'What are you seeking?' the stranger asks, and Joseph replies, 'I am seeking my brothers.' Suddenly tears welled up in Riegerman's eyes and a profound yearning arose in his soul. 'I too am seeking my brothers,' he cried. Looking around the library and realizing that no one there was really his brother, he ran directly to the Great Synagogue on Arkhipova Street, joining a line of people waiting to buy matzah for Pesaḥ. Leonid Riegerman went on to become a religious Jew, a refusenik, and one of the great heroes of our generation. Leonid Riegerman found the Torah and he found the Almighty. In a real sense, however, the Torah and the Almighty found Leonid Riegerman, and so it is with many in our time. 'It will be difficult for you, and the words of the Torah will find you' [Deut. 4:30] – in the very midst of the exile. Such is our unique *berit* (covenant) with God.

A Nation or a Religion?

*In that day God made a covenant with Abram
saying Unto your seed have I given this land.*

GENESIS 15:18

God established covenants on two different occasions with the Jewish people, the first in this week's portion of *Lekh Lekha*, and the second right after the Revelation at Sinai in the book of Exodus. At first glance these eternal, irrevocable contracts allude to the paradox of Israel: Are we a nation, bound together by a common bloodline, a shared ancestry and gene pool, whose most earnest desire is to live together as an extended family in our own land? Or are we primarily a religion, bound together by a group of laws, united not so much by where we live as by how we live, by the quality of our commitment to Jewish law and ritual passed down to us by previous generations.

The first covenant stresses lineage and land:

> In that day God made a covenant with Abram saying 'Unto your
> seed have I given this land'....
>
> Gen. 15:18

This 'covenant of the pieces' established the Jewish nation. The second
covenant is about laws and lifestyle, common rituals and rites of passage:

> And he [Moses] took the book of the covenant and read it aloud
> to the people, and they said, 'All that God has spoken will we do
> and obey.'
>
> Exodus 19:8

That covenant at Sinai established the Jewish religion.

The covenant of Abraham stresses our national identity, the borders of our land promised as our home, the fact that there will be progeny to Abraham and Sarah and all future descendants are parts of one
extended family. Generally speaking, a nation – in effect, a distinct ethnic
group which emerges from a family – shares a common language, history,
literature and celebrations. It is dependent upon a national homeland
with clearly defined borders. As long as an Englishman's descendants
live in England, they're English. But once they move across the Atlan-
tic, it's only a question of time before they adapt to their new home, all
trace of their ancestry a faint memory. Members of the family-nation
may be ignorant or critical of the cultural literature and customs, but
they belong nevertheless, as long as they remain members of the family.
Generally speaking, once they are separated from the ancestral homeland, certainly for more than two generations, they cease to belong; and
if a whole nation is separated from its homeland for a century or more,
it ceases to exist as a separate and unique ethnic entity. This is a fact of
history as well as geography; as a result, there are no longer Canaanites
or Jebusites to be found in the world.

In contrast, the second covenant in the book of Exodus stresses
not the family-nation connection as much as the religio-legal commitment. Abraham and Sarah's descendants, poised on the edge of Sinai,
outside of the border of the land promised to Abraham, are required to
accept upon themselves the Torah, the Law of Moses, the religion of

Israel. This religious structure transcends any particular land or region; the 613 commandments link the practising Jew in Sydney to the practising Jew in Singapore, much as the Catechism links the believing Catholic in Mexico to the believing Catholic in Montana. Religious identity is dependent upon adherence to a specific theology and lifestyle: a lapsed American Catholic and a lapsed French Catholic have little if anything at all in common. However, committed co-religionists in opposite parts of the world belong to a kind of international fraternity which, for example, has allowed me to feel perfectly at home spending a Shabbat with an observant Jewish family in Bangkok, Thailand or Sao Paulo, Brazil even though I could not speak the native language.

Undoubtedly, it was in largest measure our religious covenant which enabled us to survive for close to two thousand years despite our having been exiled from our ancestral homeland, a veritable miraculous phenomenon in the history of nations. And it was our familial-national identity, which kept the land of Israel and the city of Jerusalem alive in our hearts and consciousness despite our exile – and enabled us to eventually return to our homeland. Moreover, whatever the beliefs and practices of a child or sibling may or may not be, 'home is the one place where, even if no one else wants you, they will always let you in.' Each of these two aspects of our Jewishness plays a specific role in the area of conversion to Judaism. According to Jewish law, the conversion process is comprised of two essential elements for both men and women (men must also undergo circumcision, which symbolizes the casting away of gentile-dom): first the ritual immersion in living water (*mikveh*), symbolizing one's rebirth into the family of Israel and entrance into a new nationality; and second, the acceptance of commandments, demonstrating knowledge of and commitment to the laws of the Torah.

Which of the two – nation or religion – is of greater significance is a fascinating difference of opinion between the two greatest Jewish religious thinkers of our generation, Rabbi Abraham Isaac Kook and Rabbi Joseph B. Soloveitchik, and echoes an earlier difference of opinion between Maimonides and Rabbi Yehuda Halevi. In his work *Kol Dodi Dofek*,* Rabbi Soloveitchik calls the covenant with Abraham the

---

* Joseph B. Soloveitchik, *Kol Dodi Dofek* (Tel Aviv 1964).

'covenant of fate.' After all, no one asks to be born to a particular set of parents, nor is anyone queried as to with which nation he wishes to be identified. But once one is born a Jew, that becomes his/her fate. Therefore the symbol of this covenant is the *berit milah*, the rite of circumcision, because we cannot ask the eight-day-old child if he wants to be circumcised. Blood is even taken from the organ of propagation because a Jew must be ready to shed blood for his nation, often without having been given the option to decide. Indeed, no one sent off to Auschwitz was given the choice of staying behind as an Aryan.

Now if circumcision is the symbol of the covenant of fate, then Rabbi Soloveitchik suggests that Sinai becomes the 'covenant of destiny'; by choosing to follow a prescribed set of laws and customs, we are, in effect, turning our fate into destiny and declaring our willingness to live – and even suffer – for the sake of a particular ideal and lifestyle. The mission of ethical monotheism is to 'perfect the world in the Kingship of God' (from the *Aleinu* prayer);. As Jews, the second major phase in our lives begins when we're 13 years old (or 12 for girls), the age when we can choose to keep the mitzvot of the Torah, and make our own private declaration of faith and commitment. The choice is up to us.

Rabbi Kook also speaks of these two covenants, but he refers to them not as fate and destiny, but rather as the internal covenant and the external covenant.* The first, the covenant with Abraham, is the internal one, the feelings of the heart which link an individual to another individual of his/her family/nation. This has no external or visible manifestation but touches at the very essence of the individual's identity. In contrast, the covenant of Sinai is an external commitment. A person who keeps such commandments as Shabbat, Yom Tov, tefillin, synagogue attendance, kashruth, sukkah, is very much involved in the external, visible and tangible world of Torah commandments.

Maimonides defines the sanctity of Israel as linked to a life of Torah and mitzvot, and therefore Rabbi Soloveitchik, a Maimonidean, would claim that the higher covenant is the covenant of destiny, the covenant of Sinai, Judaism the religion and not Israel the nation. But Rabbi Kook, the first Chief Rabbi of Israel, who follows more in the

---

* Epistles of R.A.Y.H. Kook, 565.

footsteps of Rabbi Yehuda Halevi, believes that the deepest sanctity of Israel comes from what he calls *segulah*, our inner chosenness, our internal ethnicity, the invisible but omnipresent 'Jewish gene', the very fact that we're descendants of Abraham and Sarah. For him, Israel the nation stands supreme; a Jew who feels an inner connection and concern for all other Jews, committed to the revitalization of the Jewish nation-state, has a degree of sanctity even higher than those Jews who may be committed to ritual observances but do not feel linked to every member of the Jewish nation and the Jewish land.*

The Talmud [*Sanhedrin* 98a] speaks of the Messiah arriving on a donkey. Why a donkey? Some take this literally, others metaphorically, but Rabbi Kook explains it from his perspective of internal and external sanctity. Explains Rabbi Kook, a donkey has no external signs of purity; it neither has split hoofs nor a double digestive tract, and so doesn't chew its cud. The pig, on the other hand, doesn't chew its cud, but it has split hoofs. Nevertheless, the donkey devoid of external signs, does apparently have internal sanctity, as evidenced by the fact that its first-born must be redeemed by a priest-*Kohen*. The donkey, therefore, represents the Jew with a heightened development of family-nation consciousness. The Messiah will come on a donkey because it is largely due to Jews of the internal covenant that the Messiah will eventually come!

When I first started out as a rabbi, there was one elderly gentleman who, after each Friday night service, would confront me with heretical questions on the portion of the week. He was a classic *maskil*, an 'enlightened' Jew originally from Vilna who didn't believe in keeping any laws; he would smoke on Shabbat while immersing himself in the study of a page of Talmud. Since he was quite learned, our conversations would often take close to an hour, which caused my wife, baby daughter and Shabbat meal guests to become rather impatient. After a few weeks, I asked him in a rather exasperated tone: 'If you don't believe, and apparently my answers don't satisfy you, why do you continue to come to shul?' He responded almost in a patronizing tone, but with words that taught me a profound lesson: '*An Apikoros bin ich yoh, ober a goy bin ich nit*' (I may be a heretic, but that doesn't make me a gentile). He was telling me

---

* *Arpalei Tohar* 16.

that although he wasn't observant, he was still a member of the family, and so he felt he belonged in the synagogue for cultural national reasons if not for religious convictions. We are a religion as well as a nation: this is our complexity as well as our pride! It is virtually impossible, because of our hybrid definition, to make a clear-cut distinction between state and religion in Israel, but it is precisely because of this hybrid distinction that we alone have remained eternal among nations, despite our homelessness for almost two millennia. We are tied together by laws no matter where we live, and there are Jews who feel familially connected no matter how little of Jewish law they may practice. We must reach out to every Jew in love and acceptance, and strengthen ourselves as much as possible in every aspect of our Jewishness.

Vayera

Abraham's Silence

And it came to pass... that God did test Abraham and said to him, Abraham, and he said, Here I am! And He said, Take now your son, your only son Isaac, whom you love, and get thee into the land of Moriah; and offer him there for a burnt offering upon one of the mountains which I shall show you.

GENESIS 22:1–2

When God presents Abraham with the most difficult and tragic command to sacrifice his beloved son, Isaac, Abraham rises early the next morning, loads his donkey, calls his servants and immediately starts the journey – without a word of protest. We find no indication that Abraham considered the possibility of remonstrating with the divine, asking for a reconsideration of the injunction, a reasonable reaction given that the Almighty had just guaranteed him: 'Through Isaac shall your seed be called.' Could God have changed His mind?

What makes this question even more poignant is that Abraham

does stand up to God when he wants to. In one of the most memo-rable exchanges in the Torah, the imminent destruction of Sodom and Gomorrah brings out all of Abraham's oratorical skills as he pleads for the lives of the wicked inhabitants. 'Will the judge of the world not act justly, will the Almighty destroy the innocent together with the wicked?' he provocatively asks. And if there are at least ten innocent residents, ought the country not be spared? If Abraham was willing to defend the wicked Sodomites from a mass death, couldn't he have done at least as much for his righteous, beloved and divinely promised son?

There are a number of directions to take in explaining Abraham's silence, and I'd like to suggest three.

First of all, there is a commentary suggested by Rabbi Joseph Ibn Kaspi reminding us of the historical context of the world in which Abraham lived. True, the Torah was given for all time, but it was also given within a certain contextual and historical frame. Abraham lived at a time when the pagan world demonstrated allegiance to the idol Molokh by ritually sacrificing children. Therefore embedded within the mind of the patriarch was the terrible possibility that such a command may well reach him from his God. In a world of idolatry where children were often sacrificed to Molokh, Abraham may well have understood and even expected that he too could be commanded to do the same – and so he does not even attempt to argue. From this perspective, the com-mand of the *Akeda*, and its subsequent cancellation, irrevocably makes child sacrifice unacceptable to the Jewish religion. From this perspec-tive, the real test of Abraham comes with the second divine command emanating from the mouth of the angel, 'Abraham, Abraham…Do not send forth your hand against the lad and don't do anything against him…' [Gen. 22:12]. When the patriarch agreed not to sacrifice his son to his God, he demonstrated his break from the world of bloodthirsty idols and his true acceptance of the God of justice and compassion.

This interpretation has special poignancy when modern Israelis witness the chairman of the Palestinian Authority using young children to sacrifice themselves in the front lines of battle – urging them and pay-ing them to throw stones at Israeli citizens while shielding gun-toting Palestinians behind them to become suicidal homicide bombers. The imams promise them eternal bliss in Paradise. Clearly, such cynical use, or rather misuse, of precious children is absolutely biblically forbidden, as the final word of God at the conclusion of the *Akeda* story demonstrates.

Yet another offshoot of this interpretation is the all too common syndrome of overly ambitious, hyper-successful parents – worst case scenario in pursuit of fame and fortune, best case scenario hoping to save the world (this includes committed rabbis) – who sacrifice their children for God. In the case of a rabbi or educator, the student or congregation often come first, even at the Shabbat table. The Almighty is ultimately teaching Abraham that he dare not sacrifice his son, not even for Him!

* * *

Secondly, I've written in the past of two types of prayer – national prayer on behalf of the world and personal prayer on behalf of oneself or one's family – based on two distinct ways in which Moses beseeches the Almighty. When it comes to a prayer on behalf of the entire nation of Israel – a prayer for forgiveness following the sin of the Golden Calf – Moses pleads for forty days and forty nights, beseeching, remonstrating and even demanding that the Almighty not forsake His covenantal people. However, when his own sister Miriam is sick, he utters only five words: 'O God please heal her.' After all, God's promise guaranteed the nation's eternity, but not necessarily the health of Miriam, Moses' own sister.

What's true for Moses applies equally to Abraham. When it comes to the destruction of an entire society, a possibility that innocents will die along with the masses, Abraham pleads with all his rhetorical gifts to alter the horror of the edict. But when it comes to Isaac, his own son, he can allow himself only the minimum of words and gestures. For a people he will plead, but for himself – and Isaac is really an extension of himself – he must remain silent.

* * *

And finally, perhaps, Abraham does not argue because he is in a different relationship with God than he was when he remonstrated on behalf of Sodom and Gomorrah, a more distant relationship which does not permit the camaraderie of questioning a divine order.

Fear of God (*yirat haShem*) and love of God (*ahavat haShem*) are the two fundamental attitudes one takes toward the Almighty. The first emanates from a sense of distance from God and the second from a sense of closeness to God. Maimonides looks upon the fear of God as emanating from the existential realization of one's own smallness in the face of the Infinite, inspired by the magnificent wonders of the cosmic universe. The one who fears God is overwhelmed by the *mysterium tremendum* of divine powers, and is filled with feelings of profound reverence and awe before the majesty of divine creation (*yirat ha-romemut*). In contrast, love of God, teaches Maimonides, emanates from the desire to cleave to God as a lover, who yearns to remove any separation from himself and his beloved, whose thoughts are totally involved with her at every moment and in every situation. In commenting on the verse, 'Remember the Sabbath to keep it holy,' Nahmanides insists that the individual who serves God from love is on a higher spiritual level than the one who serves Him from fear, which is why our Sages have ruled that a positive commandment (love of God) pushes aside and overrides a negative commandment (fear of God). Nevertheless, both relationships are necessary and complement each other.

Fear of God is critical in the fabric of human existence. Those who love – either God or another human being – may sometimes rationalize away their own lapses and indiscretions with the sense that the beloved will understand, that those in love 'need not say they are sorry.' The very closeness of the relationship can breed a 'taking for granted' attitude. Fear of God brooks no exceptions, doesn't allow anyone to take any advantage. Fear of God keeps us on our toes. It keeps us brutally honest, constantly spurring us on to remain steady and steadfast despite the narrowness – the abyss on either side – of life's very narrow bridge.

Abraham was the great example of worshipping God from love. He left the comfort of his homeland, birthplace and family and entered unknown territory in order to be with God – much as a lover following his beloved. The Talmudic sages suggest that he arrived at the God idea as a result of his own intellectual understanding – and for the great philosopher Maimonides, knowledge and love are synonymous. Abraham establishes altar after altar in the name of his beloved God, of whose ethical teachings and powers of creativity he never ceases to speak – and attempt to persuade others to accept. He is close to God and he understands God – even to the extent of his realization that the Judge of all the world will never perpetrate an injustice, will consider it an anathema to destroy the righteous with the wicked. Hence, he argues with the divine on behalf of Sodom and Gomorrah.

He then sojourns to the land of Gerar where Avimelekh is king. Afraid that Sarah's beauty will endanger his life, Abraham instructs Sarah to say she is his sister. The king takes her into his harem, but then in a dream Avimelekh learns that he has overstepped his bounds, that Sarah is actually Abraham's wife. Explanations follow, and when Abraham is asked why he lied he explains, 'Surely the fear of God is not in this place….' Abraham believed that since the 'Gerareans' had no fear of God, they would be likely to murder him if he were indeed the husband of the beautiful Sarah. After all, the very first question they asked him – a stranger in town – was not whether he needed hospitality, but was about his wife!

In the end, Avimelekh makes Abraham a wealthy man. 'Behold my land is before you, dwell where it pleases you.' Abraham receives sheep, cattle, male and female slaves, even a gift of a thousand pieces of silver. Sarah is restored to Abraham. But the last words we read before the account of the *Akeda* is that Abraham lives in the land of the Philistines for many days. Indeed, the very introduction to the *Akeda* story begins: 'After these things…' – the last thing being Abraham in Gerar.

What was he doing there? Hadn't he just declared that 'surely the fear of God is not in this place…?' And nevertheless he remained behind! What happened to his own fear of God? Was it affected? Could it possibly not have been affected? Each of us is affected by his/her environment. Should the first patriarch have lived for many days in a place absent of the fear of God? Abraham will have to be tested to determine if indeed he is still worthy of becoming the father of the Jewish people.

As the events of the *Akeda* unfold, and Abraham lifts the slaughtering knife, what are the words of the angel of God? 'Do not harm the boy… For now I know that you fear God….'

A circle has just been completed, an event that began with Gerar and ends with Moriah. Abraham has proved that he still fears God despite his residence in Gerar. The entire incident of the *Akeda* bespeaks

Abraham's fear of God, his unquestioning acceptance of a divine command he could not possibly understand. His experience in Gerar had apparently caused him to work overtime on his 'fear of God' – and perhaps neglect a bit of his 'love of God.'

From this perspective, entirely new light is shed on the manner in which the *Sefat Emet* interprets the verse that describes Abraham's approach to Moriah: 'And he saw the place [*makom*] from a distance.' We must understand this to mean that Abraham saw God (*makom* is after all also taken by the Midrash as a synonym for God, who is every place) from a distance, an expression of fear of God, *yirat ha-shem*. Had Abraham perceived God from up close, he would have realized – argues the *Sefat Emet* – that the God of ethical monotheism could never possibly have wished for a human sacrifice!

Perhaps the basis for this fascinating insight of the *Sefat Emet* is the Talmudic interpretation of the prophet Jeremiah's denunciation of child sacrifice, 'which I (God) did not command, which I did not speak, and which did not approach my heart' [Jer. 19:5]:

> 'Which I did not command' refers to the son of Mesha the King of Moab...; 'Which I did not speak' refers to Jephthah; 'Which did not approach my heart' refers to Isaac, the son of Abraham...'
> *Ta'anit* 4a

And this is very much in line with Rashi, who suggests that Abraham actually misunderstood the meaning of the command of the Almighty: 'I God, never said for you to slaughter [Isaac] but only for you to lift him up' – to dedicate him to Me in life and not in death! In other words, an Abraham steeped in the emotion of fear of God, as important as such an emotion may be, is too far away to have perceived the real intention of the divine. And certainly one who feels far removed from God is hardly going to be brazen enough to conduct intimate conversations with God, to dare to argue against a divine command!

And if the first commandment to go to Israel, with which Abraham initiates his election, expresses the first patriarch's love of God, this final commandment of the *Akeda* expresses his fear of God. Only an individual who combines both religious dynamics can be the father of the children of Israel.

Especially in light of this last interpretation, there remains yet one agonizing question: why was the divine command ambiguous, leaving room for Abraham's seemingly 'misguided' interpretation? I believe that our Torah understands only too well that the future history of our people will be fraught with tragedies of exile and persecution, a holocaust war against the Jews and liberation wars to acquire the Jewish State. All of these required and requires parents to see their children burnt on the stake, to accompany their children to the IDF base...There is profound historic necessity for the fact that this last trial of Abraham pictures him as willing to silently take his only beloved son to be sacrificed on the altar of God, if he understood that such was the divine command. Given the paradoxical and ambiguous nature of the tear-drenched history of our people, Abraham and Isaac also had to serve as supreme models of those ready to give up life and future for the sanctification of the divine name.

The Ultimate Sacrifice

> *Take your son, your only son, the one whom you*
> *love, Isaac, and dedicate him there for a burnt*
> *offering [or a dedication, literally, a lifting up] on*
> *one of the mountains which I will tell you of.*
>
> GENESIS 22:2

As we have seen, there are manifold possibilities of interpreting God's most difficult directive to Abraham. But in order for us to truly appreciate the eternal quality of Torah, let us examine how the martyrs of Jewish history have taken – and drawn inspiration from – this drama of the *Akeda* (binding).

In the city of Worms, in 1096, some 800 people were killed in the course of two days at the end of the month of Iyar. In *The Last Trial*,* Professor Shalom Spiegel's study of the *Akeda*, he records a chronicle of that period that cites a declaration by one of the community's leaders, Rabbi Meshulam bar Isaac:

---

* S. Spiegel, *The Last Trial* (Woodstock, vt. 1993).

All you great and small, hearken unto me. Here is my son that God gave me and to whom my wife Tziporah gave birth in her old age. Isaac is this child's name. And now I shall offer him up as father Abraham offered up his son Isaac.

Sadly, the chronicle concludes with the father slaying the boy himself, in the presence of his wife. When the distraught parents leave the room of their sacrifice, they are both cruelly slaughtered by the murdering Christians. Spiegel quotes from a dirge of the time:

Compassionate women in tears, with their own hands slaughtered, as at the *Akeda* of Moriah. Innocent souls withdrew to eternal life, to their station on high...

The biblical story of the binding of Isaac is replayed via the Talmudic invocation of the ram's horn (shofar) each year on Rosh Hashanah, the Day of Judgment and Renewal. The shofar symbolizes the ram substitute for Isaac on Mount Moriah; God commands that we hearken to the cries of this shofar 'in order that I may remember for your benefit the binding of Isaac the son of Abraham, and I shall account it for you as if you yourselves bound yourselves up before Me' [*Rosh Hashanah* 16a]. This message of the shofar has inspired Jews of all generations to rise to the challenge of martyrdom, whenever necessary, transforming themselves into Abrahams and Sarahs, placing their precious children on the altar of *Kiddush Hashem*, sanctification of the divine name.

Indeed, there was apparently a stubborn tradition which insisted that Abraham actually went through with the act of sacrifice. After all, following the biblical command of the angel to Abraham (the *deus ex machina* as it were) – 'Do not cast your hand against the lad' [Gen. 22:19]. Where is Isaac? If indeed, his life has just been saved, why doesn't he accompany his father, why don't they go together to the lads, why don't they – father and son – return home to Be'er Sheva and Sarah together (as they have been twice described as doing – father and son walking together – in the context of the *Akeda* story)?! Moreover, when they first approached the mountain of sacrifice, Abraham tells the young men to wait down below: 'I and the boy will go yonder; we will worship and *we* will come back to you' [Gen. 22:5]. So why does the text have Abraham return alone? On the basis of this textual problem, Ibn Ezra (1089–1164) makes mention of an interpretation that suggests that Abraham literally followed God's command, slaying his son, and that God later on miraculously brought Isaac back to life. It is precisely that stark and startling deletion of Isaac's name from the conclusion of the biblical account of the *Akeda* itself, which gave countless generations of Jewish martyrs the inspiration for their sacrifice; and this is the case, even though Ibn Ezra felt compelled to deny the tradition as inaccurate: 'Isaac is not mentioned. But he who asserts that Abraham slew Isaac and abandoned him, and that afterwards Isaac came to life again, is speaking contrary to the biblical text' [Ibn Ezra, Gen. 22:1]. Ibn Ezra is obviously making reference to a commentary – which Jewish martyrdom would not allow to fall into oblivion.

The earliest referencee to this notion of Isaac's actual sacrifice is probably the Midrash Hagadol which cites R. Eleazer ben Pedat, a first generation Amorah of the Talmud:

> Although Isaac did not die, Scripture regards him as though he had died. And his ashes lay piled on the altar. That's why the text mentions Abraham and not Isaac.*

And perhaps one might argue that Isaac was so traumatized by the *Akeda* that a specific aspect of him – the part of his personality which would always remain on the altar – did die. After all, Isaac is the most ethereal and passive of the patriarchs, called by the Midrash – even after the binding – the *olah temimah*, the whole burnt offering. But this psychological interpretation and Ibn Ezra's rejection notwithstanding, the penitential Slichot prayers still speak of the 'ashes of Isaac' on the altar, continuing to give credence to the version which suggests that Isaac did suffer martyrdom. And we have already cited recorded incidents of children who suffered martyrdom at the hands of their parents, who did not wish them to be violated by the pagan tyrants.

God's command to sacrifice Isaac, and Abraham's submissive

---

*   *Midrash Hagadol*, Margulies edition, p. 360.

silence, may actually help us understand how a people promised great-ness, wealth and innumerable progeny comparable to the stars, find the courage and the faith to endure the suffering and martyrdom mercilessly inflicted upon them by virtually every Christian or Islamic society with which they come into contact.

The paradox in Jewish history is that unless we were willing to sacrifice our children for God, we would never have survived as a God-inspired and God-committed nation with a unique message for ourselves and the world. Perhaps that is why Mount Moriah, the place of the will-ingness to sacrifice, is the Temple Mount of the Holy City of Jerusalem, the place from which God will ultimately be revealed to all of humanity, the place of Jewish eternity.

Whose Sacrifice is it Anyway, Abraham's or Isaac's?

And they walked, the two of them, together.

GENESIS 22:8

Whose sacrifice at the *Akeda* was greater, Abraham's or Isaac's? Instinctively, the first answer that comes to mind is Abraham. After all, the Torah portion is introduced with the words 'And God tested Abraham.' Indeed, Isaac was the very son Abraham had waited for all his life, the affirmation of his faith, the promise of his future.

Any father, let alone Abraham, would rather die than see his child die. Had God said, 'Sir, you have a choice, either your son or yourself,' Abraham would have done what thousands of others have done – push the child toward safety and climb Moriah himself, ever grateful that Isaac would live. Nevertheless, how can we overlook the depth of Isaac's suffering? Whose life is it anyhow, whose flesh is bound to the altar, transformed into a whole-burnt offering? Father's or son's? And no matter how hard it may be to witness tragedy, can we deny that the real sacrifice belongs to the one going up in flames? Isaac is certainly no less a hero than Abraham. And it is clear that Isaac understands what is about to occur. According to Rashi he was thirty-seven years old, certainly old enough to fight his father's will or flee outright. And even if Ibn Ezra, who claims that Isaac was twelve, is more in consonance with the outline of the biblical story, Isaac still could have wept, protested, appealed to Abraham's mercy. No remonstration on Isaac's part is mentioned in the biblical account; much the opposite, even after Isaac presumably is aware of what is about to occur, the text testifies, 'And they walked, the two of them, together.'

Despite the fact that the father in all of us identifies with Abraham's sacrifice, nevertheless there does exist one essential difference between father and son, which was told to me by Rabbi Moshe Besdin.

It was the voice of God which Abraham heard commanding him to take his son, his only son, his beloved son, and to bring him as an all-burnt offering. When Maimonides wants to prove the truth of prophecy, he turns to the Binding of Isaac. Had Abraham not believed in the absolute truth of his prophecy, could he have possibly lifted his hand to slaughter his son? Would he have sacrificed his entire future as well as the future of humanity unless he was absolutely sure of the divine source of the command?

But can we say the same about Isaac? After all, Isaac heard the command not from God, but from his father.

A close look at the text between the lines and words of the Bible will provide a glimpse into the nature of the relationship between this unique father and son. There is a frightening suspicion in the mind of Isaac, a growing awareness of what is about to happen, a desire to confront his father (albeit with great delicacy), and then a profound, acquiescence, even a unity of purpose and mission. Abraham rises in the morning to take his son on the fateful journey. What they talk about, if they talk at all, is not mentioned; but on the third day, after Abraham sends away the young servants, Isaac begins to speak. And what he says, or doesn't say, is of exquisitively sensitive significance.

Professor Nehama Leibowitz has taught us that when the Torah records a dialogue and wishes to inform us of a change in the speaker, it does so by using the word '*Vayomer*', 'And he said'; after all, the Torah script is devoid of quotation marks. On the third day of their journey,

Isaac notices his father preparing the knife and wood for the offering. For the first time since the journey began the Torah records Isaac's words.

'*Vayomer*,' the text begins, 'and he said to Abraham his father....' Now we should expect to find the content of his words. But the biblical text records no such content. Instead, we get another '*Vayomer*,' but this time with a word: '*Vayomer Avi*,' 'And he said, "My father..."' But why have one *Vayomer* after another when both are referring to the same speaker, and Isaac actually said nothing at all after the first *Vayomer*? It's like having quotation marks with no quote in between them! At this point in the narrative Abraham acknowledges Isaac by saying 'Here I am, my son.' Now comes Isaac's third *Vayomer* in this context, 'And he said, "behold the fire and the wood, but where is the lamb for the burnt-offering?"'

What is the meaning of the *Vayomers*?

Apparently, Isaac suspects the true purpose of the journey from the moment his father woke him and told him they were setting out. He tremblingly waits in silence for the first three days to either hopefully hear another explanation or to get a tragic confirmation of his worst nightmare. Abraham, understandably, cannot speak. Isaac yearns to ask the question, even if it means that he will hear the worst. Anything, he thinks, would be better than this gnawing uncertainty. But how can a son ask a father, 'Are you planning to slaughter me?' Given the closeness Isaac always felt as the beloved son of a father who waited until he was one hundred years old to have a son with Sarah, how could he even begin to formulate such an unthinkable act?

On the third day, Isaac tries: *Vayomer*... – but all that came out of his mouth was 'Aaah' – he could only stutter and stammer, he was incapable of formulating such a horrific idea. At length he tries again: '*Vayomer*,' and this time he added, 'My father....' Once again he falters in mid-sentence, to which Abraham gently responds, 'Here I am, my son.' This finally gave Isaac the wherewithal to delicately suggest: *Vayomer*, and he said, 'Behold, the fire and the wood, but where is the lamb for the whole burnt offering?' Abraham's response really leaves no room for further question: 'The Almighty will provide for Himself the lamb for the whole burnt offering, my son.' If Abraham's words are devoid of a comma, he is clearly suggesting: 'for the whole burnt offering is my son.'

What is truly marvelous is the very next biblical phrase: '... so they walked both of them, together [... *yaḥdav*].' We must be struck by the ominous use of 'together' to describe a journey to which both are traveling with equal dedication despite their common knowledge that only one of them will return alive.

We must likewise be struck by the willingness of both of them to adhere to this most inexplicable command of God – despite the fact that the father heard it from God Himself and the son only heard it from his father.

And with these indisputable facts, Isaac emerges as a true patriarch, a model and paradigm for all future generations. After all, our penitential dirges (*slichot* and *kinot*) testify to the fact that Isaac is indeed the model of *Kiddush Hashem* (sanctifying of God's name, dying for one's faith and nation) throughout our blood-soaked and tear-stained history.

Did those who allowed themselves to be slaughtered, impaled on the Crusaders' swords rather than accept conversion, hear the voice of God directly? Is it not more correct to say that they were heeding their parents and teachers, the traditional texts and lessons transmitted through the generations which defined and delimited the command to give up one's life in sanctification of God's name? Abraham may be the first Jew, but Isaac is the first Jewish son, the first Jewish student, the first representative of the *mesora* (tradition handed from parent to child, from master to disciple), whose dedication unto death emanates not from his having heard God's word directly, but from his adherence to the Oral Tradition.

The essence of Judaism is not a religion based on beatific visions along the road to Damascus, or even Jerusalem. Ours is a religion whose truth is passed down from generation to generation, parent to child, master to disciple, teacher to student. And the paradigm for this begins right at the *Akeda*. Who is the first Jew? Abraham. But who is the first historic Jew, the first representative of the historic chain of being Jewish whose links are forged by the frames of commitment and sacrifice? Abraham's son, Isaac.

Isaac and Ishmael – Two Shared Destinies?

> *… And you shall call his name Ishmael… and on
> the face of all his brothers shall he dwell*
>
> GENESIS 16:12

The relationship between Isaac and Ishmael is one of the most complex – and ambiguous – in the Bible. Will they, can they, ever achieve a rapprochement? Who is really at fault – and how will their rivalry ultimately, if ever, conclude? On the one hand, the story of the *Akeda* – the Binding of Isaac – when God commands Abraham to bring his only son to Mount Moriah as a burnt offering – is one of the most difficult episodes in the entire Torah. The command to sacrifice the very child without whom there would be no descendants of Abraham and Sarah, no heir to spread the ideal of ethical monotheism, and no future nation, was a paradox that defied comprehension.

However, if we pay attention to the use of God's name in the unraveling story, the paradox becomes a little clearer. As we know, the two different names of God represent two different divine attributes;

Elokim expresses justice and the strict letter of the law, while the YHWH four-letter name of God expresses mercy and compassion.

Throughout the beginning of this episode, the Torah only uses the name of Elokim, but in the final denouement, when Abraham is commanded to refrain from the sacrifice of his son, the four-letter name of God is invoked: 'Lay not your hand upon the lad...,' commands the angel of YHWH. Why the change in attributes? What of the initial command to offer up his son? Did that only emanate from one aspect of God, from the demand for justice? And if so, why?

The *Akeda* account opens with the words: 'After these things....' What are these things? The penultimate biblical story before the *Akeda* is the account of Hagar and Ishmael sent off to the desert with minimal provisions by Abraham. I would suggest that the suffering of this mother and son is being replayed in the suffering of the father and son – Abraham and Isaac – when they ascend to Mount Moriah. Of course, there are transcendent reasons why Abraham must now undergo this particular test involving the sacrifice of his son, but the fact remains that, given the principle of 'measure for measure' – the tit-for-tat approach of biblical Jewish theology – we can discern a cause and effect link between the explicit torment of Hagar and Ishmael and the implicit torment of Abraham and Isaac.

Sarah was concerned about Ishmael's negative influence: 'And Sarah saw the son of Hagar the Egyptian, whom she had born unto Abraham, mocking.' The word used for mocking is '*metzahek*', the present tense of the future form of Yitzhak (Isaac). According to the commentaries, Ishmael's act of mockery was linked to adultery, idolatry and murder – immediate hedonistic gratification with no thought of ensuing punishment. Therefore, Sarah decides that Hagar and Ishmael are to be sent away, Yitzhak (delayed joy) dare not be mixed with the *metzahek* (joy now), and God Himself commands Abraham to listen to his wife. However, neither God nor Sarah insisted that the banished mother and son receive only minimal provisions for their desert sojourn. It was Abraham who sent them off with only 'bread and a skin-vessel of water.' Rashi notes that, at the very least, Abraham should have sent them off with gold and silver. Abraham was condemning his concubine and son to an inevitable death, and indeed they would have died had it not been for the angel who showed Hagar the well of water after hearing her and her son's cries of desperation.

A careful reading of the biblical text strengthens the parallels between Hagar's journey with Ishmael and Abraham's journey with Isaac. The exact same phrase, 'And Abraham rose up early in the morning [*va-yashkem Avraham ba-boker*],' is used when Abraham rises to give Hagar her supplies, and then again, when Abraham rises to start his journey with Isaac toward Mount Moriah. Abraham places the bread and jug of water on Hagar's shoulder, and Abraham places the wood on Isaac's back. Hagar wanders in the desert with Ishmael and Abraham goes to an uncertain place for the binding. An angel in the guise of a *deus ex machina* saves Ishmael's life and an angel in the guise of a *deus ex machina* saves Isaac's life. The striking parallelism between these accounts would suggest that the God of Justice makes Isaac the vehicle that enables Abraham to empathize, albeit only later, with the very anguish that Hagar must have experienced with Ishmael as a result of Abraham's insensitivity.

The interconnection between Abraham, Sarah, Isaac, Hagar and Ishmael is a recurrent biblical theme. Even before the banishment, once Hagar became pregnant she began to treat Sarah condescendingly: 'her mistress [Sarah] was despised in her eyes.' When Sarah complains to her husband, Abraham tells her that she can do whatever she wants with her maid – and Sarah over-reacts: 'And Sarah dealt harshly with her [Hagar] and she fled from before her.'

The commentaries pay particular attention to Sarah's harsh behavior and Abraham's benign neglect. Radak writes as follows:

> Sarai acted neither in accordance with the trait of ethical conduct, nor in accordance with the trait of piety; she was unethical because, even though Abraham relinquished his own honor and said to her, 'Do with her [Hagar] what is good in your eyes,' she should have stayed her hand out of respect for Abraham, and not have caused [Hagar] to suffer. And she didn't act out of piety or goodness of soul because it's not proper for a person to exercise all one's power against another who is in his service. A wise man says, 'How goodly is forgiveness whenever it is possible.' And

therefore what Sarai did was not good in the eyes of God. And Abraham didn't stop Sarai from treating Hagar badly, even though he knew it was wrong, in order to maintain domestic peace in the house. This entire narrative is written in the Torah in order to teach a person to 'keep away from the bad'...

Radak on Gen. 16:6

Radak refuses to condone Abraham and Sarah's behaviour toward Hagar, and his commentary reminds us how we are not to behave. Nahmanides concurs with the Radak, and goes one step further, insisting that Ishmael's descendants will do to us what Sarah did to his mother. On the verse, 'And Sarah dealt harshly with her,' he writes:

> Our mother [Sarah] transgressed by dealing harshly, and Abraham also transgressed by allowing her [Sarah] to do so. And so, God heard her [Hagar's] affliction and gave her a son who would be a 'wild ass of a man,' to afflict the seed of Abraham and Sarah with all kinds of torments.
>
> Nahmanides, ibid.

Long before the *Akeda*, Isaac and Ishmael are intimately connected with each other. Not only are they – and only they – both given names by God, but they both become significant patriarchal figures. We know that the descendants of Abraham, Isaac and Jacob will be blessed, but the fact is that Abraham's son Ishmael is blessed even before he is born. 'And the angel of God said unto her [Hagar], "I will greatly multiply your seed, and they shall not be numbered for multitude."' Isaac's son, Jacob, may become the father of twelve tribes, but this privilege is also granted to Abraham's other son: 'And as for Ishmael...behold I have blessed him, and will make him fruitful, and will multiply him exceedingly, twelve princes shall he beget, and I will make him a great nation' [Gen. 17:20].

The Torah hints that Isaac was aware of the injustice committed toward Hagar and Ishmael, and identified closely with God's consideration and compassion for Ishmael. The geographical location where Ishmael's life was saved and where God revealed Himself to the banished mother and son was Be'er-lahai-ro'i. This place becomes significant throughout Isaac's life. Rebecca initially meets Isaac, her future husband, as he emerges from his meditations in the fields 'from the way of Be'er-laḥai-ro'i....' What was Isaac doing in Be'er-laḥai-ro'i? And why is it important for the Torah to tell us this now? According to Rashi, Isaac had gone there to bring Hagar back to Abraham so that he could marry her. It was almost as if Isaac attempted to compensate for the pain she (and Ishmael) had been made to endure previously. His mother Sarah had been instrumental in sending Hagar away, but now Isaac is instrumental in bringing her back. And Rashi goes on to inform us that the identity of Abraham's second wife, Keturah, is indeed Hagar, suggesting that Isaac had successfully started the process of reconciliation.

Furthermore, after Abraham's burial, which was taken care of by both brothers equally, we read an extraordinary verse, 'And it came to pass after the death of Abraham, that God blessed Isaac his son, and Isaac dwelt by Be'er-laḥai-ro'i.' It is as though the text is teaching that Isaac becomes worthy of the ultimate blessing only after he atones for the injustice done to Hagar and Ishmael at Be'er-laḥai-ro'i.

Isaac's son is Jacob – Israel, father of the covenantal nation of twelve tribes, inheritor of the Promised Land. And there is room in that land for Isaac and Ishmael together as long as the 'wild ass of a man, whose hand is against every one,' ceases to be a *metzaḥek*, one who lusts after immediate gratification. And indeed the Sages of the Midrash teach that Ishmael does return to his father Abraham in penitence, as the Bible records: 'And Isaac and Ishmael his sons buried him at the Machpela Cave...' [Gen. 25:9, Rashi ad loc].

Conversely, God will continue to hear the pain of the descendants of Ishmael until the descendants of Isaac act toward the descendants of Ishmael in righteousness (*Yisra-el, yashar-el*, God is righteous). The destiny of Israel is apparently a function of how the descendants of these two brothers learn to relate to each other. And the ultimate destiny of our nation and the world will only be realized when the two sons of Abraham live together in peace, 'and on the face of all his brothers shall his [Ishmael's] portion fall' [Gen. 25:18].

The Power and Limitations of a Parent

*Lay not your hand upon the lad, neither do
anything to him.*

GENESIS 22:12

The *Akeda* serves as a model for one of the most important questions in contemporary family life: to what extent should a parent continue to influence, direct, or channel their adult child's life? Can the power of a parent be taken too far? Ultimately, how much control can parents continue to have in their relationships with their adult children?

It seems that God's command to Abraham to bring his beloved son Isaac as a whole burnt offering demonstrates the ultimate power of a father – the power to sacrifice his son's life to a higher ideal. We have previously mentioned the Torah commentary of Rabbi Yosef Ibn Kaspi. He maintains that the real test of Abraham lay not in God's command that he sacrifice Isaac, but rather in the second command of the angel – that he refrain from the sacrifice. We must remember, suggests Ibn Kaspi, that Abraham's social reality is rooted in the blood-drenched days of the god, Molokh, where child sacrifice was the normative expression of religious commitment. In fact, Abraham may very well have been expecting his newfound God of justice and righteousness to require that same act of devotion. From this perspective, the true test of Abraham's dedication was not his willingness to obey God and sacrifice, but rather in his ability to heed the angel and stop the sacrifice even when the knife was but an inch from Isaac's throat: 'Lay not your hand upon the lad, neither do anything to him.'

The next phrase in the same verse is usually translated as, 'For now I know that you are a God-fearing man, seeing you have not withheld [*hasakhta*] your only son from Me' [Gen. 22:12]. However, we can also understand it to mean 'For now I know that you are a God-fearing man, seeing you have not done away with [the Hebrew *h-s-kh* can also mean to remove, or cause to be absent] your only son because of Me [My command].' In the first reading Abraham is praised by the angel for his willingness to sacrifice Isaac; in the alternative reading, Abraham is praised for his willingness *not* to sacrifice Isaac.*

Rashi makes a similar point when he suggests that Abraham did not understand God's command, since the Almighty only meant for the patriarch to elevate and dedicate his son (by prayer and living commitment) and never to slaughter him.

Given these interpretations, the critical lesson being taught is not to focus on how close Abraham came to sacrificing his own son, but rather the limits of paternal power: a father is forbidden from child-sacrifice.

What happened to Isaac after the *Akeda*? We have already seen the problematic biblical report of Abraham's return from the *Akeda* without Isaac! The text reads: 'So Abraham returned [singular form] to his young men [the Midrash teaches they were Eliezer and Ishmael, who accompanied them, but did not go to the actual place of the appointed sacrifice] and they [Abraham and the young men] rose up and went together to Be'er Sheva and Abraham dwelt in Be'er Sheva' [Gen. 22:19]. But where was Isaac? Didn't Isaac also descend from the altar and return to Be'er Sheva?

Yonatan Ben Uziel, in his Aramaic translation (an interpretation

---

* See Ish Shalom, 'Akeda,' *Akdamot*, August 1996.

that embellishes the Torah) maintains that Isaac is not included as hav-ing returned home to Be'er Sheva because he went instead to the Yeshiva of Shem and Ever. In other words, at the moment of the *Akeda*, father and son magnificently joined together – 'and they walked, the two of them, together' – but afterwards it was apparently deemed necessary that they separate from one another.

Abraham returns to his household while Isaac returns to his books, to a Torah academy of solitude and study. In the vocabulary of Rabbi Joseph B. Soloveitchik, Abraham is the outer-directed, extroverted, aggressive Adam I, while Isaac is the more inner-directed, introverted, introspective Adam II. In the conceptual scheme of the mystical *Zohar*, Abraham is the outgoing, overflowing symbol of *hesed* (loving kindness), while Isaac is the disciplined and courageous symbol of *gevura* (inner fortitude). The *Akeda* is both the point of unity as well as the point of departure between father and son. Isaac enters the *Akeda* as Abraham's son; he emerges from the *Akeda* as Jacob's father (Jacob will also study at the Yeshiva of Shem and Ever). Isaac's commitment is equal to that of his father, but his path is very different. Simultaneously, the *Akeda* is the point of unity, as well as separation, between father and son, for each must respect both the similarities as well as the differences within the parent-child relationship.

The commandment to circumcise one's son is most certainly mod-eled on the symbol of the *Akeda*. After all, the basic law prescribes that it is the father who must remove his son's foreskin (even though most fathers feel more comfortable in making the more practiced *mohel* their agents). From a symbolic perspective, it is a father's (or rather parents') responsibility to transmit to the children the boundaries of what is per-missible and what is not permissible. But even though every child is a product of the nature and nurture provided by his/her parents, and the Torah teaches that a child must respect and even revere his/her parents, the existential decisions of how to live one's life, which profession to enter and which spouse to marry are decisions which can only be made by the adult child himself/herself.*

* See *Shulhan Arukh, Yoreh Deah*, Chap. 240:25, Laws of Respecting Parents, the last comment of Isserles citing the Maharik.

Paradoxically, when a parent enables a child to psychologically separate, the child will ultimately move forward. Isaac returns from the yeshiva to continue his father's monotheistic beliefs and Israel-centered life. However, we must also learn from the *Akeda* that although a father may bring his child near to the altar, he dare not sacrifice him on that altar. Our real responsibility is to allow our children to fulfill their own potential and our challenge is to learn to respect their individual choices.

Ḥayei Sara

The Blessing of Old Age:
Parents and Children

And Abraham was old, well-stricken in age…

GENESIS 24:1

The death of Sarah at the beginning of the portion of *Ḥayei Sara* leaves Abraham bereft as a single parent, looking after his home and caring for Isaac, his unmarried son. We are already familiar with their unique father-son relationship from the traumatic biblical account of Isaac's binding, where 'the two of them [father and son, Abraham and Isaac] walked together.' In addition to their shared ideals, their symbiotic relationship includes a remarkable likeness in physical appearance. Our commentaries explain this by reflecting on Isaac's miraculous birth when Abraham is almost one hundred years old. We can imagine that every town gossip cast aspersions about Abraham's paternity, hinting that a younger, more potent man must have impregnated Sarah. Just the leers and the stares would have caused unnecessary shame to Abraham and threatened Isaac's equanimity. Hence, suggests the Midrash, to prevent a trail of whispers and sly innuendos, God created Isaac as an exact double of Abraham, like 'two drops of water,' so that no one could possibly ever imagine anyone other than Abraham as the biological father.

Interestingly, one of the consequences of their physical similarity is the basis for one of the strangest comments in the Talmud. On the verse in the portion of Ḥayei Sara, 'Abraham was old, well-stricken in age' [Gen. 24:1], our Sages conclude that at this point in time, the symptoms of old age were introduced to the world [Bava Metzia 87a]. The reason? They suggest this very identical resemblance between Abraham and Isaac. The Sages describe how people seeking out Abraham would mistakenly address Isaac, and those seeking out Isaac would approach Abraham. Disturbed by the confusion, Abraham pleads for God's mercy to make him look old, and Abraham's plea is answered: a one-hundred-and-twenty-year-old man will never again look like his twenty-year-old son!

How do we begin to understand why Abraham was so upset by this case of mistaken identities? After all, what's wrong with being mistaken for your son? Doesn't every aging parent dream of slowing down the aging process and remaining perpetually young? What's the problem if father and son appear to be the same age?

We find the answers hidden between the lines of this Midrash in which the dialectic of the complex relationship between father and son is expressed. Despite our desire for closeness between the generations, a father must appear different from his son for two reasons. Firstly, so that he can receive the filial obligations due to him as the transmitter of life and tradition. This idea is rooted in the biblical commandment that the younger generation honors the elder. In fact, the last will and testament of the sage of the Middle Ages, Rabbi Yehudah the Pious, forbade anyone from taking a spouse with the same first name as that of their parents. This, explained, Rabbi Aharon Soloveitchik, zt'l, was to avoid giving the impression that a child would ever address a parent by their first name. We may be close to our parents, but they are not to be confused with our 'buddies'.

Secondly, the son must appear different from his father so that the son understands his obligation to add his unique contribution to the wisdom of the past. Abraham pleads with God that Isaac's outward appearance should demonstrate that he is not a carbon copy of his father, but rather a unique individual. After all, when Isaac becomes a patriarch himself, he will represent *gevura*, that part of God's manifestation of strength and justice which provides an important counterbalance to Abraham's *hesed* or loving-kindness. Abraham, the dynamic and creative world traveler, was a contrast to the introspective and pensive Isaac who never stepped beyond the sacred soil of Israel. With great insight, Abraham understood that unless the confusion in appearance ceased, Isaac might never realize the necessity of 'coming into his own' and developing his own separate identity.

A Talmudic discussion of the pedagogic relationship between grandparents and grandchildren illustrates the importance of a dynamic and symbiotic relationship between the generations. In discussing the importance of teaching Torah to one's children and grandchildren, our Sages insist that teaching your own child Torah is equivalent to teaching all your child's unborn children down through the generations [*Kiddushin* 30a]. R. Yehoshua b. Levi adds that 'teaching one's grandchild Torah is equivalent to having received it from Sinai.' He proves this by quoting from two consecutive verses in Deuteronomy: the first highlights the commandment to '…teach thy sons, and thy son's sons' and the following verse begins with, 'The day that you stood before the Lord your God in Horev-Sinai…' [Deut. 4:9, 10]. The message is crystal clear: our parents are our link to Sinai, the place of the initial divine revelation of Torah. When the younger generation learns Torah from the previous generation, it is as though they were receiving the words from Sinai. Such is the eternal bond which links the generations and one of the powerful reasons for children to respect and learn from their parents.

Interestingly, in that same Talmudic passage, R. Hiya bar Abba makes a critical word change in R. Yehuda's interpretation. R. Hiya states, 'Whoever hears Torah from his grandchild [not whoever teaches his grandchild] is equivalent to having received it from Sinai'! What does it mean for a grandchild to teach his grandfather Torah? Obviously, this will make any grandfather proud, but this concept also reveals that the line from Sinai to the present can be drawn in the opposite direction. Not only do grandfathers pass down the tradition to their children and grandchildren, but grandchildren pass up the tradition to their forebears. In contemporary times, this could certainly refer to the phenomenon of the *ba'alei teshuva*, the return of the younger generation to the traditions, where in many cases, the grandchildren literally are teaching their grandparents. But it might also be alerting us to the additional insights into Torah that we can and must glean from the younger generations.

Consider one of the most puzzling Talmudic passages which describes how, when Moses ascended on high to receive the Torah from the Almighty, the master of all prophets found God affixing crowns (*tagim*) to the holy letters of the law [*Menahot* 29b]. When Moses inquired about their significance, God answered that the day would arrive when a great Sage, R. Akiva the son of Joseph, would derive mounds of laws from each twirl and curlicue. Moses asked to see and hear this rabbinic giant for himself, and the Almighty immediately transported him to R. Akiva's Academy. Moses listened, but felt ill at ease almost to the point of fainting; the arguments used by R. Akiva were so complex that they eluded the understanding of the great prophet. However, when a disciple asked for R. Akiva's source, and he replied that it was a law given to Moses at Sinai, the prophet felt revived.

How is it possible that Moses could not understand a Torah lecture containing material that was given to him at Sinai? The answer is embedded within the same Talmudic text. Moses was given the basics, the biblical words and their crowns, the fundamental laws and the methods of explication and extrapolation (hermeneutic principles). R. Akiva, in a later generation, deduced necessary laws for his day, predicated upon the laws and principles which Moses received at Sinai.

This is the legitimate march of Torah which Maimonides documents in his introduction to the interpretation of the Mishna, and it is the methodology by which modern-day responsa deal with issues such as electricity on the Sabbath, brain-stem death and life-support, and in-vitro fertilization. The eternity of Torah demands both the fealty of the children to the teachings of the parents, as well as the opportunity for the children to build on and develop that teaching. This duality of Sinai enhances our present-day experience.

Abraham prays for a distinctive old age to enable Isaac to develop his uniqueness. Sons and fathers are not exactly the same, although many fathers would like to think that they are. Only if sons understand the similarity, and if fathers leave room for individuality, can the generations become truly united in Jewish eternity.

The Significance of a Grave

My lord hearken to me: a piece of land worth four hundred shekels of silver, what is that between you and me.

GENESIS 23:14

A significant part of this Torah portion deals with Abraham's purchase of the Hebron grave-site from the Hittites in order to bury Sarah, his beloved wife. In painstaking detail, the text describes how the patriarch requests to buy the grave, how the Hittites wish him to take it for free, and – when Efron the Hittite finally agrees to make it a sale – he charges Abraham the inflated and outlandish sum of four hundred silver shekels. The Midrash seems perplexed: why expend so much ink and parchment – the entire chapter 23 of the book of Genesis – over a Middle-Eastern souk sale? Moreover, what is the significance in the fact that the very first parcel of land in Israel acquired by a Jew happens to be a grave-site? And finally, how can we explain the irony of the present day Israeli-Palestinian struggle over grave-sites – the Ma'arat HaMakhpela in Hebron where our matriarchs and patriarchs are buried and Joseph's grave-site in Shekhem – which were specifically paid for in the Bible by our patriarchs?

In order to understand our biblical portion, it is important to remember that throughout the ancient world – with the single exception of Athens – the only privilege accorded a citizen of any specific country was the 'right' of burial, as every individual wanted his body to ultimately merge with the soil of his familial birthplace. Abraham insists that he is a stranger as well as a resident (*ger toshav*) of Het; he lives among, but is not one of, the Hittites. Abraham is a proud Hebrew; he refuses the 'right' of burial and demands to pay – even if the price is exorbitant – for the establishment of a separate Hebrew cemetery. Sarah's separate grave-site symbolizes her separate and unique identity. Abraham wants to ensure that she dies as a Hebrew and not a Hittite.

Interestingly, the Torah uses the same verb (*kikha*) to describe Abraham's purchase of a grave-site and to derive that a legal engagement takes place when the groom gives the bride a ring (or a minimum amount of money).* Perhaps our tradition is suggesting that marriage requires a husband to take ultimate responsibility for his wife – especially in terms of securing her separate and unique identity – even beyond her life and into her grave.

This *parasha* reminds me of two poignant stories. First, when I was a very young rabbi, one of the first "emergency' questions I received was from an older woman leaning on a young Roman Catholic priest for support. She tearfully explained that her husband – who had died just a few hours earlier – was in need of a Jewish burial place. He had converted to Catholicism prior to having married her, and agreed that their children would be raised as Catholics. The Roman Catholic priest was, in fact, their son and she had never met any member of her husband's Jewish family. Even though they lived as Catholics during thirty-five years of their married life, his final deathbed wish had been to be buried in a Jewish cemetery....

Second, when my good and beloved friend Zalman Bernstein z'l was still living in America and beginning his return to Judaism, he asked me to find him a grave-site in the Mount of Olives cemetery. With

* Cf. *Kiddushin* 2a-b.

the help of the *Hevra Kadisha* (Sacred Fellowship) of Jerusalem, we set aside a plot. When he inspected it, however, he was most disappointed: 'You cannot see the Temple Mount,' he shouted, in his typical fashion. I attempted to explain calmly that after 120 years, he either wouldn't be able to see anything anyway, or he would be able to see everything no matter where his body lay. 'You don't understand,' he countered. 'I made a mess of my life so far and did not communicate to my children the glories of Judaism. The grave is my future and my eternity. Perhaps, when my children come to visit me there, if they would be able to see the holiest place in the world, the Temple Mount, they will be inspired by the Temple and come to appreciate what I could not adequately communicate to them while I was alive…'

For each individual, their personal grave-site represents the past and the future. Where and how individuals choose to be buried speaks volumes about how they lived their past lives and the values they aspired to. Similarly, for a nation, the grave-sites of its founders and leaders represent the past and reveal the signposts of the highs and lows in the course of the nation's history. The way a nation regards its grave-sites and respects its history will determine the quality of its future.

Indeed, the nation that chooses to forget its past has abdicated its future, because it has erased the tradition of continuity which it ought have transmitted to the future; the nation that does not properly respect the grave-sites of its founding patriarchs will not have the privilege of hosting the lives of their children and grandchildren. Perhaps this is why the Hebrew word, *kever*, literally a grave, is likewise used in rabbinical literature for womb. And the Hebrew name *Rvkh* (Rebecca), the wife of Isaac who took Sarah's place as the guiding matriarch, is comprised of the same letters as *hkvr*, the grave and/or the womb, the future which emerges from the past. Is it then any wonder that the first parcel of land in Israel purchased by the first Hebrew was a grave-site, and that the fiercest battles over ownership of the land of Israel surround the graves of our founding fathers and mothers? And perhaps this is why our Sages deduce the proper means for engagement from Abraham's purchase of a grave-site for Sarah – Jewish familial future must be built upon the life style and values of our departed matriarchs and patriarchs. The grave is also the womb; the past is mother to the future.

What Makes Laban Run?

> *And Rebecca had a brother, and his name was Laban, and Laban ran out unto the man, unto the well.*
>
> GENESIS 24:29

Laban is undoubtedly one of the most perplexing characters in the Torah. On the one hand, the Pesaḥ Haggada focuses on Laban as someone even more wicked than Pharaoh himself:

> Pharaoh merely attempted to murder the male children, whereas Laban sought to uproot every thing – the entire nation.

Apparently our Sages are saying that our greatest enemies are not necessarily the Pharaohs who threw the male children into the Nile, or the Nimrods who threw Abraham into the fiery furnace for believing in one God. Rather, oftentimes it is those much closer to us, sometimes even 'members of the family' who, in their own devious and assimilating ways, present a far greater danger to our survival than our sworn enemies.

Yet despite the Haggada's corroboration of the wickedness of Laban, he nevertheless serves as a model for many of our marriage customs. The very words with which he blesses his sister Rebecca, just prior to her departure to meet her betrothed Isaac, is what every groom says to his bride prior to the wedding ceremony, when he places the veil over the bride's head in the ceremony known as 'the *badeken*' (Yiddish for 'a covering'):

> Our sister, be thou the mother of myriads of ten thousands, and let thy seed inherit the gate of those that hate them.
>
> Gen. 24:60

Moreover, Laban's argument – when he deceived Jacob by giving him in marriage his elder daughter, Leah, rather than the preferred and betrothed younger daughter, Rachel (for whose hand the ardent suitor had worked for seven years) – that 'in our locality we do not give the younger before the older' [Gen. 29:26] stands as legitimate custom amongst traditional Jewish families to marry off the older daughter before the younger. Why would the Torah honor Laban by having his actual words serve as the introduction at such a significant moment in every couple's life, and by maintaining a custom which he, in effect, initiated in an act of deception? How do we reconcile the contemptible Laban of the Haggada with the model Laban for marriage ceremonies?

Perhaps the answer can be found in a fascinating statement of R. Haim b. Attar, in his commentary *Ohr Haḥayim*. He directs us to an insight of the Sages that when the Torah refers to righteous people, their 'names' (the word '*shem*' means both name and fame) precede them. In other words, with regard to the righteous, the verse will read, 'and his name was … so and so,' as we find in the case of Boaz, the judge of Israel, destined to redeem Ruth: '… a man of wealth, of the family of Elimelech, and his name was Boaz' [Ruth 2:1]. But when it comes to the wicked, their individual given name precedes the word 'name', as we find regarding Nabal – where the Torah writes, 'Nabal was his name …' [I Sam. 25:25]. Given this distinction made by the Sages, one would have expected that Laban, the anti-hero of the Haggada, certainly deserves a negative assignation similar to that of Nabal. However, the Bible in this portion introduces him: 'And Rebecca has a brother, and his name is Laban' – the word 'name' preceding the individual given name, as in the case of the righteous.

Ohr Haḥayim explains the Torah's adulatory means of introducing Laban in terms of a significant moral responsibility he demonstrated. We have to remember that in Laban's world – and to this day in much of the Middle East – strangers do not speak to young women in the street. It wasn't simply a question of decorum, but a principle that held the social structure together. But if the rule was broken and a young woman did speak to a man in the street, her brother would make it his business to find out what was going on. And if she entered the house wearing jewelry – a nose ring, or a bracelet – the family would immediately grow suspicious that something illicit had transpired, or was about to. If we follow the words in the verse closely, we note that '*Ushmo Lavan…*', the usual appellation of a righteous person, is followed by the phrase describing Laban's running outside, which was certainly a noble action on his part. After all, he was protecting his sister's honor and chastity.

The following verse continues with the narrative and describes that when Laban

> …saw the earrings and bracelets upon his sister's hands and when he heard the words of Rebecca, …he said [to the stranger]: 'Come in, blessed be God, why do you stand outside…?'
>
> Gen. 24:30, 31

Ohr Haḥayim explains that here the truer and perhaps even more natural colors of Laban's character are coming to the fore. Only after he 'sniffs' gold, silver, and diamonds does he extend his hospitality, his calculating mind figuring out how he can benefit from the entire affair. Nonetheless, even though Laban is devious, his instinctive response regarding Rebecca is nonetheless recognized as positive. He was first and foremost concerned about the honor of his sister.

I'd like to suggest an expansion of *Ohr Haḥayim* as to why the Torah includes Laban with the righteous. An overview of Laban's behavior in the Torah reveals that not only does he 'protect' his sister in our portion, but that whenever he relates to his immediate family we note a thematic consistency of sensitivity and concern – albeit at the expense of others. This may well be why our Sages eternalized Laban's words of blessing to his sister; although Laban has a mean, corrupt streak in general, when it comes to his own family, his dedication and devotion know no limitations. We see this demonstrated in relation to Rebecca, but the same is true when he consciously tricks the love-struck, hard-working Jacob into marrying Leah. For Laban, everything is permissible for the sake of bringing his less attractive, weak-eyed, elder daughter under the marriage canopy. Later, when Jacob wants to return to the land of his forefathers, the major stumbling block in his path is his father-in-law. From the perspective of Laban, Jacob's decision to return to his father's house is bringing unnecessary danger and financial insecurity upon his daughters and grandchildren. It is a foolhardy journey. After all, Esau may well be lying in wait to ambush the brother who took the blessings. Moreover, there is no family business back there in Canaan, no partnership that Jacob can join. Here in Laban's house he genuinely believes Jacob has everything he could possibly need: a good job, a good income, a nice house, even respect from the local council. Hence, Laban will stop at nothing to prevent Jacob's departure.

And this is precisely the problem. From one point of view, his dedication to family is honorable and praiseworthy. In fact, we emulate him in our marriage ceremonies. But Laban's narrow vision is a source of grave danger to Jewish destiny. With Laban at the helm, we will never return to Israel, never turn toward God and listen to His words. Instead, we'll happily sit with our paychecks and allow Jewish destiny to be perverted and sidetracked. We'll be assimilated, transformed, converted from the world of ladders connecting heaven and earth with ascending and descending angels to the world of Wall Street and investment, cattle and livestock. Laban is a runner. From the very first moment we're introduced to him, we see him on the move, running. But we must remember that his destination is not the same as ours, that he is moving on a totally different track. For us to join him would mean forsaking our God-given destiny.

Abraham is the Rabbi because Sarah is the Rebbitzen

> *And the life of Sarah was a hundred and seven*
> *and twenty years; these were the years of Sarah's*
> *life. And Sarah died in Kiryat Arba; that is*
> *Hebron, in the land of Canaan; and Abraham*
> *came to mourn for Sarah, and to weep for her.*
>
> GENESIS 23:1–2

Abraham may have been the first patriarch, the founder of
Israel, the monotheist who brought a new vision of God to the world,
but if Sarah had not been Sarah, Abraham could not have been Abraham.
This realization of Abraham about his wife is the implicit message of the
portion of *Ḥayei Sara*, and it's what paves the way for the last significant
act in Abraham's life: making Eliezer take an oath to find a wife for Isaac.

The first hint that something unusual has taken place after Sarah's
death is the way the Torah charts Abraham's reaction. Ordinarily when
it comes to mourning the dead, which response should come first, the

eulogy or the tears? One would think that the immediate response to the shocking finality of the death of a loved one is grief and pain, a feeling of such overwhelming emotion that it can only be expressed in tears. And only afterwards, when the mood has settled and a measure of inner quiet and acceptance has returned, can the person who has been weeping offer some kind of eulogy, words that assess the uniqueness of the deceased and his/her special qualities.

However, in the portion of *Hayei Sara* the exact opposite takes place. When Sarah dies in Hebron, we read how Abraham comes to '...eulogize Sarah and to weep for her' [Gen. 23:2]. First a eulogy, and only then tears!

Why the reversal? Let's consider Abraham and Sarah while both were still alive. Without doubt theirs was an 'ideal marriage', although not necessarily ideal in what we usually think of as the 'perfect marriage', where the couple looks lovingly into each other's eyes. Rather theirs was a marriage rooted in ideals: the teaching of the existence of one God of justice and compassion, and expressing that belief by extending loving-kindness to all strangers. Both husband and wife were heroic personalities with awesome visions. As the Midrash writes, Abraham and Sarah shared responsibility in taming the Wild East: Abraham converted the men from idolatry to monotheism, and Sarah converted the women. But in the end, despite whatever greatness Abraham may have achieved, Sarah was recognized by God as being the greater personality. After all, when Sarah suggests that Ishmael must be sent away because he is a bad influence on Isaac, and Abraham vacillates, God decides: 'Everything which Sarah tells you, listen to her voice' [Gen. 21:12]. This is what leads our Sages to say that Sarah was on a higher prophetic level than was Abraham [Rashi, ad loc].

Over the course of the years, however, familiarity does demand its price. Even the most perceptive of men can take their better half for granted. She can be the most beautiful woman in the city, but he is so involved in their joint mission that he doesn't notice. She may well be a prophetess, but his ongoing relationship with God causes him to see prophecy as an everyday occurrence. It doesn't necessarily mean that Abraham wasn't close to Sarah; on the contrary, he was so close to her that she had virtually become his alter-ego, flesh of his flesh, bone of his bone. We see this clearly expressed in the incident shortly after Abraham enters the stage of world history at the age of seventy-five. A famine forces him to head down to Egypt to seek food, but the ramifications of the journey immediately strike him. 'Now I realize that you are a beautiful woman [*yefat toar*]' [Gen. 24:11], Abraham says to Sarah. Danger has awakened him, for the Egyptians will surely lust after her and kill the husband of such a beautiful woman. But only at that point does he take notice of her beauty. Until then, he had accepted it as a matter of course, just as he accepted the openness of their home, the dedication of her activities, the cleverness of her approach.

Intellectually, Abraham certainly understood exactly where Sarah stood in his life, the person whose idyllic home (Sarah's tent) provided the holy atmosphere for their joint spiritual work. But it is understandable that he might lose sight of Sarah's unique stature and distinctive achievements, that he might come to take her for granted.

Hence, when he first heard of her death, he was undoubtedly upset. But it was only after he began to assess the multiple commitments and accomplishments of her life in the preparation of the eulogy that he really began to cry. It was the realization of how indispensable she really was that gave rise to bitter tears of grief which could never be consoled; Abraham, following the eulogy, clearly understood that his life and mission could never be the same again.

Thus, these tears of Abraham never come to an end. True, Abraham marries again and even has children, but the Torah does not elaborate. The sixty-two years of his spiritual journey come to a complete end with the death of Sarah. It's as if her death is also the death of Abraham's religious creativity, although he outlives Sarah by thirty-eight years in which he remains strong and virile; we are told by the Bible that he remarries and even has more children [Gen. 25:1–6], but Abraham's achievements for his new faith recorded in the Torah are only achieved in the lifetime of his wife. When she dies, the major part of him dies as well. And if the Torah now turns its spotlight away from Abraham, it only confirms that without his wife, Abraham's life is no longer worthy of being mentioned. Indeed, God no longer enters into recorded dialogue with Abraham after Sarah's passing.

In fact, the last act of Abraham that the Torah records emerges directly from Sarah's death. Once Sarah is buried in the field which Abraham buys, we read that Abraham turns to Eliezer and charges his servant to return to Haran and seek a wife for Isaac. Why now? Wasn't Abraham interested in grandchildren earlier?

But this last request of Abraham emerges directly from the tears after the eulogy. Now that he has a deeper understanding of the significance of Sarah in his own life, he realizes that Isaac must marry a woman who will be able to reach the stature of Sarah. No small task, but anything less will thwart the effort to create a third generation that will carry the message of the One God to the world.

Not only does Abraham give this charge to Eliezer, but we read that Eliezer departs on his journey '… having all goodly things of his master's in his hand' [Gen. 4:10]. Rashi explains that these 'goodly things' is a blank check which might be needed to convince a reluctant family of the wealth of their prospective son-in-law, Isaac.

But the verse can also be read literally. 'Having all goodly things of his master's in his hand' means that everything Abraham accomplished, everything he was, all that he had become because of his wife Sarah – was now placed into the hand of Eliezer with the request that he find a similar wife for Isaac. The whole future of the Jewish people depends on the woman Isaac will marry.

The succession from Sarah to Rebecca is emphasized by the Torah itself. 'And Isaac brought her into his mother Sarah's tent, and took Rebecca, and she became his wife; and he loved her. And Isaac was comforted for his mother' [Gen. 24:67]. Rashi explains that when Sarah was alive three miracles distinguished her tent: the light from the Sabbath candles (*shalom bayit*, household tranquility) lasted from week to week; there was blessing in her dough, (generous hospitality with more than enough for all); and the clouds of the Divine Presence rested upon her tent (purity in personal life). All this ceased upon her death. But when Rebecca married Isaac, all three miracles resumed.

Thus we see how the Torah effectively closes the pages of Abraham's spiritual life with a flashback to Sarah. The text focuses on her tent. Abraham's tears were not the result of a spontaneous burst of emotion; they grew in proportion to his understanding of the greatness of his wife, without whom the people of Israel would have never emerged.

Pre-Arranged vs. Romantic Marriages

> *And Abraham said to the eldest servant of his*
> *house... Put I pray thee, thy hand under my thigh,*
> *and I will make thee swear by the Lord, the God*
> *of heaven and the God of earth, that you shall*
> *not take a wife to my son of the daughters of the*
> *Canaanites, amongst whom I dwell, but you shall*
> *go to my country, and to my kindred place, and*
> *take a wife to my son Isaac.*
>
> GENESIS 24:2–4

The Torah presents us with two models of marriage – the arranged marriage of Isaac and Rebecca in the portion of *Ḥayei Sara*, and the romantic love-at-first-sight model of Jacob and Rachel two portions later.

The two are very different. Jacob's love was such that he worked for fourteen years in order to marry his beloved Rachel. Not only was Jacob enthusiastic about his love, but he consulted with his wives, calling to Rachel and Leah to consider tactics for regaining what their father Laban has taken from him. Jacob's open line of communication is the very antithesis of the non-communication that seems to prevail between Isaac and Rebecca. This is not to say that all is grim between Rebecca and Isaac. If it were, their act of lovemaking would not have revealed to King Avimelekh that this 'brother and sister' who arrived in his land seeking food are in reality husband and wife. And the word used to describe the act is '*metzaḥek*', (literally, playing) which Rashi specifies as sexual intercourse. And earlier, the Torah's descriptions of their marriage are extraordinary in terms of tenderness.

> And Isaac brought her into his mother Sarah's tent and took Rebecca, and she became his wife; and he loved her. And Isaac was comforted for his mother.
>
> Gen. 24:67

Rashi notes that Rebecca's entry into Sarah's tent revives the light and blessings that were extinguished with the death of the first matriarch, casting Rebecca into an exalted position. The text specifically states that Rebecca comforted Isaac and that he loved her. Nevertheless, seemingly missing from their lives is the deep connection that only comes from authentic communication. What better evidence of the distance between them can there be than the argument surrounding the *bekhora*, the spiritual blessings a parent bequeaths to the next generation.

Differences between parents may exist, but if the father prefers Esau, and the mother prefers Jacob, ought there not be a recorded discussion, and an opportunity to examine the true nature of their sons' characters in order to arrive at a united decision? Instead, Rebecca resorts to ruse, casting studious Jacob into a role of deception for which he is totally unsuitable. Not only does he perpetrate an act which will haunt him for the rest of his life, but what begins as a split between brothers comes to signify the far greater division between Jews and gentiles throughout history.

The Netziv, in his commentary *Ha'amek Davar*, probes why Rebecca resorts to deception. Realizing that Isaac was not suited to find his own mate, Abraham sent his trusted servant, Eliezer, to scout the land for a suitable wife. Eliezer returned with Rebecca. The Torah records the first encounter between Isaac and Rebecca. Isaac had been meditating in the fields, and with the approach of Eliezer and the bride-to-be, he raised his eyes: 'When Rebecca looked up and saw Isaac, she fell from the camel' [Gen. 25:5]. The Netziv explains that she fell because she had never seen a religious personality before. So awesome was the sight of Isaac transformed by prayer that she must have been knocked off her feet, literally. Compared to the lying and cheating world of her father, Betuel, and her brother, Laban, Isaac projected a vision of purity with which Rebecca had no previous experience. When Eliezer revealed the man's identity, she took the veil and covered herself, not only as a sign of modesty, but as an expression of her unworthiness. From that moment on, the veil between them was never removed.

Granted that the veil comes to symbolize the distance between their worlds, why couldn't Isaac bridge the gap? When told to put away the knife that was poised at Isaac's neck, Abraham certainly celebrates, but Isaac remains in a state of shock. In fact, a part of him always remained behind on Mount Moriah, as hinted at in the final verse of the *Akeda*. 'Abraham returned to his young men, and together they went to Be'er Sheva, and Abraham dwelt at Be'er Sheva' [Gen. 22:19]. Why isn't Isaac mentioned? Very likely the verse alludes to the fact that only Abraham came down, but Isaac, or part of him, remained behind on the altar. Thus it's not surprising that the traumatized Isaac became a silent, non-communicative survivor.

We know little about the sibling relationship between Isaac and Ishmael. Ishmael is, after all, the banished son of the banished wife, Hagar. But God did reveal Himself to Hagar and Ishmael at Be'er-lahai-ro'i, and guarantee greatness to Ishmael. Isaac seems to be brooding over God's relationship to Ishmael, searching for a similar revelation in the same spot it occurred to his brother.

But all of this is never expressed: it is suggested in Isaac's travels, although not in his words. Isaac seemingly has no difficulty communicating with God (our Rabbis tell us that he even originated the Minha prayer*), but he does have difficulty communicating with his brother and with his wife. If a couple cannot communicate, the result can sometimes be tragic. I don't know if the Torah prefers the marriage of Jacob

---

* Cf. *Berakhot* 26b.

and Rachel over the marriage of Isaac and Rebecca. But we do know who communicates and who doesn't. Was Jacob happier for it? Probably. After all, he is the father of the twelve tribes, while Isaac fathers two brothers whose split is irrevocable.

Toledot

With Whom to Make Treaties

> *And they said, we saw indeed that the Lord was with you and we said: let there now be an oath between us, between us and you, and let us make a covenant with you.*
>
> GENESIS 26:28

On what basis, and with which type of people, are we encouraged to make treaties? A careful reading of the relationships between Abraham, Isaac and Avimelekh – and especially a study of Chapter 26 in *Toledot* – provides a significant answer to these questions, which also contains a crucial message for the government of Israel today.

Some background: We first met Avimelekh in Chapter 20 in *Vayera*, when Abraham wandered over to Gerar, the area where Avimelekh ruled. Gerar was the land of the Philistines, which is part of the divinely promised borders of Israel. Abraham referred to Sarah as his sister, and she was immediately taken into Avimelekh's harem – without anyone asking her or her 'brother's' permission [Gen. 20:2]. Clearly he was a lascivious and cruel despot, who certainly would have murdered any husband of Sarah. After he was given a dire warning in a dream sent by God, Avimelekh played the innocent victim, asserting that the fault lies with Abraham since he [Avimelekh] acted 'with purity of heart and innocence of hand' [Gen. 20:5]. Abraham correctly explains: '...there is no fear of God in this place, and I would have been murdered because of my wife' [Gen. 20:11].

Chapter 21 proceeds to tell us about the birth of Isaac and the banishment of Ishmael and then returns to describe a meeting between Abraham, Avimelekh and his general, Piḥol. Avimelekh insists that Abraham swear he will not act falsely by taking away his land during the lifetime of his grandchildren and great-grandchildren. Abraham agrees [Gen. 21:24], but then Abraham chastises Avimelekh for having stolen his well. Yet again, Avimelekh plays the innocent victim, remonstrating that 'I didn't know who did this thing, you didn't tell me, and I never heard of it until today' [Gen. 21:26].

Despite Avimelekh's apparent duplicity as a woman-snatcher and well-stealer, Abraham nevertheless makes a treaty with him. Abraham gives him sheep and cattle as well as seven more ewes as a sign that he dug the well at Be'er Sheva (literally 'the well of the oath'). It is remarkable that it is Abraham who does the giving: he receives nothing, although the covenant, the oath, is taken by both of them.

Then with a brief segue 'And it happened after these things...', we read about the terrifying command by God that Abraham offer his only son as a whole burnt offering. Rashbam cites a Midrash suggesting that the sacrifice of Isaac was a punishment to Abraham for his treaty with Avimelekh. Entering into a treaty with a treacherous individual for a number of generations is irresponsible. Abraham has no right to take such a risk and jeopardize his children's lives. More to the point, says Rashbam, Abraham had no right to give away Isaac's patrimony, a portion of the promised land of Israel. Hence, concludes this commentary, God commands Abraham to sacrifice his son; if Abraham was willing to 'treaty away' his son's inheritance to a rogue, Abraham apparently does not value his son anyway.

This context brings us to *Toledot*, where the most important thing we learn from history is that we never learn from history. Now, it is Isaac,

Abraham's son, who is forced by famine to go to 'Avimelekh, the King of the Philistines, to Gerar' [Gen. 26:1]. Immediately, the people of the area ask about his wife and – for self-protection – he too refers to Rebecca as his sister. We discover that Avimelekh is also a voyeur; he looks into Isaac's window and sees him 'playing' with his wife! Yet again, Avimelekh feigns innocence, calling Isaac the deceiver. 'What is this that you did to us by claiming she was your sister? One of my people almost slept with your wife!' [Gen. 26:10]

Isaac goes on to amass a vast accumulation of wealth, including cattle, sheep and servants. He is still living in Gerar, 'And the Philistines were jealous of him' [Gen. 26:14]. This is the same Avimelekh and these are the same Philistines with whom Abraham made his covenant. Nevertheless, 'the Philistines stopped up all of the wells which were dug by the servants of his father,' and Avimelekh forces Isaac to move away because 'his wealth was amassed from them' [Gen. 26:16]. Isaac passively leaves, but nevertheless insists upon re-digging the wells of his father which had been destroyed. To add insult to injury, Isaac now digs two new wells in his new location – only to have the Philistines arguing with him over the ownership of the water.

The finale of this incident is difficult to imagine. After all that has transpired, Avimelekh comes to Isaac flanked by his general Piḥol and *ahuzat me-re'ehu* – a group of friends – in order to sign another treaty with him. Isaac is understandably surprised, seeing that they have 'hated him and exiled him.' The fork-tongued Avimelekh argues, 'we have done only good towards you because we sent you away in peace.' The Philistine king apparently believes that if a Jew is banished – but is permitted to flee with his life intact – the Jew ought be grateful! And, despite Avimelekh's history, Isaac has a feast with him and they swear yet another oath together. Isaac now renames the place Be'er Sheva in honor of this second oath-treaty.

Is the Torah then teaching us to continue to make treaties, even though our would-be partners have a history of duplicity and treachery? I believe the very opposite to be the case. 'The actions of the ancestors are repeated in the lives of their children.' Unfortunately, Jews are always over-anxious to believe that their enemies have become their friends and the leopard has changed his spots. The very next verse in the Torah – the closing of the story of Isaac and Avimelekh but seemingly without any connection to it – reads:

> And Esau was forty years old and he took as a wife Yehudit the daughter of Be'eri the Hittite and Bosmat the daughter of Eglon the Hittite. And this was a bitterness of spirit to Isaac and to Rebecca.
>
> Gen. 26:34–35

Now, the one clear prohibition insisted upon by the Patriarchs was that their sons not take Canaanite or Hittite wives. I believe that the Torah is telling us that if Isaac makes a treaty with an inappropriate partner, his son will enter into a marriage with an inappropriate partner.

Just as Abraham is punished for his treaty with Avimelekh, so is Isaac punished for his treaty with Avimelekh. The land of Israel is too important and the preservation of a Jewish future is too vulnerable for us to take risks and make treaties with unconscionable and dishonest rulers. A treaty is only possible when it is made with a partner who fears God in the same way that we do.

Rebecca's Choice: Deception for the Sake of Heaven

> *And Rebecca spoke to her son Jacob, saying... And now, my son, obey my voice according to which I command you...*
>
> GENESIS 27:5, 7

One of the many glories of the Bible is that it recognizes the complex personality especially of great individuals, and the fact that strength and weakness, virtue and vice, can sometimes both reside in the very same soul. Even more significantly, that which may superficially appear to be dishonest – an act of deception – may very well provide the necessary ingredient which ultimately creates grandeur. It is this understanding which supplies the real motivation for what appears to be Rebecca's deception according to the profound interpretations of the Malbim and Rabbi Samson Raphael Hirsch.

The most obvious question which strikes us, as we read the Torah portion, is why Rebecca had to deceive her husband by dressing her younger son Jacob in the garb and in the skins of her older son Esau? Why could she not merely have explained to her husband that Esau, although he was the elder brother, was simply not worthy of the birthright? From a textual perspective, this doesn't seem to have been a difficult task at all. After all, right before Isaac summons Esau requesting venison meat as the hors d'oeuvre of the blessing, the Bible specifically records that Esau had committed the one great sin of the patriarchal period: he married two Hittite women, which was 'a bitterness of spirit to Isaac and to Rebecca' [Gen. 26:35]. Moreover, Rebecca could certainly have argued that the son who had been willing to sell his birthright to Jacob for a mere bowl of lentil soup, could not possibly be worthy of the mantle of Abrahamic leadership. Furthermore, Rebecca had heard from the Almighty that 'the elder son would serve the younger' [Gen. 25:23] during her frighteningly difficult pregnancy. So why didn't she make her convincing case to her husband after coffee one evening rather than resort to an act of trickery?

Malbim suggests that indeed such a conversation between husband and wife did take place. And after Rebecca marshalled her arguments, Isaac then explained to his wife that he was as aware of Esau's shortcomings as she was. In fact, he understood that the spiritual blessing of family leadership, the blessing of Abraham which we know as the birthright, must certainly go to Jacob; indeed when Jacob is later forced by the wrath of his deceived brother Esau to leave his home and go into exile with Laban, after his father warns him not take a wife from the daughters of Canaan, he is blessed with the messianic dream of becoming a congregation of nations and he is given the blessing of Abraham, to inherit the land of Israel [Gen. 28:3, 4]. But, argues Isaac, he must make a split between the birthright of spiritual leadership which rightfully belongs to Jacob and the physical blessing of material prosperity and political domination which he has decided to give to Esau:

> May the Lord give you from the dew of the heavens and the fat [oil] of the land and much grain and wine ... Be the political master over your brother and may the daughters of your mother bow down to you.
>
> Gen. 27:28–29

The more spiritual brother must receive the religious-spiritual birthright (*bekhora*) and the more physical brother must receive the material-political blessing (*berakha*). After all, argues Isaac, the bookish, naive, and spiritual Jacob (*ish tam, yoshev ohalim*) would not begin to know how to maneuver in an economically driven, militaristically guided society. Give Esau the oil and the sword; give Jacob the books and the Temple.

Rebecca strongly disagrees. She understands that the world at large and the human nature of individuals dare not be so simplistically divided between the spiritual and the material, God and Caesar. If religious leadership is to emerge supreme, it requires the infrastructure of economic stability; in an imperfect world of aggression and duplicity, even leading spiritual personalities must sometimes reluctantly wage war against evil in order for the good to triumph. Rebecca understands the world of reality; after all, she comes from the house of Laban and Bethuel, two masters of deceit and treachery.

It is fascinating that, in the next generation, Jacob's wife, Rachel, alongside her great spiritual gifts of kindness and humility (remember that she gave the secret signs to her sister under the nuptial canopy in order not to embarrass Leah), also had the practical ability to steal the household gods. In the ancient world of Mari and Nuzu – ancient peoples contemporaneous with the patriarchs – these gods belonged to the inheritor of the birthright. When Rachel stole the gods she was securing her husband's rights, because after all it was Jacob who was responsible for Laban's material success. She also knew how to cover up her actions when her father began his search. It is no accident that her son Joseph rises to greatness not only because of his great moral qualities but also because of his practical wisdom and his ability to take advantage of every situation.

We should also remember that the King Messiah, the progenitor of whom is King David, is both the sweet singer of songs with a voice of Jacob as well as the great warrior of Israel with hands of Esau. Indeed, when Samuel the prophet anoints David, the young shepherd-singer is described as 'a red faced man (*admoni*) with beautiful eyes and goodly appearance' [1 Sam. 16:12]. Edom is also another name for Esau, who was also born an *admoni* (ruddy-complexioned) and who ate the red lentil pottage. King David's strength as well as his weakness apparently was derived from that aspect of Esau which was part of his personality. Every Jacob must learn to utilize, tame and ultimately sanctify the necessary hands of Esau, without which it is impossible to triumph.

But the profound complexity of our Torah continues its lessons. Yes, Jacob justifiably received both blessing and birthright (*berakha* and *bekhora*) from his father, but we cannot – and he cannot – forget that this occurred as a result of his act of deception. Jacob, therefore, has to pay a heavy price. He must flee from his parents' home in order to escape Esau's wrath, and is thrust into exile with the treacherous Laban.

And in addition to all of the problems faced by someone on the run, Jacob has the added dilemma of looking at himself in the mirror. His deception was orchestrated by his mother, perhaps even ordained by God, but, nonetheless, something inside him has been forever tainted. This feeling of guilt never leaves him. Twenty years later, when Jacob is about to return to his birthplace as a mature older man – as a husband and a father – he realizes that unfinished business between Esau and himself still remains.

Conscience-stricken, he acts totally subservient and obsequious, beseeching his brother, '*kah na et birkhati*' [Gen. 33:11] which literally means 'take my blessing,' as he hands over a large portion of his material acquisitions. After all these years, Jacob wishes to make amends by returning the very blessings he undeservedly had received from his father. 'And one must restore the stolen object which one has taken' [Lev. 5:23], demands biblical morality.

But Jacob even goes one step further. He is so remorseful about his youthful act of deception that when presenting his final will and testament to his children, Jacob himself acts according to his father's intention. He grants Judah the spiritual blessings of the nation's leadership, and to the sons of Joseph, Ephraim and Menashe – the physical blessings, the double portion of the *bekhorah*, the fat of the land, physical increase, material prosperity.

However, perhaps children are generally doomed to repeat the mistakes of their parents. What Jacob does is certainly understandable: in his search for forgiveness, he feels he must return to his father's original place and reject his mother's vision of unity. But in principle, Rebecca was right. This split of the blessing and birthright between Judah and

Ephraim planted the seeds of division in the Jewish people, between Judah's concentration on religion and the Holy Temple, and Ephraim's celebration of luxury and lawlessness. However, Rebecca dreamt of a different world of unity, where Torah and technology, yeshiva and military service, could dwell together.

The Truth Behind the Masquerade

Now Isaac loved Esau, because he did eat of his venison, and Rebecca loved Jacob.

GENESIS 25:28

Т he tragedy which haunts Jacob until the end of his life, the transgression which informs the rest of the book of Genesis – indeed, all of subsequent Jewish history until this very day – is Jacob's deception of his father in order to wrest the blessings meant for Esau. In 'measure for measure' fashion, Laban gives Jacob the unloved daughter under the marriage canopy because 'it is not done in our place to give the younger before the elder' – setting the stage for the bitter rivalry of the wives which led to Reuven's heinous crime against his father. Jacob is further deceived by his sons when they present him with Joseph's blood-soaked coat of many colors, leading Jacob to mistakenly conclude, 'he has been torn apart by a wild beast' – which further sets the stage for the subsequent deception of Joseph's brothers by the Grand Vizier of Pharaoh after the sale of Joseph into Egypt. Moreover, the enmity between Jacob's children and Esau's children (Israel vs. Rome) as well as the internal strife and sibling hatred among the children of Israel themselves reverberates throughout Jewish history and plagues us even now. What would impel the 'wholehearted' Jacob, the studious dweller of tents, to fall prey to an act of deception and pose as his brother in disguise for the sake of the blessings – even if it was his mother who made the suggestion! And what makes the ruse even stranger to comprehend is the fact that it was bound to be uncovered. After all, Esau would appear sooner or later with the venison in hand, and the wrath of father Isaac was certain to fall upon the head of impostor Jacob. So why does he do it?

I believe a fascinating answer may be found within the complexity of the parent-child, father-son relationship, which is so profoundly depicted between the lines and embedded within the parchment folds of the amazing book of Genesis. From the very first verses in our portion of *Toledot*, the stage is set for the sibling rivalry between the twin brothers Jacob and Esau. It is important to take careful note of how the Bible testifies that Isaac loved Esau because of *tzayid b'fiv*, which literally means 'because the hunt (or entrapment) was in his mouth,' and Rebecca loved Jacob [Gen. 25:28]. Every child yearns for – and deserves – unconditional love from his/her parents. After all, the child did not ask to be born into the world; the most potent armor he/she can receive as protection against the irrational forces expelled by both environment and society is the protective love – no matter what – of concerned, committed parents. To paraphrase Robert Frost, a home is the place where, when everyone else closes the door on you, they will always welcome you in with a warm embrace. And within the patriarchal society which was Jacob's world, Jacob especially yearned for the warm embrace of his father.

Tragically, he didn't receive it. Rebecca loved Jacob, period; apparently this meant unconditionally. But that was not enough. Jacob felt unloved, rejected, by his father – who did love his brother Esau. Jacob desperately yearned for this love – and there was even a way for him to acquire it. After all, Isaac did not love Esau unconditionally; he loved him because the hunt (entrapment) was in his mouth. Esau fed his father the venison meat he so dearly loved ('Esau's venison meat was in Isaac's mouth'), and the mellifluous speech of the lawyer-politician-trickster was Esau's gift-of-gab ('Esau's entrapment via words was the gift of speech in Esau's mouth'). If only.…

Permit me a story to help elucidate the unfulfilled need which caused an emptiness in Jacob's heart, the aching angst with which only the child who feels himself unloved and rejected by the favored parent can ever identify.

My wife and I have a respected and beloved friend, a survivor of the Holocaust, a beautiful and intelligent woman blessed with a strong sterling character, a stunningly frank but generous disposition, and a rare ability to express herself in prose and poetry. During one of our many conversations in which she would reminisce about her childhood, she revealed that one of the happiest recollections of her life was the day in which she was forcibly removed from her family and taken by the Nazis to an extermination camp. Responding to our shocked expressions, she described a family situation in which her older sister was the favored, *frum* (religious) daughter and she was the rejected, rebellious one. If there was one pat of butter and one pat of margarine, her sister would get the butter and she would get the margarine. 'After all,' her mother would explain, 'Miriam is exhausted from davening with such concentration; you skipped a few corners with the prayer-book in your hand, so you can do with less.'

What was even more difficult for her to bear was her mother's complaint whenever she was angered by her younger daughter's conduct: 'You probably aren't my own biological daughter! Your sister was born at home, whereas you were born in a "clinic." The doctors probably exchanged my real daughter with you …' Obviously, this was not a usual refrain spoken by the mother, but was only engendered by our friend's occasional rebellion. But as the Yiddish proverb goes 'A slap departs, a word still smarts' (*A patsch dergeht, A vort bashteht*).

In 1942 the Nazis came to her hometown of Bendine, and rounded up the children. Only she and her parents were at home. Her father tried to steady his trembling hands by writing a *kvittel* (petition) to the Gerer Rebbe; her mother threw herself at the feet of the Nazi beasts, begging them to take her and spare the life of her precious child. Our friend said she felt absolutely no fear, even when they loaded her onto the cattle car; she could feel only joy, joy in the knowledge that her mother truly loved her after all, joy in the confirmation that she was indeed her parent's own and beloved daughter, joy in the discovery that she was at last accepted and not rejected.

I would argue that Jacob desperately wanted to feel his father's love, even if but for a brief period. If he supplied the venison meat, if he truly expressed the words 'I am Esau your first-born,' then perhaps Isaac would love him just as he loved Esau of the venison, just as he loved Esau of the mellifluous verbal entrapment. Indeed, Jacob yearns to be Esau – because then he could hope to gain paternal acceptance and affection. And so begins Jacob's odyssey, first searching for an Esau identity in Laban's house and business for twenty-two years and then finally succeeding in exorcizing Esau at the River Yabbok in order to become reconciled with his own true self. But Jacob's journey will only be completed, and the Lord will only become his God, when he eventually returns in peace to – and is at peace with – his father's house – and as Jacob-Israel, but not as Jacob-Esau.

Perhaps Esau is the Prime Deceiver!

> *Perhaps my father will feel me, and I shall seem to him as a deceiver, and I shall bring a curse upon me, and not a blessing.*
>
> GENESIS 27:12

Isaac is about to render judgement. Jacob has just left his father's tent garbed in goat skins, pretending to be his twin brother, Esau, and has deceived his father into giving him the blessing. The real Esau comes in. We have every right to expect an angry reaction from a father who understands he has been duped. After all, this is not merely an innocent lie; the younger son has taken advantage of his father's blindness. Discovering his son's cunning and guile, Isaac would certainly have been justified had he turned the blessings into curses, just as Jacob feared he would if he was ever found out.

From our perspective, Jacob's fear is legitimate, his anticipated punishment justified. But instead, the opposite occurs: At the moment of discovery, Isaac declares: 'Moreover, he [Jacob] shall be blessed'

[Gen. 27:33]. Blessed? After this deception?! Something is amiss. It simply doesn't follow.

In order to understand Isaac's response, we have to step back and consider the central subject of the story. Even a hasty reading leaves our heads spinning from all the apparent deceptions. Everybody deceives everybody. Esau perceives that he has been deceived by Jacob twice; once when Jacob took advantage of Esau's hunger from the hunt to buy the birthright from him for a mess of pottage, and a second time when he assumed his elder brother's identity to receive the blessings from his father. Isaac is deceived by Jacob and Rebecca. But Isaac too is deceived by Esau. And I would maintain that it is this latter deception which is really the mother of all subsequent deceptions.

No doubt there have always been those who love to attack Jacob, portraying Esau as the oppressed victim, a cynical twist on the traditional biblical perspective. I even had a classmate who wanted to name his son Esau, arguing that Esau and not Jacob deserved the patrimony and patriarchy. And given the times we live in, I could easily imagine the creation of a Society to Restore Esau's Maligned Name, an Esau anti-defamation league. After all, didn't Jacob snap up Esau's birthright with a bowl of soup, and then, with the aid of his mother, a quickly prepared goat stew, and some of Esau's old clothes, steal the blessing from Isaac, deceiving two people with one meal?!

But if we're going to speak about deception we have to start at the beginning. Even before any of the entanglements between Jacob and Esau unfold, the Torah has clearly defined the vast differences between these two twin brothers:

> And the boys grew, and Esau was one who knew how to trap, a man of the field, while Jacob was a whole-hearted man, dwelling in tents.
>
> Gen. 25:27

The Hebrew words suggest a double entendre, a connotation that Esau knew how to entrap, or deceive, as well as to trap animals. After all, his knowledge of trapping stands in opposition to Jacob's whole-heartedness, suggesting that each description relates to character rather than profession.

Picking up on this, Rashi cites the Midrash which extracts from the biblical suggestion that Isaac favored Esau because 'his hunt was in his mouth' (*ki tsayid b'fiv*) – not only because Isaac liked Esau's venison but also, and perhaps primarily, because Esau had developed the skill of entrapment with his tongue. He tricked his father into thinking he was extremely punctilious in keeping the commandments by asking such questions as to whether or not salt requires tithing [Rashi on Gen 25:28]. Hence, the Midrash is suggesting that Isaac was initially entrapped by Esau's clever 'fork-tongued' questions, by the son who said the right things at the right time to the right people. Esau spoke as if he were Jacob!

Indeed, the very fact that the Torah gives a reason for Isaac's love while Rebecca's love is reason-less supports this contention. Isaac loves Esau because of his deceptive tongue; the more perceptive Rebecca loves Jacob because he is Jacob. Isaac was manipulated, deceived into favoring Esau.

And should there be any doubt as to what kind of Esau we're dealing with, the Torah next presents us with a hungry Esau who wants lentil soup from his brother, Jacob. Soup in exchange for your birthright, negotiates Jacob. Clearly, Esau should have refused such outrageous terms, going over to the cupboard himself, measuring out a cupful of lentils as he got the water to boil. Does Jacob deceive Esau, or is he rather testing Esau's true priorities: soup now or a birthright later, inherited upon Isaac's death. Jacob has proven to his own satisfaction that the unworthy Esau had only been talking a good game to impress a naïve and unsuspecting father.

With this act of selling out, the lines are drawn. In broader terms, one brother represents the forces that are unable to delay gratification, and the other brother represents the forces that can, and do. Obviously for the future survival and redemption of the Jewish people, the blessing must go to the brother who has mastered delaying physical gratification for a greater good. The problem, however, lies in the fact that Isaac is so imbued with the values of honesty with which he grew up in the home of his father Abraham that he cannot possibly imagine that his own son has been lying to him all his life.

But Rebecca sees the world and Esau with different eyes. First of all, God Himself (as it were) had communicated to her that two nations were in her womb, and that the elder would serve the younger. But, most to the point, Rebecca grew up with Laban, the Aramean, a word linguistically connected with *rama'i*, deceiver, and its repetition three times in the opening verse of this Torah portion suggests that Rebecca knew only too well the sounds of a person who speaks with a forked tongue. From this perspective, Rebecca's suggestion to Jacob that he pose as Esau takes on an altogether different significance. Rebecca's real aim is not to deceive Isaac into blessing Jacob; she knows that the ruse will soon be discovered – because, after all, Esau is bound to enter his father's tent with the venison meat in short order. As Rabbi Samson Raphael Hirsch suggests, Rebecca merely wishes to demonstrate to her naïve husband that he is capable of being deceived by his son, that his inner vision is not as perceptive as he thinks.

The matriarch must demonstrate to her husband that he is capable of being tricked; if so, he may have misjudged his sons all these years. He thinks he knows the true Esau. Rebecca will attempt to prove to him that Esau deceived him all along, that it is Jacob who deserves being Esau (the first-born) in his eyes!

Thus when she overhears Isaac beckoning to Esau, she realizes that she can put into effect a plan that will open up Isaac's eyes once and for all. Would she ever have answered Jacob's fear of being cursed by saying, 'upon me be your curse…' [Gen. 27:13] had she not understood Isaac's heart perfectly, and known that as soon as he discovered that he was capable of being deceived, he would also understand that the same deception practiced against him by Jacob this night had also been practiced by Esau against him all these years.

And this is precisely what happens. Esau's arrival with the venison produces a great trembling in Isaac, possibly evoking the trembling he felt on the *Akeda*. He realizes that just as his father once nearly sacrificed him, Isaac has unconsciously been sacrificing Jacob in favor of his hunter-deceiver brother, overlooking the son given over to study and morality in favor of the son who craves animal blood and entrails.

Rebecca, sister of Laban the Aramean deceiver, saw it all along. Isaac realizes at last that he is capable of being fooled. Hence, anger directed at Jacob is not appropriate. On the contrary, Jacob is the true heir to the blessing, which is why the key phrase is, 'Moreover, and he shall be blessed' [Gen. 27:33].

The truth overrides whatever emotional attachment Isaac may still have for Esau. Jacob is not the deceiver. Esau is, and has been all along.

When Man Disposes, God Proposes

> *And Jacob said to his mother Rebecca, Behold*
> *Esau my brother is a hairy man, and I am a*
> *smooth man. Perhaps my father will feel me and I*
> *shall be in his eyes as an impostor...*
>
> GENESIS 27:11–12

All of our prior explanations and rationalizations notwith-standing, we still remain with a wife deceiving her husband and a son deceiving his father. And the commentaries, as well as the biblical text itself, seem uncomfortable with the subterfuge. Rashi points out that when Isaac addresses Jacob with the question, 'Are you my son Esau?' he answers, 'I am,' paused a bit, and then said 'Esau is your first-born,' technically having avoided the bold-faced lie of misrepresentation. The *Ktav v'Hakabbalah** also finds more than one textual indication hinting at Jacob's heavy heart in this entire matter. He alerts us to the fact that

---

* Y. Meckelburg, *Haktav v'Hakabbalah* (Jerusalem 1985). Originally published in Frankfurt in 1880.

two Hebrew words can be used to indicate the concept of 'perhaps' or 'lest' – *'ulai'* or *'pen'*; the substantial difference between them is that while *'ulai'* connotes an inner desire for the possibility to take place, *'pen'* indicates that the individual is extremely reticent about the possibility ever transpiring. Thus Jacob's complaint to his mother that 'perhaps my father will feel me and I shall be in his eyes as an impostor…' should have utilized the adverb *'pen'* because of Jacob's obvious reluctance to his being discovered by his father. Nevertheless, the Torah employs the adverb *'ulai,'* close to *ulevai* (literally, would that it be so), indicating that Jacob's inner desire was that the deceit should be discovered before it's too late.

Nonetheless, when all is said and done, the fact remains that a deception took place; Rebecca orchestrated it and Jacob perpetrated it. Do we then, as students of the Torah, deny this deception, painting the episode in a hue of translucent colors, or somehow confront the deceptions and ask what the Torah wants to teach us by recording it in such a forthright manner?

Professor Nehama Leibowitz provides a most profound answer to our question. She postulates the 'double track' theory of Jewish theology, suggesting that the Bible speaks on two separate tracks or planes: the human and the divine. On the human level, there is absolutely no justification whatsoever for deception. Jacob ends up working seven years for his beloved Rachel, only to be deceived by Laban who substitutes the elder sister for the younger under the marriage canopy. When the son-in-law takes his father-in-law to task, Laban responds: 'It is not done in our place to give the younger before the elder' [Gen. 29:26]– a clear denigration of Jacob's previous act of usurping his elder brother's place.

Years later Jacob's own sons will deceive him, claiming that his beloved Joseph was torn to death by a wild animal, and Joseph's exile in Egypt leaving his father Jacob bereft of a beloved son will correspond to the number of years that Jacob spent away from his own father when he was forced to leave as a consequence of his deception – measure for measure. Moreover, just as Jacob posed as someone else before his father Isaac, so does Joseph pose as the Grand Vizier of Egypt before his father Jacob; Jacob deceived his brother and Joseph deceives his brothers. The Torah doesn't want to whitewash the facts: Esau and

Isaac were deceived by Jacob, so Jacob must pay the penalty by being deceived by others.

As ordained by biblical morality, our matriarch Rebecca also pays a heavy price for having orchestrated the deception. Her beloved younger son Jacob must leave his parent's home and be separated from his adoring mother. Indeed, the Bible never even records Rebecca's death – although it does record the death of Deborah, the nurse-maid of Rebecca and apparently the *au pair* who actually brought Jacob up. It seems that Jacob came to bear resentment towards the mother who enticed him into deceiving his father; the Midrash even alludes to the fact that Rebecca's burial was never made public lest people come to curse her [Gen. 35:8 and Rashi ad loc].

So much for the human plane. On the divine plane, however, a totally different picture emerges. Jacob may be condemned for lying and Rebecca may even be cursed for orchestrating the deception – but it was as a result of these actions that the Jewish people emerged not as the children of Esau (which would have been a non-starter), but rather as the children of Israel, dedicated to God and morality. A parallel situation occurs in the stories of Joseph. One of the most heinous crimes in the Bible is the brotherly hatred which results in Joseph's being sold as a slave into Egypt by his brothers. Indeed this sin of fraternal strife has haunted us throughout our history, even until this very day.

Nevertheless, in the climactic scene which develops into Joseph's revelation of his true identity and a real rapprochement between the brothers, Joseph declares:

> I am Joseph your brother whom you sold into Egypt. And now do not be sad or angry [at yourselves], since it was for the preservation [of Israel] that God sent me before you.
>
> Gen. 45:4–5

Joseph understands that in addition to the apparent sequence of events in the world below which resulted in his near-murder and eventual exile to Egypt, another, invisible supernal design was transpiring simultaneously from above:

> So now it was not you that sent me hither but God. He has made
> me Pharaoh's vizier, director of his entire government and dicta-
> tor of all Egypt.
>
> Gen. 45:8

How does Joseph know this, and what's the significance of turning a
sibling feud into a cosmic plan?

When Joseph was sent by his father to locate his brothers somewhere in the region of Hebron, and they were nowhere to be found, the
Torah records how an anonymous individual directed him to Dotan
where his brothers actually were. But isn't it strange that the Bible would
find it necessary to record a simple request for proper direction, and
even stranger that the Midrash should identify the one who gave the
directions as the angel Gabriel? But, as Nahmanides explains, Joseph
could have easily justified returning to his father. He knew the potential
danger in his brothers' wrath and jealousy; it would have been normal
for him to turn back, explaining that he tried to locate them but he had
no idea where they were pasturing the flocks.

> Although Joseph had sufficient reason to return to his father,
> justifying his failure in locating them, he persisted for the honor
> of his father.
>
> Nahmanides on Gen. 37:15.

And Nahmanides continues to give a second reason:

> This teaches us further that God's decree is true and human effort
> is illusory; God prepared a guide, who didn't necessarily under-
> stand his function, in order to bring Joseph into [his brothers']
> hands, in order for the wisdom of the divine to emerge supreme.

What the brothers perpetrated against Joseph was a heinous
crime; from the moral perspective of human actions, everything should
have been done to prevent it from transpiring. The brothers were guilty,
and they had to be punished. But on the divine plane, the tragic sale
of Joseph eventually brought the Jews to Egypt, and not only saved the

House of Jacob from death by Canaanite hunger, but also set the stage for the pattern of persecution and redemption which was to become the hallmark of our national destiny.

There is a Yiddish saying: 'a human being proposes and God disposes.' The Bible teaches that when significant human beings err, the Almighty will often utilize the transgression to bring about the divine plan of ultimate redemption. Our personal challenge is to link ourselves so completely to the Jewish nation that even our sins will become sanctified if only retrospectively and on the plane of the divine.

Vayetzeh

The First Monument to Life and Eternity

> *And Jacob rose up early in the morning and took*
> *the stone that he had put under his head and set it*
> *up for a monument and poured oil on the top of it.*
> GENESIS 27:18

Vayetzeh opens with Jacob's journey into exile. He is leaving his Israeli parental home and setting out for his mother's familial home in Haran. His first stop, as the sun is setting, forces him to sleep outdoors in the fields outside Luz – the last site in Israel he will occupy before he begins his exile. He dreams of a ladder standing (*mutzav – matzeva*) on land with its top reaching heavenwards, 'and behold, angels of God are ascending and descending on it' [Gen. 28:12]. God is standing (*nitzav*) above the ladder, and promises Jacob that he will return to Israel and that this land will belong to him and his descendants eternally. Upon awakening, the patriarch declares the place to be 'the House of God and the gate of heaven' [Gen. 28:17]. He then builds a monument from the stones he has used as a pillow and pours oil over it.

This monument – (Hebrew, *matzeva*) is the first one in Jewish history. Until this point, the great biblical personalities have erected altars (*mizbaḥot*, sing. *mizbeaḥ*), to God: Noah when he exited from the ark, Abraham when he first came to Israel, Isaac when he dedicated the city of Be'er Sheva, and Jacob on two significant occasions. An altar is clearly a sacred place dedicated for ritual sacrifice. But what is a monument? An understanding of the first monument in Jewish history will help us understand the biblical attitude towards life and death – and even the true significance of the land of Israel.

Jacob's experience leaves us in no doubt: a monument is a symbol of an eternal relationship. It is the physical expression of a ladder linking heaven and earth, the land of Israel and the Holy Temple of Jerusalem (House of God) which connects the descendants of Jacob to the divine forever. A monument is a gateway to heaven, a House of God on earth. The land of Israel, with its laws of tithes, Sabbatical years and Jubilee, magnificently expresses the link between humanity and the Almighty, and the promise of Jacob's return from exile bears testimony to the eternity of the relationship between the people and the land of Israel.

Furthermore, a monument is made of stone – the Hebrew word for stone is *even*, comprised of the letters *aleph-bet-nun*. This is also a contraction of parent-child (Hebrew, *av-ben*) which also uses the letters *aleph-bet-nun* symbolizing the eternity of family continuity. And the monument is consecrated with oil, just as the Redeemer will be consecrated with oil – and herald eternal peace and redemption for Israel and the world.*

Jacob then spends two decades with his uncle Laban, who does his utmost to assimilate his bright and capable nephew-cum-son-in-law into a life of comfort and business in exile. Jacob resists, escaping Laban's blandishments and eventually secretly absconds with his wives, children and livestock to return to Israel. Laban pursues them, and they agree to a covenant-monument: 'And Jacob took a stone, and set it up for a monument' [Gen. 31:44]. Here again, we have the expression of an eternal promise: Abraham's descendants will never completely assimilate – not even into the most enticing Diaspora. The text continues:

---

* In Hebrew, *Messiah* literally means 'the one anointed with oil.'

> And Jacob said to his brethren, gather stone, and they took stones
> and made a heap…. And Laban called it [the monument] Yegar-
> Sahaduta, but Jacob called it Gal-Ed.
>
> Gen. 31:44–47

The wily Laban wants the monument to bear an Aramean name, a symbol of the gentile part of Jacob's ancestry while Jacob firmly insists upon
the purely Hebrew inscription of Gal-Ed – the eternal, Israelite language.

When they take their respective oaths at the site of the monument, the deceptive Laban still endeavors to manipulate: 'The God of
Abraham and the god of Nahor, the gods of their fathers, judge between
us' [Gen. 31:53]. Jacob refuses to give an inch; this monument must
give testimony to the eternity of his commitment to Israel, the faith and
the land: 'But Jacob swore to the fear of his father Isaac' [Gen. 31:53].
Jacob's response is a polite – but emphatic – rejection of Laban's attempt
at assimilation.

Although this monument is erected with Laban after Jacob leaves
his home, it is nevertheless still established in exile; therefore it is not
anointed with oil. Whatever important role the Diaspora may have
played in the history of Israel – as long as we maintained our unique
values and lifestyle – the oil of redemption will only emerge in the land
of Israel. When Jacob returns to Bet-El, the House of God, he will erect
another stone monument in order to fulfill his oath. Understandably,
that monument – erected to God in Israel – will be anointed with oil.

In the next sequence, tragedy befalls Jacob's family when the
beloved Rachel dies while giving birth to Benjamin. 'And Rachel died,
and she was buried on the road to Efrat which is Bethlehem. And Jacob
erected a monument on her grave; it is the monument of the grave of
Rachel until this day.'*

Many of our commentaries question why Jacob didn't continue
the relatively short distance – perhaps twenty miles – to bury his beloved
wife in the Ma'arat Ha Makhpela in Hebron, the ancestral burial place.

---

* Incidentally, this explains the origin of ceremoniously erecting a monument
over the graves of our loved ones; obviously it reflects the desire to link the
world of the present to the world of eternity.

The midrashic response, cited by Rashi, is that when the Jews would be carted off to their first exile in Babylon, they would pass by the monument at Rachel's tomb and pray that the matriarch's spirit intercede on their behalf before the Almighty. God hears her prayers, and promises Jewish return:

> ... Rachel weeps for her children, thus does God say: 'Stop your voice from weeping and your eyes from tears. There is a reward for your deeds ... a hope for your future: the children shall come back to their border.
>
> Jer. 31:15–16.

Rachel's grave is a truly fitting place for a monument, a link between heaven and earth. It represents the eternity of the Jewish spirit and our eternal relationship to the land of Israel.

*   *   *

Max Nordau became the world leader of Zionism after the death of Theodore Herzl. He was a Viennese physician who was not an observant Jew and had no previous connection to the Zionist movement. What made him a committed believer in Jewish return? He writes in his memoirs that a Hassidic family whose young daughter had been stricken with a mysterious disease came to him for a diagnosis. He diagnosed the malady and prescribed the cure. The grateful family returned, promising – despite their poverty – to pay whatever they owed him because he had saved their daughter's life. He smiled and suggested that she kiss him on the cheek as a fitting payment. The young girl, who had just reached the age of twelve, blushed as she explained that she could not kiss a grown man. He then suggested that she tell him the Torah lesson she had learned that morning as substitute payment. She cited the midrash I have just written about Rachel's grave site. Max Nordau writes in his diary that if, after close to two thousand years of exile, Jewish children still learn about and believe in a Jewish return to Israel, then the Jews will certainly return. At that moment, Max Nordau became a committed Zionist.

Can One Really Come Home Again?

> *If God will be with me, and will keep me in this*
> *way that I go, and will give me bread to eat, and*
> *clothing to wear, so that I shall come back to my*
> *fathers house in peace, then the Lord shall be my*
> *God and I shall erect a monument.*
>
> GENESIS 28:20–21

What does it really mean 'to return whole, in peace, (*beshalom*) to one's parents home? Is it really possible to 'come home' again? The Torah portion of *Vayetzeh* speaks volumes about parents, adult children and what it really means to come home.

Rabbi Yeshoshua Baumel, in his collection of halakhic inquiries called *Emek Halakha*, writes the following fascinating responsum. A certain individual vowed to give a hundred dollars to a local synagogue if his son came back '*beshalom*' – usually understood to mean whole-alive, in one piece, from the war. As it turned out, the son returned very much in one piece; the only problem was that he brought along his gentile wife, whom he'd married in France, as well as their child. The father now claimed that the conditions of his vow had not been met since the forbidden marriage constituted a breach of the '*beshalom*'. The synagogue rabbi and board of trustees disagreed, claiming that as long as the son had returned home from the front without a war wound, the father owed the hundred dollars. Both parties agreed to abide by Rabbi Baumel's ruling.

Rabbi Baumel ruled that the father was required to pay the money to the synagogue. He ingeniously based his ruling on a mishna in the little known Tractate *Tvul Yom* [Chap. 4 mishna 7], where we learn that if a person vows to give wine or oil from his cistern as an offering to the priests (*teruma*), but stipulates 'let this be a heave-offering provided that it comes up whole (*shalem*); then we take his intention to have been that it be safe from breakage or from spilling, but not necessarily from contracting impurity'. As Rabbi Baumel explains, apparently according to a sage of the Mishna who determines the normative halakha, the concept of '*shalom*' only refers to physical wholeness, without a breakage of spilling; in the instance of ritual impurity, the loss is not in the physical essence of the object but is rather in its religio-spiritual quality, and this latter defect cannot be considered a lack in '*beshalom*'. Moreover, the son's 'impurity' may only be temporary, since the possibility always exists that his wife may undergo a proper conversion [*Emek Halakha*, Chap. 42].

I believe that we need not go all the way to a mishna dealing with heave offerings in order to define the words 'to return to one's father's home *beshalom*'. Our biblical portion deals with the patriarch Jacob, setting out on a dangerous journey far from home, who also takes a vow saying that if God protects him and he returns to his father's house in peace *beshalom*, he will then erect a monument to the Lord. The definition of '*beshalom*' in the context of Jacob's vow might shed more direct light on the question asked of Rabbi Baumel, and might very well suggest a different response.

It should be noted that although Jacob leaves his Uncle Laban's home and employ at the conclusion of Chapter 32 of the book of Genesis, he wanders all over the Land of Canaan until the end of Chapter 35, when he finally decides to return to his father's house. Why doesn't he 'go home' immediately? Is the Bible telling us that Jacob himself understood that he had not yet achieved the '*in peaceness*' of his vow, and that until Chapter 35 he was not yet ready to return? I would submit that Jacob was waiting for the peace which comes from his being accepted by his father, the peace which comes from a loving relationship between father and son. Without this sense of parental acceptance no child can truly feel whole.

Indeed, no one in the Torah has more problematic relationships than Jacob. He has difficulty with his brother, with his father-in-law, with his wife Leah, and with his sons. But the key to all his problematic relationships lies in his problems with his father, Isaac. Unless he repairs that tragic flaw, unless he feels that his father has forgiven him for the deception which haunts him throughout his life, he knows that he will never be able to 'return to my father's house in peace.'

Thus we can read the series of events that begins with Jacob's departure from Laban at the end of Chapter 32 and his reunion with his father three chapters later as a crucial process in Jacob's development vis-a-vis his paternal relationship. It begins with a confrontation between the brothers in which Jacob bends over backwards to appear subservient to Esau, repeatedly calling him *my master*; plying him with gifts, urging him to 'take, I pray, my blessing' – all to the end of returning the fruits of the deception to the rightful biological first-born. Then, the Bible records how Jacob attempts to start a fresh life in Shekhem, only to have to face the rape of his daughter, Dina. His sons, Shimon and Levi, deceive their father and sully his name by destroying all the male inhabitants of the city. And then in the very bloom of her life, Jacob's beloved Rachel dies in childbirth, as a result of her having deceived her father and stolen the household gods. It certainly seems as though Jacob is being repaid in spades for his having deceived *his* father, Isaac!

Then we encounter the worst betrayal of all, the terrible act of Reuven having usurped, or interfered with, the sleeping arrangements of his father. Whether we understand the words literally, that Reuven actually had relations with his father's concubine, Bilha, or whether we follow the interpretation of the Midrash, that Reuven merely moved his father's bed from Bilha's tent to the tent of his mother, Leah, after the death of Rachel, it was a frontal desecration of the father-son hierarchy, a son's flagrant invasion of the personal, private life of his father.

Until this point, Jacob's life is a steady accumulation of despair. But this act of Reuven's is the worst humiliation of all. Just knowing that

Reuven even contemplated such an act could have led Jacob to lash out; fathers have responded violently for much less.

We now find one of the most striking passages in the Torah – not because of what it says but because of what it does not say. The literal reading of the biblical text records that Reuven went and slept with Bilha, his father's concubine. 'And Israel heard about it… (*vayishma Yisrael*)' [Gen. 35:22]. Not only does the biblical sentence end here, but what follows in the parchment scroll is a complete break in the Torah writing. It is not just a gap of white space that continues on the same line, but it is rather a gap which continues until the next line, a *pe'tuha* which generally signals a complete change in subject and a new beginning. Yet the cantillation for the last word before the gap, "Yisrael', is not a *sof pasuk* (period) as is usually the case before such an open space between texts, but is rather an *etnahta* (semi-colon), indicating a pause, but not a total interruption from the previous subject. I would suggest that between the lines the Torah is telling us that Jacob heard of his son's deception, is enraged, may even be livid with anger, but holds his wrath inside, remains silent – and thinks a great deal, perhaps amidst tears.

Undoubtedly, we would expect to find the verse after the long space (of Jacob's ruminations) telling us that Jacob banishes his scoundrel son, Reuven, disinheriting him from the tribes of Israel. Much the opposite, however. The text continues by presenting us with an almost superfluous fact. 'Now the sons of Jacob were twelve' [Gen. 35:23] – including Reuven. Then come four verses listing all the names of the twelve sons, at long last followed by the verse, 'And Jacob came unto Isaac his father to Mamre, to Kiryat Arba, which is Hebron…' [Gen. 35:27].

We are given no details about this ultimate reunion between son and father, Jacob and Isaac, bringing to a close more than two decades of separation and alienation. Apparently now – and not before – Jacob is finally ready to come home. But why now? Is it not reasonable to assume that the last event which the Torah records, the cause of understandable tension between Jacob and his son, Reuven, is the most significant reason for Jacob's reconciliation with his father Isaac? I would suggest that the blank space following Jacob's having heard of his son Reuven's indiscretion might have begun with rage, but it concluded with resolve for rapprochement. Jacob thinks that Reuven's arrogance is beyond contempt, but can a father divorce himself from his son? What do I gain from banishing my own flesh and blood? Is it Reuven's fault that he acted the way he did? Am I myself not at least partially to blame for having rejected my first-born Reuven in favor of the younger Joseph? Perhaps he was trying to tell me – albeit in a disgraceful and convoluted way – that he was my rightful heir. Or perhaps he was acting out his belief that Leah, and not a servant of Rachel, deserves to be the primary wife and mother, yielding the rightful first-born son. So does Jacob agitate within himself. And he decides at last that if he can and must forgive his son for his deception towards him, it is logical to assume that his father, Isaac, who was also guilty of preferring one son over the other, must have forgiven him for his deception as well.

Now, finally, Jacob is ready to return to his father's home in peace… He has made peace with his father because he believes his father has made peace with him. Finally he can make peace with himself.

When does a son return to his father *beshalom*? Only when the father accepts the son, and the son accepts the father, in a personal and emotional sense as well as in a physical one.

So, does the father in our responsum have to pay the money to the synagogue? Only if he is ready and able to accept his son and his new wife *beshalom*. And that depends on the father and on the son in all the fullness, complexity and resolution of their relationship – past, present and, only then, future.

May We Bargain with God?

> *If God will be with me... from all that God gives me I shall tithe.*
>
> GENESIS 28:20–22

Let's make a deal. God, you restore my health and I'll donate $100,000 to the new wing of my local hospital. Or, let's put it another way:

> If God will be with me, and guard me on this road that I am going, and give me bread to eat, and garments to wear, and restore me in peace to the house of my father, then the Lord will be for me as God, and this stone which I have made a monument will be a House of God, and from all that God gives me I shall tithe.
>
> Gen. 28:20–22

Is Jacob's conditional vow, in its standard format of an *if* clause followed by a *then* clause, the way to engage with the Almighty? Is it proper to say, If God will do such and such, then He will be my God? Is such an exchange an authentic expression of divine service, or is it an attempt at divine manipulation? And, if making a deal with God is not proper religious conduct, what are we to make of Jacob's conditional vow?

To help us address these questions, we need to consider a discussion in the Talmud where the Sages address a similar issue:

> If a person says, 'I will give this *sela* [monetary gift] to charity so that my son may live,' he is a complete *tzaddik* [righteous person].
>
> *Pesaḥim* 8a

Apparently it would seem that 'making deals with God' is meritorious. However, according to Rabbenu Hananel, the proper textual reading should be not *tzaddik* but rather *tzedek* (charity). This rendering would maintain that the individual who gives charity in such a manner cannot be regarded as a *tzaddik*, as a righteous person. Rather we can only regard the gift itself as *tzedek*, a gift of righteousness and charity. Rabbenu Hananel wants us to understand that such a conditional vow does not vitiate the gift, but does render the giver less praiseworthy.

Ba'alei HaTosafot also question the accepted reading of 'he is a complete *tzaddik*' [*Pesaḥim*, ad loc]. After all, there is a theological principle set forth in Ethics of the Fathers [Chapter 1, Mishna 3] that teaches that a person should not be like a servant who serves his master in order to receive a reward, but rather ought serve his master with no thought of reward. Hence, the Ba'alei Tosafot (as well as Rashi) explain the talmudic teaching to refer to an instance in which the individual is not making his charity a conditional gift. After all, the Hebrew doesn't state 'on the condition my son lives,' but rather 'so that my son will live.' The father will give the charity in any case; he is merely expressing the prayer that the merit of the good deed will help towards his son's recuperation. Clearly, even if his son should die, God forbid, he would not take back the charitable contribution. Had he made his gift conditional on his son's recovery, he would not be considered righteous at all!

From the perspective of these commentaries, the talmudic passage ultimately teaches us that every action brings with it varied and complex motivations and it is unnecessary to delve into all of the motivations of the person performing a good deed. However, as long as the *sole* motivation is not individual reward, we need not investigate any further.

From the above discussion, a vow to the Almighty that is *conditional* upon the attainment of an individual reward is meaningless. Certainly a vow which stipulates acceptance of God only if personal well-being is experienced can hardly be considered meritorious. Therefore, how can we justify Jacob's vow?

Rashi clarifies the conditions of the verse, thus mitigating our theological problem considerably:

> *If* God … will guard me in this path … and He will give me bread to eat and clothes to wear and will return me in peace to the house of my father, and the Lord will be for me as a God, *then* this stone which I have made a monument will be a House of God, and from all that God gives me I shall tithe.
>
> Gen. 28:20–22

Rashi explains that 'the Lord will be for me as a God' is part of the *if* clause, not the *then* clause. And the list of specifics in Jacob's *if* clause are not new demands that he is now bringing as a deal before God; it is rather a list of God's own previous promises. After all, God has already declared:

> I am with you, and will watch over you wherever you go, and will bring you back to this land, for I will not leave you until I have fully kept this promise to you.
>
> Gen. 28:15

Jacob is saying that if God does everything He said He would, if God is acting as *his* God in accordance with the divine promises, then Jacob will return to Bet El, erect a Temple to God and tithe everything he owes to God. If he is prevented in some way from returning to Israel, he will obviously be unable to erect a monument in Bet El; and if he has no physical substance, there will be nothing to tithe. Hence, this is not a deal but a logical result of the situation at hand.

Nahmanides accepts Rashi's premise that Jacob is not striking a bargain with God but is rather expressing the natural results. However, in one important respect he disagrees with Rashi; he does regard the phrase 'the Lord shall be for me as a God' as part of the *then* clause: '*if* You [God] will return me to the land of my fathers, *then* the Lord shall be for me as a God.' For Nahmanides it is clear that if Jacob were to remain outside Israel, he would ipso facto be exiled from his God. After all, the Talmud declares, 'Whoever lives outside the land of Israel, it is as though he has no God' [*Ketubot* 110b]. For as long as Jacob will be forced to wander in the homeland of Laban, Diaspora to Jacob, he will have no God. Hence his statement, 'If you bring me back to Israel, then You will be for me as a God' is plain and straightforward. Jacob means exactly what he says; if he never returns to Israel, he will have no God!

How are we to understand this startling idea? Since the essence of the Torah is keeping the commandments, the Midrash further amplifies the talmudic statement cited above by explaining that only in Israel does the performance of the commandments have real value. In fact, the only reason we keep the commandments in the Diaspora is so that they not be forgotten when we eventually return to the true home of the Jewish people and the true place for Torah observance – the land of Israel. According to Nahmanides, this applies to all of the commandments, and not only to the laws that are related to the land and its produce, such as tithes and the Sabbatical year. He argues that even the genuine observance of Shabbat can only take place in Israel.*

But isn't God everywhere? Why shouldn't a Jew in New York, Johannesburg, London or Paris be able to keep those commandments which are not dependent on the land of Israel – like the tithes and the Sabbatical year – just as well as a Jew in Efrat?

I believe that Jacob's dream of the ladder rooted on earth, whose top extends heavenwards, contains the key to a proper understanding of Nahmanides' position. Judaism posits a 'this-worldly' religion, that attempts to suffuse every aspect of earthly culture and endeavour with a touch of the divine and a taste of heaven. We are not to escape this world in our quest for the divine, but are enjoined to bring God down into this world. Jerusalem is not a city of God, but a city of humanity, and Jewish law extends far beyond the precincts of the Temple or the synagogue. The angels ascend the ladder in order to ultimately descend,

---

* See Rashi on Deut. 11:18.

and to bring with them a sanctity which can and must infuse the kitchen and the bedroom, the market-place and the wheat field, the prayer house and the sporting fields. And it is only in Israel that Judaism has the right and the challenge to influence every aspect of society; only Israel is, after all, a Jewish state. I believe this to be Nahmanides' position.

I'd like to suggest another interpretation of Jacob's vow. There are two major names of God in the Torah: *Elokim*, which reflects God's quality of truth and judgment, and the four letter name of God (*YHWH*), which expresses God's attribute of love and compassion.

With this in mind, Jacob's vow to God means that under all circumstances he will serve God as *Elokim*. But, if the things God promised will come to pass and Jacob will be cared for by God in a personal and compassionate way, then a Lord of compassion will be revealed to him as his God.

Having given this interpretation, we must remember that the young Jacob learnt a great deal by the end of his life. I am reminded of a significant prayer attributed to Rabbi Nachman of Bratzlav, when he was only a child:

> Dear God, I do not ask You to make my life easy; I do ask You to make me strong.

Jacob experienced very little divine compassion in his life – he is hurt by the lack of a father's love and appreciation; he is forced to flee his homeland to escape a vengeful brother; he works for two decades for a scoundrel uncle; he loses a young beloved wife; and he is separated for twenty-two years from his favorite son, whom he thinks is dead. Although he manages to return to Israel, the end of his life is spent in exile. Nevertheless, an aged Jacob blesses his grandchildren:

> May the angel who has redeemed me from all evil bless these children.
>
> Gen. 48:6

The God of justice has indeed become his God of compassion and redemption – not because his life was made easy, but because he found the inner strength to confront, and overcome, all obstacles. That fortitude is ultimately the greatest gift we can ask of the Divine, and is the greatest expression of His compassion towards us.

What You Dream is Who You Are

> And he dreamed, and behold a ladder set
> up on the earth, and the top of it reached to
> heaven; and behold the angels of God ascending
> and descending on it. And, behold, the Lord
> stood above it, and said, I am the Lord God of
> Abraham your father, and the God of Isaac, and
> the land on which you lie, to you will I give it, and
> to your seed.
>
> GENESIS 28:12–13

To what extent do we believe in dreams? And what is the significance of Jacob's dreams?

There are very few things in life as significant as dreams. Tell me your dreams and I can generally assess not only who you really are, but also what you may eventually become. The Bible understands this and therefore records many dreams of the most significant founders of our faith. The Talmud understands this, and therefore devotes almost an entire chapter* to a discussion of the significance of dreams and proper methods of their interpretation. Shakespeare understood this and therefore declares, 'We are such stuff that dreams are made of.' Perhaps he should have said: 'Dreams are the stuff that we are made of.' Freud understood this, and he therefore made dream interpretation the pivotal point in our self-understanding and the foundation of modern psychoanalysis. But how many of us are given the privilege of realizing our dreams? How many times do we dream great dreams only to have them result in bitter disappointment! When the gap between dream and reality is too great, depression and frustration are the usual result. Let us analyze the dreams in the portion of *Vayetzeh*, the dreams of Jacob. We will learn a great deal about Jacob's personality. We will see what happens when great dreams are dashed against the rocks of despair. But we will also see how it is possible to think that one's dreams have been frustrated when in reality they have been realized to a far greater degree than we ever thought possible; after all, our dreams are us and we are our dreams.

Jacob begins his exodus from his father's home with the most lofty dream possible. He falls asleep on the stones of Bet El and dreams of a ladder rooted in the ground and reaching up to the heavens with angels ascending and descending. Indeed, he dreams the ultimate dream of Israel's destiny: the connection between the unification of heaven and earth. If Judaism and Torah have any message at all to convey to the world, it is the possibility of bringing together the divine and human, the spiritual and the material. These were the lessons he imbibed from his father and grandfather. This was the goal of the birthright which he so zealously sought for his own. And he sets out to the great world beyond his father's house in the hope of perfecting that world in the kingship of the Almighty, bringing God's rule to every place on earth.

But Jacob falls on hard times. He meets up with his uncle Laban who not only teaches him the business of shepherding and flock-gathering, but also teaches him business trickery at the same time. Jacob lives with Laban for more than two decades. At first he must use deception in order to hold his own with his devious employer; in time the bright nephew even out-Labans his clever uncle and becomes a fairly

---

* The ninth chapter of the Tractate *Berakhot*.

wealthy man in his own right. Our Sages testify to the fact that he has not forgotten his early traditions despite his distance from his parent's home: "With Laban have I dwelt," and the 613 commandments have I kept'* [Rashi Gen. 32:5]. He still observes the rituals, gives at least lip service to the prayers and customs. But what of his earlier dream…? Jacob may have amassed a fortune, but he did not unite heaven and earth. Indeed, he seems to have completely forgotten his youthful dream and aspiration. After twenty-two years with Laban he has substituted dreams and – despite his external practices – has become a very different personality than what he had been when he first arrived. After two decades, he dreams another dream:

> And I saw in a dream and behold rams coming upon the sheep speckled, spotted and striped.
>
> Gen. 31:10

Jacob dreams of livestock, of the stock market and of material success devoid of any spiritual component. So his dream continues with the charge of the divine messengers:

> I have seen everything that Laban is doing to you. I am the God of Bet El…now rise, leave this land and return to the land of your birthplace.
>
> Gen. 31:13

Leave this land of Laban; leave this land of livestock. Return to the land of your fathers and the dream of your fathers. Laban may not have influenced your actions, but he certainly perverted your dreams!

But two decades in the prime of one's life is a very long and significant period. Jacob must have been devastated when he realized what had become of himself and his dreams. He must have seen himself as an abject failure. He must have questioned whether he would ever succeed in achieving his aspirations. He knows he must leave Laban before it is too late – but perhaps it was already too late. Remarkably, however,

---

* The Hebrew word *'garti'* has the same letters as *'taryag'* 613.

the time with Laban was not only spent in successful business ventures. The entire portion of *Vayetzeh* deals with Jacob's wives and children, his loves and disappointments, the development of his family. When he leaves Laban's home, he has yet a third dream:

> And Jacob went on his way and he was met there by angels of God…and he called the name of that place *Mahanayim* [divine encampments of God's messengers].
>
> Gen. 32:3

The portion concludes almost the way it began. Jacob again meets angels of God but this time the movement is not vertical from earth to heaven; instead there are two distinct encampments, family compounds, one outside Israel and the other in Israel. Perhaps the dream is saying that when one concentrates on family and develops a family dedicated to God and Torah in Israel and not to materialism in Laban's house of exile, this is the best way of uniting heaven and earth. Perhaps the dream is saying that our angels – messengers of God – are not to be found in the heavens but rather on earth, in our families and in our businesses, in our study halls and in our vacation spots. Indeed, we must become angels on earth, and then the world will be a sanctuary in which God may dwell comfortably.

Jacob's children learn from their father's failures as well as from his successes. They cannot help but be impressed with the fact that he has the strength and courage to leave Laban's wealth behind and to return home to Israel. They cannot help but be inspired by their father's ability to recapture his lost dream. And ultimately Jacob's greatest success is in the perfection of his twelve sons, the twelve tribes of Israel. The Midrash puts it very succinctly calling Jacob the most chosen of the patriarchs:

> Abraham was compared to a mountain – the mountain he climbed for the binding of Isaac. Isaac was compared to a field – the fields of the land of Israel in which he meditated and in which he planted and developed. But Jacob was the most chosen of all, for he was compared to a household – the household of Israel.
>
> *Midrash Raba*

*   *   *

Since our family made *aliya* to Israel in the month of Menahem Av, 1983 (thank God, the best decision of our lives), I have become somewhat of a 'reformed alcoholic' urging almost every Jewish Diaspora audience I address to think seriously about making Israel their home. However, as the rather paltry *aliya* statistics from North America testify, the response to my plea is generally less than overwhelming. And it is even more difficult to convince someone who once lived in Israel, and experienced difficult circumstances, to return home, particularly if they have been successful in the Diaspora. This is exactly the situation that confronted Jacob our patriarch – yet he returns to Israel.

Indeed, the very symmetry found in the portion of *Vayetzeh* – opening with Jacob's hurried departure from the land of Israel, and ending with his return to those same borders twenty years later – serves as a prophetic guide to the entire experience of *aliya* to this very day. Just like many of us who make *aliya* in later life are motivated by concern for our children and our desire to see them grow up in our Jewish state, Jacob's decision to return to Israel was made the moment he became a father to the child who counted most to him. 'And it was, when Rachel gave birth to Joseph, Jacob said to Laban, "Let me leave that I may go to my place and to my land"' [Gen. 30:25].

The decision to settle in the land of Israel is never an easy one, and even when the decision has been made, it doesn't mean that we're on the plane next week. However, the fact that it takes time and effort to put all the pieces together shouldn't discourage us – because this too is precisely what happened to Jacob. Remarkably enough, in a portion 148 verses long, the decision to return takes place in the first half of *Vayetzeh*, which means that the rest of the portion – more than 76 verses – is devoted to the actual details of his getting back, the ups and downs, the problems and obstacles that deter him along the way.

The fact that he nevertheless does manage to return – despite the inertia of habit and the comfort of his new home – is the reason, I believe, why Jacob is called the 'chosen among the patriarchs'. Abraham obeys the divine command to come to the land, and Isaac's divine voice never allows him to leave the land. Jacob, however, is the patriarch who is forced by family conflict to depart from Israel, and in doing so, he assumes the dubious honor of becoming the first Diaspora Jew. Unlike the experiences of his father and grandfather, Jacob's travels are the ones with which most of us can personally identify.

Is there any guarantee that *aliya* will work? Disappointments will develop, the pocket will hurt, and even the most idealistic soul may find his/her values at odds with those of the government. But if our sights are set on preserving the Jewish heritage of the future generations, if we wish to live a whole, complete life characterized by Jewish values and deeds, and if our dream for our future is creating a society with the capacity to merge heaven and earth, then the only place with even the remotest possibility of making that happen is in the land of our past and future, the State of Israel.

It Is Not What You Have, but What You Are!

And he carried away all his cattle, and all his
goods which he had acquired, the cattle of his
getting, which he had acquired in Padan Aram to
go to Isaac his father, in the land of Canaan.

GENESIS 31:18

Where would a middle-aged Jacob, with responsibility for four wives and thirteen children, find the courage to leave the comfort of his father-in-law, a successful business, and relative security, for the land of Israel devoid of financial prospects? Moreover, coming home to Israel meant facing an angry Esau demanding material remuneration for the stolen blessing and be ready, willing and able to attack his brother. One thing is certain: such an act of bravery required a strong ego and a sense of self which enabled him to assert his identity and to courageously tackle the challenges of his new surroundings. And if we can discover Jacob's formula, it would greatly benefit every one of us.

The one message the Torah does convey – albeit between the lines – is that real self confidence cannot come from material possessions alone. In fact, it is the opposite: unless the individual is comfortable with 'who he is' as opposed to defining himself by 'what he has', he will never be able to stand up to life's tests, temptations and tragedies. Almost from the very beginning of their lives, Esau is characterized as one who 'knows the hunt, a man of the fields' while Jacob is 'a whole person, a dweller in tents' [Gen. 25:27]. A hunter traps and captures external material objects which he both consumes and saves (the animal furs and skins, for example, which he can later barter or sell); a dweller in tents, explain our Sages, is an idiom for a student in a Torah academy.* This is a person who achieves an internal store of knowledge and develops a moral and ethical personality. The hunter concentrates on what he has; the dweller in tents values what he knows and who he is. If the hunter loses his game, he is left with nothing; the dweller in tents can always rely on his inner resources.

There is a midrash, turned into a Yiddish folk song, that expresses this idea in a charming way. Three individuals set out by ship on a long journey. The first brought his merchandise to sell – a large box filled with diamonds. The second also brought his merchandise – a crate filled with silk garments. The third had no baggage, but claimed that his merchandise was superior to the others. A storm broke out at sea, and the diamonds and silks had to be cast overboard. Ultimately there was a shipwreck; the three hapless passengers found themselves penniless and friendless in a strange environment. In short order, however, the third traveler was discovered to be a proficient Torah scholar, and was asked to become the spiritual leader of the Jewish community for as long as he chose to remain in that town. 'I told you,' he said to his incredulous companions, 'I had the best merchandise. Torah is the best merchandise. *Toireh is die beste s'choireh.*' You can lose what you have; material possessions are extrinsic to your essential being. Essentially, you are what you know, and what you believe in.

It would seem that Jacob started out with the proper values and the right priorities. Even his earliest dream was a spiritual one, of angels ascending and descending, of connecting heaven and earth, of returning to Israel, and of erecting an altar to God. However, he was jealous

---

* Gen. 25:27, Rashi and Seforno ad loc.

of his older brother, Esau, and especially of the fact that '[father] Isaac loved Esau, because of the hunt in his mouth' [Gen. 25:28]. We can hardly blame young Jacob for desperately wanting to win his father's love and approbation; we can even understand his feeling that the way to achieve that love was by amassing material possessions, by adopting deceptive characteristics in order to acquire those possessions ('the hunt' – or entrapment – 'in his mouth' can also be taken to mean that Esau was fork-tongued and double-dealing) – in short, by attempting to become as much like Esau as possible. And so Jacob deceives his father in order to receive the blessing – material prosperity, 'the dew of the heavens, the fat of the land, and much grain and wine' [Gen. 27:28], and successfully apprentices himself under the master deceiver himself, Laban.

And indeed, Jacob 'made it' in terms of material success:

> And the man increased exceedingly, and had large flocks and maid-servants and men-servants and camels and asses.
>
> Gen. 30:43

But then, disaster struck:

> And Jacob beheld the countenance of Laban, and, behold, it was not with him as it had been before.
>
> Gen. 31:2

Now, if one is dependent upon one's material possessions for one's self esteem, then one likewise becomes dependent upon the individual who is responsible for that material prosperity; hence, in this instance, Jacob felt completely dependent upon Laban. As the Talmud teaches:

> R. Yohanan and R. Elazar both said: when an individual is dependent upon other human beings, his face changes like a *kroom*… What is a *kroom*? When Rav Dimi came, he said: There is a bird in the cities on the other side of the sea, and its name is kroom. And when the sun shines, it changes into many colors.
>
> Berakhot 6b

At this moment, something must have snapped in Jacob. He realizes that he dare not be dependent upon someone else's good graces for his own well-being. He must become his own person, his own man, with internal resources of identity, strength and courage. Jacob is now ready to hear the divine message: 'And the Lord said to Jacob: Return to the land of your fathers and your birthplace; I will be with you' [Gen. 31:3]. Now Jacob understands that if God is with him, he doesn't need Laban to be with him, and if God loves him, he can even do without his father's love – no matter how great the pain might still be. And Jacob informs his wives of the divine command for them to return home – as well as of his new-found, and now-to-be-discarded, dream of streaked, speckled and grizzled cattle. Jacob is now ready to reject the Esau ideal of material acquisitions as life's highest priority; Jacob must return to his childhood home in Israel, to his childhood dreams of angels, to his childhood values of internal knowledge, morality and identity.

And so the new-old Jacob – Israel – has the wherewithal to return to his roots, to divest himself of his possessions and to face the spirit – or demon – of Esau as an independent being with his independent lifestyle and life's goal:

> ... and he sent over (the stream) all of the possessions that he had. And Jacob was left alone; and there wrestled a man with him....
>
> Gen. 32:24, 25

He has no difficulty giving over his material goods to Esau ('take my blessing') and when Esau declares that he doesn't require them because he has 'much' (*yesh li rav*), Jacob responds that he has 'everything' (*yesh li kol*) [Gen. 33:9–11]. And indeed he does have everything – ego strength, independent knowledge, morality, and the sense that God is with him. Armed with such a strong identity, Jacob has the courage to face whatever challenges life may bring.

Vayishlaḥ

The Search for God and the Search for Self

And he said, Your name will no longer be called
Jacob, but Israel, for you have striven with God
and with men, and have prevailed. And Jacob
asked him and said, 'Tell me, if you would, your
name.' 'Why do you ask after my name?' And he
blessed him there. And Jacob called the name of
the place Peniel because I have seen God face to
face and I have survived.

GENESIS 32:29–31

Is it religiously valid to attempt to find one's own God – or is it sufficient to accept the God idea handed down by parents and/or tradition? Certainly, if the individual can develop his own unique contact with God, his divine service will be genuine and spontaneous, rather than mechanical and formal. But a search, after all, is fraught with pain and anguish. And what if the Almighty still remains elusive, even after a lengthy quest?

We begin the *Amida* prayer with the words: 'Praised art thou, our

God and God of our fathers.' Rabbi Yisrael Ba'al Shem Tov explains that it is preferable and worthy to attempt to discover one's own God and to establish a personal relationship with Him. Until that occurs, however, one must still serve the God of one's fathers.

In studying the biblical portions of *Toledot*, *Vayetzeh* and *Vayishlaḥ*, we can trace an undeniable pattern which reveals that the underlying theme in Jacob's life is his search for God – *his* God, and not only the God of his father.

One might suggest reasons as to why, at least in Jacob's case, the mere acceptance of his father's God would be difficult, if not impossible. If Jacob truly felt unloved, even rejected, by Isaac, it would be problematic for him to connect with his father's God. And when his mother's ploy deceives his father, this would only serve to intensify the anguish of separation from the patriarch that Jacob must feel. Jacob wasn't sure who he really was, or more importantly, who he wished to become. After all, if his father loved Esau, perhaps he should become more fork-tongued and aggressive, more Esau-like. Perhaps then he would gain his father's love and God's love!

Jacob's jealousy and guilt vis-a-vis Esau certainly got in the way of his ability to establish a meaningful relationship with the God of his father Isaac. It is certainly the wrath of his brother Esau that forces the underlying purpose of Jacob's journey to become a personal search for God and – if only subconsciously – the God of his mother in her birthplace. After all, if his father had rejected him, at least his mother accepted him. Moreover, his mother's family was much more Esau-like – cunning and smooth-tongued – than his father's.

The first episode recorded when he leaves home is the dream of the ascending and descending angels in which God suddenly appears to Jacob. The words God chooses are significant: 'I am the Lord, God of Abraham, and the God of Isaac ...' [Gen. 28:13]. But not yet the God of Jacob.

How does Jacob respond when he awakes? 'Surely God is in this place, and I did not know' [Gen. 29:16]. The general understanding of this verse is that Jacob, not realizing that God is in this place, is taken by surprise. But the simple meaning of '*lo yodati*' is that Jacob does not yet know Him, his God. He knows what he must do to serve Him and he knows what to say in order to pray to Him, but he has not yet experienced his own personal God. We see this point underscored when Jacob makes his vow, which is usually understood to mean that if God will feed and clothe him, then Jacob will accept the Lord as his God [Gen. 28:20, 21]. Obviously it is difficult to accept such a materialistic 'deal' with the divine. Perhaps we must view the phrase in question as belonging to the 'if' clause of the oath; '*if* God will ... guard me, give me bread to eat ... and I return in peace to my father's house and if the Lord will become *my* (*li*) personal God, *then* this stone will ... become a House of God ....' Jacob is asking for a personal God, that the Lord become *his* God. Jacob is asking, in addition to his physical needs, that God provide him with his most sought after spiritual need, that he experience a personal God. Then Jacob will know that his search shall have borne fruit, and he will be able to truly build a house for God and give tithes.

But in order for Jacob to find his personal God, he must first come to grips with his own personality, with his own inner and truest self and identity. He must discover who *he* is before he is to find his God.

For the next twenty years Jacob lives with Laban's household. In the process of raising a family and establishing a financial foothold, he loses sight of his earlier spiritual vision. He is more Esau than Esau, more Laban than Laban. Not only does he not find his own God, he runs the risk of even losing the God of his father. Although he is very successful and aggressive, he has lost, and deeply misses, his earlier dream of uniting heaven and earth. He knows he must return to his father's land and home, to his true self. When we next find him making an oath, it is with Laban upon his departure. But he still cannot speak of his own God, the God of Jacob; he can only take an oath by 'the God of Abraham and the Fear of Isaac' [Gen. 31:53]. Now he knows who he once was and must once again become – but he isn't there yet.

Ultimately, Jacob understands that he cannot successfully find God without first being himself – and that requires frontal confrontation with Esau. Will Esau stand in the way of God's promise to Jacob and his seed? Can Jacob atone for the guilt he feels vis-a-vis Esau, and exorcise the jealousy he feels towards this favored brother? Addressing God, Jacob says, 'O God of my father Abraham, and the God of Isaac ...' [Gen. 32:10], but still no mention of the God of Jacob.

And because of what follows, it becomes clear that the wedge between Jacob and himself, between Jacob and his God, was Esau. Only after Jacob can successfully separate himself from Esau will he be able to confront his own God. On the night before he is scheduled to meet his brother in the flesh, the Torah records how Jacob remained alone and wrestled with an unidentified stranger over whom he prevailed. Identified by our Sages as the spirit of Esau, Rabbi S.R. Hirsch suggests that it may well have been the Esau within Jacob who is haunting the patriarch with guilt and jealousy.

Jacob receives the victory name Yisrael (Israel) from the stranger; he has prevailed against men and God. In what way? He has finally confronted the twin personality within himself: the Esau he desired to become in order to try and gain his father's favor and achieve momentary materialistic enjoyment – and succeeded in removing Esau and Esauism from within himself. He is ready to take the wealth he received from Laban during his Esau stage and return it to Esau when they meet on the morrow: 'take my blessing' (which I received under false pretenses) he will say – and he is ready to accept himself as he was even vis-a-vis his father. He is therefore ready to return home not as Jacob-Esau but as Jacob-Israel.

And only after he has successfully wrestled with the stranger – exorcising the pain and guilt created by his jealousy and deception – is Jacob finally rewarded by seeing God face to face. Apparently it was Esau, or the spiritual struggle he symbolized, that had previously stood in his way. After his mastery over the spirit of Esau, Jacob calls the place of the encounter Peniel, 'because I have seen the Lord face to face, and my soul has been saved' [Gen. 32:31]. Jacob exorcised Esau – and in the process found both himself and his God. His struggle and search ended in victory.

If what we've been describing is correct, we should now be presented with Jacob's personal God. The text describes that Jacob '...came in peace [*shalem*] to the city of Shekhem...' [Gen. 33:18]. The verse can also read 'whole' – and indeed he is now his whole, complete and independent self. And so he erects an altar to his own God, indeed calling it '*Kel Elokai Yisrael*' [Gen. 33:20] God, the God of *Israel*. Finally God is not just the God of his grandfather and of his father, but He is also the God of Israel, the God of the pristine and purified Jacob, his own personal God, whom he has discovered after many travels and through much pain. The circle is complete, the search for his own God is over. Thus empowered, Jacob is ready to face the third stage of his life, the transformation of twelve sons into twelve tribes of Israel. And now we can pray in the *Amida* to the personal God of each of our patriarchs, the God of Abraham, the God of Isaac, and the God of Jacob.

Esau Revisited – Identity Without Continuity

And Esau ran to meet him, and embraced him,
and fell on his neck, and kissed him, and they
wept.

GENESIS 33:4

Years ago, a college classmate provocatively announced that he planned to name his first son after the most maligned figure in the entire Torah: Esau. And the truth is that on the basis of a literal reading of the biblical text (*p'shuto shel mikra*) a case could be made to defend Esau. In fact, we're doing Jacob, his twin brother, a disservice by ignoring Esau's positive behavior. Only by presenting the best possible portrait of Esau, and then probing where the cracks lie, can we achieve an authentic portrait of Jacob.

Let's consider Esau's defense. After we are introduced to Esau as Isaac's favorite son since 'the hunt was in his [Isaac's] mouth' [Gen. 30:28], we are immediately taken to the fateful scene where Jacob is cooking lentil soup when Esau came home exhausted from the hunt. The hungry hunter asks for some food, but Jacob will only agree to give his brother food in exchange for the birthright. Who is taking advantage of whom? Is not a cunning Jacob taking advantage of an innocent Esau?

Then there is the more troubling question of the stolen blessing. Even without going into the details of how Jacob pretends to be someone he's not, Esau emerges as an honest figure deserving of our sympathy. After all, Esau's desire to personally carry out his father's will meant that he needed a long time to prepare the meat himself. Indeed it was Esau's diligence in tending to his father that allowed enough time to pass to make it possible for his younger brother to get to Isaac's tent first. Surely, Rebecca must have realized the profound nature of Esau's commitment to his father, for she masterminded Jacob's plan.

Additionally, Esau possessed qualities that many people admire, particularly in America where the spirit of the Wild West lives on. Esau was a hunter and was not afraid to go out into the unknown. He spoke the language of the buffalo and the Apache. He was a frontiersman: reading tracks, smelling the wind and listening with a sensitive ear. In nineteenth-century England he would have explored Africa. Had he lived in Spain, he would have been at the right side of Columbus. Esau may not be a scholar, but he is nevertheless a larger-than-life, self-made man whose exploits are the stuff of legends.

On his return from the field, Esau realizes that Jacob has already received the blessing originally meant for him. His response cannot fail to touch the reader. Poignantly, Esau begs of his father,

> 'Have you but one blessing, my father? Bless me, even me also, O my father.' And Esau lifted up his voice and wept.
>
> Gen. 27:38

Does this sound like someone whose name should be shunned forever? We all know the pain of arriving somewhere a moment too late, begging for the door to be reopened. But we've missed our chance. We walk away, disappointed and heartbroken, and in Esau's plea for a blessing we feel his immense pain, and hear our own pain. At this moment, Esau is Everyman and we all weep with him.

Isaac does give him a blessing that ensures he eventually becomes the head of Edom, a powerful nation identified by our Sages as the progenitor of Rome; and, in the final forty-three verses of *Vayishlaḥ*, we find the civilization created by Esau: its wives, children, grandchildren, chiefs and generals, are meticulously recorded by our Bible.

But it is the beginning of *Vayishlaḥ* that clinches our pro-Esau case. Jacob finally returns to his ancestral home after an absence of twenty years. Understandably, Jacob is terrified of his brother's potential reaction, and so in preparation, Jacob sends messengers ahead with exact instructions as to how to address Esau. Informed of the impending approach of Esau's army of four hundred men, he divides his household into two camps, so that he's prepared for the worst. But what actually happens defies Jacob's expectations: Esau is overjoyed and thrilled to see him. The past is the past. 'And Esau ran to meet him, and embraced him, and fell on his neck, and kissed him, and they wept' [Gen. 33:4]. Even if Esau is the villain, shouldn't this moment of reconciliation redeem him? And what a redemption: the two halves of Isaac coming together in an embrace of peace and love and hope. Jacob accepts a cool reconciliation, refusing Esau's offer of their traveling together. Jacob is somehow constrained to travel a different path. At Jacob's behest, the brothers separate once again.

The defense rests. Thus described, Esau hardly seems worthy of the official censure of Jewish history as the personification of the anti-Jew. In fact, my college friend had good reason to name his son after Esau.

So, why are our Sages so critical of him? I would suggest our analysis so far overlooks something central in Esau's character. Yes, there are positive characteristics of Esau to be found in many Jews across the Diaspora. Many are aggressive, self-made people who weep when they meet a long-lost Jewish brother from Ethiopia or Russia. They have respect for their parents and grandparents, tending to their physical needs and even reciting – or hiring someone to recite – the traditional mourner's Kaddish for a full year after their death. Financial support and solidarity missions to the State of Israel, combined with their vocal commitment to Jewry and Israel, reflect a highly developed sense of Abrahamic (Jewish) identity, just like Esau seems to have. Esau feels Abrahamic identity with every fiber of his being.

But when it comes to commitment to Abrahamic (Jewish) *continuity*, to willingness to secure a Jewish future, many of our Jewish siblings are found to be wanting – just like Esau. Undoubtedly, one of the most important factors in keeping us 'a people apart', and preventing total Jewish assimilation into the majority culture, has been our unique laws of kashrut. Refusing to break bread with our non-Jewish work colleagues and neighbors has imposed a certain social distance that has been crucial for maintaining our identity. But Esau is willing to give up his birthright for a bowl of lentil soup. Hasn't the road to modern Jewry's assimilation been paved with the T-bone steaks and the lobsters that tease the tongues lacking the self-discipline to say no to a tasty dish? Like Esau, the overwhelming majority of Diaspora Jewry has sold its birthright for a cheeseburger.

Esau's name means fully-made, complete. He exists in the present tense. He has no commitment to past or future. He wants the freedom of the hunt and the ability to follow the scent wherever it takes him. He is emotional about his identity, but he is not willing to make sacrifices for its continuity. Primarily, it is on the surface, as an external cloak that is only skin-deep. That's why it doesn't take more than a skin-covering for Jacob to enter his father's tent and take on the character of Esau. Indeed, Esau is even called *Edom*, red, after the external color of the lentil soup. Esau has no depth; he is Mr. Superficial!

And what's true for a bowl of soup is true for his choice of wives. Esau marries Hittite women. And that causes his parents to feel a 'bitterness of spirit' [Gen. 27:35]. No wonder! The decision of many modern Jews to 'marry out' has reached an American average of 52%! The 'bitterness of spirit' continues to be felt in many families throughout the Diaspora. Even those who marry out and continue to profess a strong Jewish identity cannot commit to Jewish continuity. Perhaps Esau even mouthed the argument I've heard from those I've tried to dissuade from marrying out. 'But she has a Jewish name! She even looks Jewish!' He may have said, 'Her name is *Yehudit* [literally, a Jewess, from Judah]; she has a wonderful fragrance [*Basmat* means perfume]' [Gen. 26:34].

On the other hand, Jacob's name is a future-tense verb meaning 'he will triumph at the end.' Jacob is constantly planning for the future, anticipating what he must do to perpetuate the birthright. Similarly, if we want to continue as a people we have to realize two things from the lesson of our almost-forefather Esau: don't sell the birthright cheap, and to guarantee a Jewish future, one has to plan strategically.

Who Are the Real Terrorists – Shimon and Levi or Shekhem and His Subjects?

> *And it came to pass on the third day when they
> were in pain, the two of the sons of Jacob, Shimon
> and Levi, Dina's brothers, took each man his
> sword and came upon the city unresisted...*
>
> GENESIS 34:25

The rape of Dina, and the violent revenge meted out on the men of Shekhem by Shimon and Levi in *Vayishlaḥ* [Gen. 34] has all the elements of a best-selling novel: illicit sex, intrigue, terrorism, murder and mayhem. In summary, Shekhem, the Prince of Hivi, rapes Dina, the daughter of Jacob, and then desires to marry her. He arranges a meeting of the families: the prince and his father, King Hamor on one side of the table, patriarch Jacob and his sons on the other. It is clear during the meeting of the families to discuss the wedding plans, that Dina is still being held captive in Shekhem: Jacob's sons suggest that if the entire male population of Shekhem agree to be circumcised, they would agree to the marriage – and even to business and social relationships between the two large and extended families. They make the consequences of a failure to agree to their conditions crystal clear:

> If you will not listen to us to become circumcised, *then we shall take our daughter and leave.*
>
> Gen. 34:17

Obviously, Dina is still behind Shekhem's closed doors.

The men of Shekhem agree. On the third day following the sensitive operation, when they are considerably weakened, Shimon and Levi kill all of the males of Shekhem with their swords. One way to justify their actions is that because the wedding negotiations were being held under the specter and sword of Dina's captivity, it was obvious that the primary goal had to be to free Dina. And to unreservedly prove the point, after Shimon and Levi slew everyone 'they took Dina from the house of Shekhem and they left.' Now we understand why the Torah records that the brothers made their offer of circumcision '*be-mirmah*' – with deceit. They certainly understood that circumcision alone was not sufficient to join a gentile to the Abrahamic family. Their purpose was single-mindedly to free Dina. Therefore, they formulated a proposition that required the most sensitive of operations, hoping that it would be refused and Dina would be sent home. But were it to be accepted, they would at least have the opportunity to arrange for Dina's escape without serious opposition from the recuperating Shekhemites. The brothers (without Shimon and Levi) were only interested in freeing Dina, not in punishing the citizens of Shekhem. We also understand now why Jacob's sons do the talking rather than Jacob himself (since filial respect would seem to demand that the patriarch conduct the negotiations). Obviously, Jacob wished to distance himself as far as possible from subterfuge – although he certainly understood the necessity of getting Dina back.

Shimon and Levi went one giant step further. They believed that all of the citizens of Shekhem must be punished for countenancing a captive's rape. If not, any daughter and granddaughter of Jacob's will be considered fair game by the gentiles!

Who is the guilty party? Shimon and Levi or Shekhem? Shekhem transgressed the natural and universal laws of morality by raping a Jewish maiden and holding her captive; therefore Shekhem is the terrorist. And the only way such terrorism could be stopped is by the townspeople themselves declaring such an activity unacceptable and bringing the perpetrator to justice – even if he is their prince, and even if some of them would be beheaded for their opposition. But no such action is recorded on the part of the population. This compels Shimon and Levi to do what they believe is in the moral interest to teach these (and all would-be) terrorists a lesson. They utilize the weakened state of the citizenry on the third day of the circumcision as the perfect opportunity to slay all the residents of Shekhem and to free their sister.

The Torah itself seems to justify the actions of Shimon and Levi. Even when Jacob chastises them, saying,

> You have sullied me, causing me to stink among the inhabitants of the land. I am small in number and I shall be destroyed, me and my household...
>
> Gen. 34:30

his argument is a tactical rather than moral one. And the last words of the chapter – the closing line of the incident – is the justification of Shimon and Levi: 'Shall he [Shekhem] be allowed to make our sister into a harlot?' [Gen. 34:31]. Even from a practical perspective Shimon and Levi win the day, since the Torah testifies a few verses later that 'the fear of God descended upon the neighboring cities, and they did not pursue the sons of Jacob' [Gen. 35:5]. Jacob's fears did not transpire. Shimon and Levi understood from the beginning that their action would serve as a critical deterrent.

But what about the innocent Shekhemites they murdered? Is that not an act of terror? Fascinatingly enough, the universalist philosopher Maimonides does not think so – because he does not believe the citizens of Shekhem to be at all innocent, and so he rules in support of Shimon and Levi. Maimonides sets down the principle that 'Moses bequeathed the 613 commandments only to Israel'; however, this great twelfth-century jurist-philosopher also recognizes the universal message of our Torah to all of humanity. Therefore he continues,

In a similar fashion, Moses was commanded to enforce the seven commandments of Noah upon every human being – and whoever does not accept them, must be killed.

Maimonides, Laws of Kings, 8:10

Maimonides explains this harsh statement when he defines the seventh Noahide law, which he maintains is to establish law courts:

And how are the gentiles commanded to establish law courts? They are required to establish judges and executors in every area of habitation to rule in accordance with the enforcement of the other six commands, to warn the citizenry concerning these laws, and to punish any transgressor with death by the sword.

And the other six laws are not to murder, not to commit adultery, incest or rape, not to steal, not to eat the limb of a living animal, not to blaspheme God and not to serve idols. Maimonides then concludes:

And it is on this basis that all the people of Shekhem were guilty of death [at the hands of Shimon and Levi, sons of Jacob]: because Shekhem [their prince] stole [and raped] Dina, which they saw and knew about, but did not bring him to justice....

Maimonides, Laws of Kings, 9:14

Maimonides is teaching us that unless humanity accepts a fundamental morality – 'Thou shalt not rape, thou shalt not murder' – a free humanity will not endure. The Torah of the seven Noahide laws must be accepted by everyone. Those who do not accept these principles and have the capability to destroy, are automatically in the category of 'those who come to murder innocent people,' and 'must be killed before they can wreak their havoc.' All of Shekhem shares in the guilt of their prince if they did not bring him to justice. All who harbor, aid or abet terrorists share in their guilt. There are no innocent citizens of terrorist societies. Had the Germans declared the destruction of Jewish property unacceptable after Kristallnacht, the Holocaust would have ended before it began. Obviously, it is under pain of imprisonment or death that subjects of

North Korea or Syria dare stand up to their inhumane governments. But it was only after people like Solzhenitzyn in the Soviet Union were willing to risk punishment and even death by protesting the enslavement of Communism that the world was saved from imminent destruction. The only way for terrorism to be stopped is by not allowing it to continue unpunished; the only way for civilization to endure – especially in a global village with mass weapons of destruction – is by insisting on the acceptance of the seven Noahide laws of humanity by every citizen of the world. And whoever remains silent in the face of his government's terror becomes an accomplice to that terror and must be held accountable for his participation in evil-doing.

What remains difficult, however, are the final words of 'blessing' uttered by Jacob to Shimon and Levi on his death-bed:

> Shimon and Levi are a sibling twosome, vessels of violence are their wares ... Through their anger they killed a man and through their willfulness they uprooted an ox ... Cursed be their anger because it is impudent and their ire because it is harsh. I shall separate them throughout Jacob, I shall scatter them throughout Israel.
>
> Gen. 49:5–7

This harsh condemnation of their actions by their own father seems to contradict our discussion justifying their actions. And indeed, many of our biblical commentaries (such as Nahmanides ad loc, for example) would disagree with Maimonides' assessment and condemn Shimon and Levi for taking the law into their own hands and murdering citizens who did not actively perpetrate the crime without due process!

Rabbi Yaakov Kaminetzky, however, in his masterful book of biblical commentary *Emet Le-Yaakov*, provides a fascinating insight in support of Maimonides. Yes, Jacob shouts recriminations at his sons Shimon and Levi, but he nevertheless bequeaths to them a most significant blessing. Levi is the father of the priests and Levites, the clerical leadership of Israel, the High Priests and Temple guardians. And Shimon (according to the Midrash) will provide the teachers and principals, the educators and the *Roshei* Yeshivot. When Jacob is truly disappointed in one of his sons – as in the case of Reuven – he withholds the birthright, he gives him no prize of inheritance. So from the perspective of the bequests granted Shimon and Levi, Jacob seems to be quite proud of them. If this be the case, then how can we understand his sharp words?

Explains Rabbi Kaminetzky: Shimon and Levi acted courageously and correctly, zealously and fearlessly. The honor of their sister had to be upheld, and society had to rid itself of terrorist-rapists and their collaborators. Shimon and Levi took the law into their own hands, acting without due process or consultation with their father, because it was the only way they could have succeeded, given the circumstances at the time. Yet Jacob had to fulminate against them so that they not make zealotry a way of life and so that others – more given to hotheadedness – would not derive permission to perform even more extreme actions with less provocation. Shimon and Levi had to act – and their father Jacob had to admonish them.

Perhaps this is even hinted at in Jacob's final words: 'I shall separate them throughout Jacob, I shall scatter them throughout Israel.' The priests live in the various cities of refuge, and educators must go wherever there are students needing or willing to be taught by them. The quality of zealousness is a necessary spice for national pride and honor, but as is generally the case with condiments like salt and pepper, small doses enhance the taste while concentrated quantities will ruin the dish! Shimon and Levi dare not be concentrated in one place. A little of them scattered throughout Israel will provide the necessary pride to enable the children of Israel 'to stand straight and tall (*komemiyut*) in their land.'

Vayeshev

What Constitutes Guilt?

> *And there passed by Midianite merchants, and*
> *they drew and lifted up Joseph out of the pit, and*
> *sold Joseph to the Ishmaelites for twenty shekels of*
> *silver, and they brought Joseph down to Egypt.*
>
> GENESIS 37:28

Who bears the ultimate responsibility for a criminal act? Is it the person who plans the crime, or the one who pulls the trigger or stabs with the knife? Is it the agency that sets up the act, the terrorist inciters, the mercenary for hire, or even the disinterested parents or apathetic society that nurtured the evil intent leading to the villainous deed? An ambiguous verse in *Vayeshev* dealing with the sale of Joseph initiates a difference of opinion amongst biblical commentators that have relevance to this important question.

Let's consider this scene of déjà vu. We know that Isaac was actually blind when he gave the blessing to his favored son, Jacob. Now, we find Jacob is equally blind in his relationships with his own sons, for 'Israel [Jacob] loved Joseph more than all his children, because he was the

237

son of his old age, and he made him a coat of many colors' [Gen. 37:3]. This infuriated his brothers. 'And when his brothers saw that their father loved him more than all his brothers, they hated him, and could not speak peaceably to him' [Gen. 37:4]. The Talmud declares:

> A person must never favor one child among the others; because of a piece of material worth two *selahs* that Jacob gave to Joseph more than his other children, his brothers became jealous of him and the matter degenerated until our forefathers were forced to descend to Egypt.
>
> *Shabbat* 10b

Apparently, our Sages felt that Jacob bore 'ministerial responsibility' for the tragedy of the brothers, although his sin was certainly inadvertent. Jacob suffers grievously for his mistake in family management, believing for twenty-two years that his beloved son is dead. But he certainly is not the main culprit.

Joseph doesn't do anything to assuage his brothers' feelings: he recounts his dreams that flaunt his superiority and eventual domination over the other family members [Gen. 37:5–11]. Then, in a fateful move, Jacob sends Joseph to Shekhem to see 'whether all is well with his brothers, and well with the flock' [Gen. 37:14]. Sighting Joseph from a distance and clearly aggrieved by their father's favoritism, Joseph's brothers conspire in their hearts to kill him. They tear off his coat of many colors and cast him into a pit. Shortly afterwards, the brothers spy an approaching caravan, prompting Judah to suggest that since killing isn't profitable, they should rather sell Joseph to the Ishmaelite caravan and tell their father he was devoured by a wild beast.

Undoubtedly, the moment Joseph is sold into slavery is one of the turning points in the Torah. It is considered the most heinous crime of the biblical period – the sin of sibling hatred foreshadowing the Jewish divisiveness that led to the destruction of the Second Holy Temple and its aftermath of tragic exile and persecution.

However, when we examine the verse recording the sale of Joseph, its hard to figure out who actually sold the hapless brother.

> And they [the brothers] sat down to eat bread, and they lifted
> up their eyes and saw a caravan of Ishmaelites coming. And
> Judah said, Come, let us sell [Joseph] to the Ishmaelites. And
> there passed by Midianite merchants, and they drew and lifted
> up Joseph out of the pit, and sold Joseph to the Ishmaelites for
> twenty shekels of silver. And they brought Joseph down to Egypt.
>
> Gen. 37:27–28

Although the brothers spotted Ishmaelites, it seems that it was the Midianite traders who actually passed by and captured Joseph in order to sell him. After all, the phrase, 'they drew up and lifted him out' seems to refer to the Midianites.

So, who actually pulled Joseph out of the pit to sell him? Rashi [ad loc] suggests that it is the brothers of Joseph, *'bnei Yaakov,'* and not the Midianites. Rashi draws on Joseph's comment twenty-two years later when he reveals himself to his brothers: 'I am Joseph whom you sold into Egypt.' Rashi argues that the initial biblical verse describing the sale seems ambiguous precisely in order to inform us that Joseph was sold many times before ending up in Egypt: the brothers sold him to the Ishmaelites, the Ishmaelites to the Midianites, and the Midianites to the Egyptians.

Nahmanides agrees that it was the brothers who did the selling, but suggests that the Midianite traders hired the Ishmaelite caravan drivers, thus explaining the usage of both nations interchangeably.

In contrast, Rashbam maintains that the brothers were not the ones who actually pulled Joseph out of the pit, and therefore not the ones that sold him, Yes, the brothers put him into the pit, abandoned him and certainly would have sold him had the opportunity arisen. However, before the brothers had a chance to sell him, Midianite traders came by, pulled Joseph from the pit and sold him to the Ishmaelites. The twenty silver shekels lined the pockets of the Midianites, not the pockets of the brothers. According to Rashbam, the brothers had nothing to do with the actual sale. However, this leaves us with the problem: how do we understand Joseph's declaration to his brothers, 'I am Joseph your brother whom you sold into Egypt'? [Gen. 45:4].

I think that this difference between interpretations may be under-stood as conflicting views regarding the nature of responsibility. Rashi understands the initial verse to mean that the brothers themselves lifted Joseph from the pit and personally sold him, because otherwise it contradicts Joseph's words later on, 'I am Joseph whom you sold.' For Rashi, the words are facts, not metaphors, and although responsibility can have all kinds of shades and meanings, ultimate responsibility can only fall upon the person who actually carries out the deed. According to Rashi's logic, since Joseph held the brothers responsible, they must have executed the actual act.

Rashbam's concept of responsibility differs. He argues that although the brothers did not actually pull him out of the pit and sell him, nevertheless they must still share responsibility for the events that unfolded as a result of the sale. Their initial act of casting their brother into the pit was done with murder in their hearts. Rashbam casts guilt upon everyone who shares in unleashing the forces of evil, even those whose hands remain clean while others do the actual dirty work.

I share the view of Rashbam. One must do something – not merely think something – in order to be responsible, but the one who sets the ultimate crime in motion by his action, even though he might not have perpetrated the act of the sale itself, must nevertheless cert-ainly take responsibility. Hateful intentions cannot create culpability, but placing an individual in a vulnerable position – like casting him into the pit – inciting others to participate in that hatred as well as actively aiding and abetting the perpetrators of the crime, certainly makes one a partner in crime who must assume a share of the guilt.

But there is a twist in this portion, and Joseph engages in a little historical revisionism. A much wiser and more mature Joseph looks upon this incident from the perspective of Jewish history, *sub specie aeternitatis*, under an eternal gaze. From his vantage point, twenty-two years later, he continues 'But now do not be sad, and let there not be reproach in your eyes because you sold me here; it was in order that you might live that God sent me [to Egypt] before you ... to ensure your survival in the land and to sustain you [for a momentous deliverance]. And now, it was not you who sent me here but God...' [Gen. 45:5–8]. Hence Joseph may very well be holding the brothers responsible for the sale even though it may have been the Midianites who actually committed the transaction – not only because he wishes to implicate them in guilt, but mostly because he wishes to involve them in redemption. For Joseph, the act that began as a crime, concluded – owing to divine guidance and Joseph's own quick-wittedness – as the salvation of the family of Israel. Joseph is anxious to restore family unity – and to look upon the sale from a divine perspective.

The brothers are responsible both for the crime, as well as for the good that resulted from the crime. Although Jewish tradition never forgave the brothers for their cruelty to their brother (witness the *Eleh Ezkera* dirge which traces the Hadrianic persecution which cruelly took the lives of ten great rabbis back to the sale of Joseph), Joseph praises God for having extracted salvation from sin; triumph from transgression.

Jews, Not Reuvs

> *And Judah said unto his brethren: What profit is it*
> *if we slay our brother and conceal his blood?*
>
> GENESIS 37:26

A Jew's identity – at least as far as the word Jew itself is concerned – is related specifically to descendants from the tribe of Judah. The other ten tribes, led off into captivity, were lost to history. Thus the vast majority of Jews in the world owe their very existence to one tribe, Judah. The only others who survived come from the tribe of Levi; these are fewer in number, and they – the regular Levites and the more elevated sons of Aaron, the *kohen*-priests – ministered in the Holy Temple, and retained their special lineage to this very day. The mere fact that a person can still call himself a Jew 3,500 years after Sinai and despite close to 2,000 years without our own homeland, is no small miracle. He/she is one of the rare ones, a delicate and miraculous survivor sustained and nurtured and kept alive despite exile, wars, pogroms, and assimilation. To understand what it is that allows a Jew to survive despite all the forces against him, we ought to turn to the founder of this particular line, Judah himself. What special traits did he possess which were absent from his brothers? Apparently, father Jacob-Israel identified his uniqueness as well, having granted him – and not his first-born brother Reuven – the gift and birthright of messianic majesty: 'the scepter shall not depart from Judah…and unto him will gather the community of nations' [Gen. 49:10]. We still pray every day for a ruler in Jerusalem from the House of David – a descendant of Judah!

What serves to especially sharpen our query is the fact that – at the moment of truth, when an angry and jealous mob of brothers cast the hapless favorite son Joseph into a pit (according to the Midrash, filled with snakes and scorpions) – Reuven and Judah each react, with Reuven's words appearing to be the more courageous and edifying. It turns out that Reuven steps into his role as first-born and acts accordingly, as he attempts to abort the brothers' evil design: 'Let us not kill him…Shed no blood…Cast him into this pit…but lay no hand upon him…' [Gen. 37:21]. His plan, as the text seems to tell us and which Rashi confirms, is that Reuven's intention was to return to the pit afterwards and to personally restore Joseph to their father.

Reuven, however, never gets the chance to execute his possible rescue. The text records that Judah sights a caravan of Ishmaelite traders in the distance, and suggests to his brothers that there is no point to murdering Joseph when they could just as easily earn money from his sale:

> What profit [*mah betzah*] is it if we slay our brother, and conceal his blood? Come and let us sell him to the Ishmaelites, and let not our hand be upon him, for he is our brother and our flesh….
>
> Gen. 37:26

Judah's proposal is accepted, and Joseph joins the caravan as a slave in tow, the silver that his head brought now in the pockets of the brothers. We then read how Reuven returns, finds an empty pit, 'and rent his garments' [Gen. 37:29]. His despair is deep and painful:

> The child is not and I, whither shall I go?

And now the others have no choice but to invent a story about animals having torn apart their brother Joseph – for how can they possibly admit to their father that they sold his beloved son into slavery?

If we compare the responses of Reuven and Judah, the heroic one seems to be the response of Reuven. He risks his brothers' wrath when he initially stops them from carrying out an act of murder, and devises an alternative plan which, albeit dangerous, might allow him to bring about a rescue. Judah, on the other hand, is crass and commercial, turning it all into a question of profit. He speaks like an opportunist, a cool businessman. He sees a good deal, a group of traders in the distance and so convinces the brothers to get rid of their nemesis and enjoy a material advantage at the same time. In this light his concluding words 'for he is our brother and our flesh' sound hypocritical. If Judah indeed harbored fraternal feelings for Joseph, how could he subject him to the abject slave conditions and to the thousand gods of Egypt?!

Nevertheless, Jacob chooses Judah as the recipient of the birthright, rejecting Reuven: '…unstable as water, you will no longer be first…' [Gen. 49:4]. Thus our question is, Why Judah, and not Reuven? Why are we called Jews and not Reuvs?

Let's examine Judah from two perspectives. One way of interpreting the text is that Judah was wrong by citing the profit motive, and had the blessings of Jacob been given the following week, Reuven, and not Judah, would probably have received the birthright. But Judah's life didn't end at the side of the pit. He continued to grow and evolve. He is the archetypal *ba'al-teshuva*, the classic penitent. When he impregnates his daughter-in-law Tamar, we see the greatness of a person able to admit his mistake, despite the personal risk and shame involved in revealing his guilt. Indeed, he says publicly, 'She is more righteous than I' [Gen. 38:26]. And when we follow Judah's development to the point when he offers himself as a slave to the Grand Vizier of Egypt in exchange for Benjamin's release into the arms of their aged father, we see just how far a distance Judah has travelled. Jacob's words regarding his fourth son, '…from the prey, my son, you have gone up…' [Gen. 49:9] confirms the ascent of Judah from jealous veniality to altruistic heroism. And perhaps it is just this ability to pick oneself off the ground and raise one's head up high, to redeem one's past, to recreate one's life, not to be victimized by fate but to rise above it, which made Judah the most worthy namesake for his Jewish descendants.

But there is also a second way to view Judah: perhaps he is not so much a penitent as practitioner, a shrewd realist who understands the art of compromise. As far as Judah is concerned, leaving Joseph inside the pit (especially if it was really filled with snakes and scorpions) was tantamount to leaving him to die a cruel death. When Judah saw the Ishmaelites in the distance, he seized the opportunity to save his brother. In order to be heard by his angry and jealous brothers, he understood that he had to conceal his pure-hearted motivations under the guise of a profit-making venture. Although he realizes that sending Joseph off to Egypt poses an obvious danger, it is a paltry risk when compared to the certainty of death by starvation in the pit. Reuven may have had the best intentions for Joseph, but intentions alone are not enough. 'Let us not kill him,' Reuven declared, but his words fell on deaf ears. Judah, on the other hand, understood that his brothers had murder in their hearts and therefore he couched his plea in accordance with the politicians' 'art of the possible'. It is for this reason that he used a word which would be likely to strike a responsive chord in his brothers' hearts: *betzah*, profit, money, cash. His goal was to do whatever it took to divert their passion for blood. Since Judah was effective in his very first test of leadership, as an individual who was able to sway nine very angry men away from their intention to murder, it is Judah who becomes worthy of receiving the birthright from Jacob-Israel.

These opposite interpretations of Judah at the pit are echoed in a later Talmudic debate surrounding the attitude of our sages towards arbitration and compromise, using a cognate term for compromise – *botzea* – which is derived from *betza* (profit). R. Meir insists that it is forbidden to compromise or arbitrate, that the law must express absolute purity. Indeed, he who blesses the compromiser – Judah, who used the word *betza* – is to be scorned by God [Psalms 10:3]. Moreover, R. Eliezer asks: 'if one stole a measure of wheat, ground and baked it and then performs the ritual act of separating the *halla*, what blessing does he make?' And the answer he gives is that in such a situation the individual crass enough to make a blessing on stolen goods is to be scorned by God.

And he, too, cites the aforementioned verse from the Psalms, giving it a slightly different twist: 'the one who steals (*botzea*) and blesses is to be scorned by God' [*Sanhedrin* 6b]. Clearly, these sages are telling us that Judah's statements in our Torah portions are duplicitous, a comparison being made between his ignoble speech to his brothers and a man pronouncing a blessing over stolen cake. How can Judah have declared 'he is our brother, our flesh' and then turn around and sell his 'brother' to the highest bidder! Judah the crook is attempting to whitewash his crime with a blessing! 'Whoever praises the one who said '*betzah* – profit' is to be scorned by God!'

But the final word in the Talmud is not given to this opinion. We go on to learn R. Judah b. Korcha's definitive statement, 'Settlement by arbitration is a meritorious act ... [*mitzvah livtzoah*].' Hence there is also a second way to view Judah's actions, from the lens of the sage who honors arbitration and compromise. This implies that Judah had to compromise in order to save Joseph's life, and so he must be praised for his wisdom.

We even find halakhic decisors taking two views regarding the question of making a blessing over 'forbidden' food. Maimonides rules that whoever eats forbidden food should not make a blessing, neither before nor after the meal [*Mishneh Torah*, Laws of Blessings, 1:19]. This ruling would be in line with the idea that a hypocrite should be scorned, that Jewish law must be followed in an absolute fashion. But the Ra'avad rules differently, distinguishing between a blessing made over a ritual performance (*birkat hamitzva*) and a blessing made because of the intrinsic pleasure one derives from a particular object (*birkat hanehenin*). The Ra'avad would agree that it is forbidden – and hypocritically foolish – to attempt to perform a ritual act for God with an object acquired by devious methods; the individual who makes the blessing of having performed God's commandment over such an object is in reality blaspheming God! He does not do a mitzvah but a mockery! But an individual who derives enjoyment from a cheeseburger, for example, ought at least thank the Almighty for his pleasure, even though Jewish law forbade him from eating the cheeseburger in the first place!

I remember how, many years ago, a fourteen-year-old girl at a youth seminar told me that she was the opposite of most Jews she knew: in those days many Jews kept kosher at home and ate non-kosher food on the outside (at least their dishes would go to heaven!). However, *she* ate only strictly kosher outside the home, but had to make certain compromises when she ate at her parents, who were not willing to keep a kosher kitchen. I ruled that she ought to make the proper blessings even when eating at home, using the Ra'avad as an indisputable source for my decision. Today this young girl has grown into one of the most effective 'Rebbetzins' in North America. The truth is that you have to do the best you can, and a half a loaf is better than none. 'All or nothing' may be the ideal in a perfect world, but it hardly applies for us today. Why does Judah become the leader of the brothers and then the leading tribe of the nation? Penitence and compromise, the ability to rise after a fall and to realize that striving only for the absolute may well prevent one from being very good, albeit not quite perfect.

Dreams and Visions

*We were binding sheaves in the field, when my
sheaf suddenly stood up erect. Your sheaves
formed a circle around my sheaf, and they bowed
down to it.*

GENESIS 37:7

The sibling rivalry between the eleven sons of Jacob and their
brother Joseph results in their casting him into a pit and selling him to
Egypt. What was the source of such bitter hatred and enmity?

On one level, Jacob's favoritism expressed towards the elder son
of his beloved wife Rachel was the obvious cause, exacerbated by the
young Joseph's dreams. Predictably, the brothers are aghast at the dream's
grandiose message: Does Joseph desire to be king and rule over them?

He then divulges a second dream, populating it with the sun, the
moon, and eleven stars all bowing down to him. Even Jacob, whose own
life was transformed by the dream of the ladder, scolds his son. 'Do you
want me, your mother, and your brothers to come and prostrate ourselves on the ground to you?' [Gen. 37:10].

From this perspective, it is more than obvious that the dreams served as an incendiary device, and biblical language affirms this position. After all, what follows the account of the second dream is Jacob sending Joseph to where his brothers have gone to graze their flocks near Shekhem. When Joseph is spotted from the distance, a plot against him unfolds: 'Here comes the dreamer... Let us kill him and throw him into one of the pits...' [Gen. 37:19–20].

On the fundamental level (*p'shat*), the arrogant dreams catapult the plot forward. But Joseph's dreams should not be regarded exclusively, or even primarily, as manifestations of sibling rivalry. On a deeper level, the dreamer may have generated the sibling rivalry not only because of their message of superiority, but also and perhaps even primarily because of their inherent ideology. Indeed, the argument between the brothers may well have been far deeper than familial jealousy; it may well have been a profound conflict between two different philosophies and two antithetical ways of life. The key to understanding the difference in *Weltanschauung* between Joseph and his brothers may lie in a more sophisticated interpretation of his dreams.

The brothers are shepherds, their lives are their flocks. This was true of their forebears, Abraham, Isaac and Jacob. But Joseph dreams of sheaves of corn, the symbol of agricultural society. His dream may well allude to an ideological rivalry between the new world of the farmer and the old world of the herdsman, the nomad, the shepherd.

The very first instance of sibling rivalry in the Bible, a rivalry which results in the first murder, emerges from the struggle between these two different ways of life. '... and Abel was a keeper of sheep, and Cain was a tiller of the ground' [Gen. 4:3]. Both bring offerings to God, Cain the fruit of the earth and Abel the first-born of his sheep. But only Abel's offering is pleasing to God, enraging Cain, and the result is the murder of Abel.

The worlds of shepherding and of farming are fundamentally different. The shepherd preserves and maintains the status quo. He shears the wool and extracts the milk, providing himself with food (cheese, butter) and clothing without destroying or essentially changing the livestock in his charge. The shepherd has time to rest, pray, meditate, compose poetry. He weaves an inner harmony with nature.

Farming is the opposite. In the evolution of civilization, it is a major step forward. The farmer's job is to transform nature. Nature does its share, but that is not enough to make whole wheat toast. The Mishna specifies eleven stages in the manufacture of bread, all of which are forbidden on the Sabbath because they create a basic change in the natural world as it is: sowing, plowing, reaping, gathering, threshing, winnowing, sorting, grinding, sifting, kneading and baking [*Mishna Shabbat* 7:2]. Indeed, there is a time honored custom to place our ten fingers on the *hallot* right before making the blessing over bread at the Sabbath meals, explained by most commentaries as reminding us of the ten words in the '*Hamotzi*' blessing. The *Zohar*, however, the mystical interpretation of the Bible, provides another explanation. Bread is the symbol of the partnership between humans and God, and the *halla* is the result of divine beneficence plus human effort and change. It should not be surprising that bread, not meat or fish or wine, is called the staff of life, and that the blessing over bread obviates the necessity of making blessings over other foods consumed during the meal. Bread does not grow on trees, and never will; the transformation from seed to pumpernickel is up to the human being to effectuate.

What Rabbi Joseph B. Soloveitchik defines as Adam II, "reflective person," the individual who fits in with the natural order of the universe, finds its counterpart in the contemplative existence of the shepherd. The shepherd is conservative; he wants things to remain as they are. Adam II is placed into the garden of Eden to save, protect and conserve it. The shepherd is perfectly content to leave the world as it is, seeing his major task in continuity and preservation.

The revolutionary is the farmer. He is the experimenter, the transformer. Placed into the world to subdue it, he makes it yield its secrets, whether they be technological, biological or atomic. He is the prototype of Rabbi Soloveitchik's Adam I, functioning as a partner with God, creating and aggressively producing a world very different from the one he was given by the Creator. His major task is to improve and change.

Joseph's brothers, being shepherds, are for the old way of life. They stand for the conservative way, and are suspicious of change. The land of Israel is also a perfect place for shepherding, with its mixture of desert and oases providing areas for leading the sheep without having to be constantly concerned about their destroying the crops. Egypt, on the other hand, as 'the gift of the Nile' is the land – and sophisticated center – of agriculture, and seems to be the foreign focus of Joseph's distant and even heretical dream. Joseph, unlike his brothers, is symbolic of a psychology of advancement, the transformation of the nomadic existence of the tribes into an agricultural and eventually industrial nation, which must deal with new societies and challenges. And if it takes the family to foreign places, so be it. After all, it is the Abrahamic mission to be a blessing for all the families of the earth.

The imagery of the second dream not only expands this theme, but takes it to a higher level. The sun, moon and stars are not just familial symbols of mother, father and children, but should also be understood literally. The heavens are the zenith of Joseph's aspirations. He desires to conquer the cosmos. It is not only the sheep of Canaan but the entire universe which he sees as his sphere of concern. In neither dream is there any veneration of, or even consideration for, past traditions and a former way of life.

The rebuke mingled with respect which Jacob expresses upon hearing of Joseph's dreams foreshadows the blessing he eventually gives his sons. He gives the blessing but not the birthright to Joseph because he is sensitive to the intrinsic danger of his dream. One may reach for the stars, but one dare not forget one's foundation, the matrix that bore us. Joseph gets the *brakha*, the material part of the blessing, the freedom to fly jets, to build laboratories and turbo engines and spaceships. Judah is the devoutly religious son whose very name expresses divine praise and who publicly admits transgression with his daughter-in-law Tamar. The Midrash teaches that he established an academy of Torah learning in Goshen prior to Jacob's arrival in Egypt [Gen. 46:28, Rashi ad loc]. It is Judah who gets the *bekhorah*, the spiritual leadership which will eventually inspire the ingathering of the nations to Jerusalem.

But neither Judah nor Joseph can prevail alone. Our tradition speaks of two messiahs, Messiah son of Joseph and Messiah son of David (who emerges from the seed of Judah). Judah guards the traditions of the past, protecting what is holy and good and worth holding on to. Judah is the Torah scholar, the master of Jewish law. Joseph will apply that law to new situations and conditions, confronting technology, philosophy and psychology, to achieve the biblical dream of uniting heaven and earth. These two brothers need each other, for one without the other is incomplete. A world of only Josephs could lose sight of the old in the adoption of the new, and a world of only Judahs could strap Judaism into a web of irrelevancies. Ultimately it is Judah, and not Joseph, who is the progenitor of the Messiah; Joseph must utilize his skills to provide the necessary universal and scientific infrastructure for Judah's spiritual vision.

Hanuka, which always falls out during these Torah readings, also represents the struggle between two forces: a Hellenistic Jewish mindset, which found in Greek culture and philosophy the more progressive direction for Judea and which would have transformed Jerusalem into a Greek city-state (*polis*); and the Hasmoneans, who would rather have given up their lives than give up the traditional Torah's commandments, and were against any change whatsoever. In many ways, this struggle has resurfaced today between modern-day 'secularist' Hellenists who define progress in terms of the norms of a permissive Western society, and Maccabean religionists who are suspicious of every idea which emanates from a source other than the Torah.

The truth lies in a synthesis between the two – in the ability of Josephs and Judahs to work together to take the best of Western culture and incorporate it under the rubric of Torah Judaism. It is the beauty of Japheth (Greece), in the Tent (Torah) of Shem. In Rabbi Abraham Isaac Kook's words, 'the old must be made new, and the new must be sanctified.'

Miketz

The Ability to Listen to Dreams of Others as Well as to Our Own

> *And Pharaoh said to Joseph, I had a dream last night, and no one is able to interpret it....*
>
> GENESIS 41:15

There is an unusual symmetry in the portion of *Miketz* as well as in *Vayeshev*, both of which deal almost exclusively with the rise and fall – *Vayeshev* – and fall and rise – *Miketz* – of Joseph.

Vayeshev begins with an introduction to Joseph. Not only is he talented, brilliant and handsome, but he is the beloved son of the beloved wife, Rachel. As the apple of his father's eye, physically as well as spiritually, he can do no wrong. Little wonder that his father adores him and adorns him with the much-prized cloak of many colors.

Yet, by the end of the portion, Joseph is in prison. It is the final degradation in a series of degradations that began shortly after earning the hatred of his brothers for his loose tongue and provocative dreams as a result of which he was cast into a pit and sold into slavery in Egypt.

Miketz finds Joseph still in prison, but almost immediately we witness his miraculous rise and emergence as a world leader. The former seventeen-year-old dreamer becomes Grand Vizier (second only to the Pharaoh) and Secretary of Treasury, Labor and Agriculture all rolled into one. Pharaoh may be the symbolic head of Egypt, the god of the Egyptian 'pantheon', but because of his total trust in Joseph, the son of Jacob now effectively rules the land, a prime minister without the possibility of anyone casting a no-confidence vote against him.

Rabbi Isaac Bernstein ingeniously suggests the method behind the symmetry. The favored and beloved Joseph is doomed to begin his downward descent because, although he dreams grand dreams, he is totally self absorbed; his sole interest lies in communicating his dreams of self-aggrandizement to others. By the beginning of *Miketz*, Joseph is listening to the dreams of others and using them to help the others. Once one begins listening to other people's dreams one is ready to ascend upwards and achieve true leadership.

I would develop this idea further by suggesting that the real key to Joseph's interpretation lies in his new-found ability to carefully listen. Remember that the prophet Elijah receives a vision from the Almighty at the end of his life teaching him that the Divine Presence is to be found in a small silent voice, *Kol demama daka*. How can a *voice* be silent? The adviser's voice must be silent in order to listen very carefully to the words of the supplicant. Proper advice which has God's own stamp of approval can only emerge from careful listening to and empathizing with the individual who speaks out of desperation and travail. Only when one understands what the questioner really wants, can one offer him/her proper advice. Prophecy is based in no small measure upon one's ability to listen.

When the wine steward revealed his dream – and dreams are always a key to the hidden and often subconscious thoughts and aspirations of the dreamer – of 'squeezing grapes into Pharaoh's cup, and then placing the cup in Pharaoh's hand' [Gen. 40:11], it became clear to Joseph that the wine steward only wanted to continue to serve his master, that he had no trace of a guilty conscience, and so he would be found innocent and returned to service.

The chief baker's dream, on the other hand, is very different. He dreams of birds snatching the loaves of bread from the basket on his head. The birds, or nature, are 'out to get him' – and usually people who suffer from paranoia have reason to feel guilty. Joseph listened well and surmised that the chief baker was indeed guilty and so would be hanged within three days.

Similar was the case of Pharaoh's dream. Joseph understood that Pharaoh's chief concern was the economic well-being of Egypt, and this subject had to be the point of a dream which repeated itself so often to the man most responsible for Egypt's well being. And if Pharaoh was frightened of economic disaster – by the way, a cyclical occurrence in Egypt which Joseph was certainly aware of – the best way for Joseph to overcome that concern was to present a plan of prevention:

> 'Now therefore let Pharaoh seek out a man understanding and wise, and set him over the land of Egypt in the seven years of plenty. And let them store up all the food of those good years that come, and pile up corn under the hand of Pharaoh...that the land shall not be cut off through the famine.' And the thing was good in the eyes of Pharaoh....
>
> Gen. 41:33–37

The Joseph of *Miketz* did not shout his dreams to others whom he saw as his servants; he rather listened carefully to the dreams of others, and was ready to be of service to them wherever possible. Only this changed Joseph could be expected to rise and remain on top.

The content of Joseph's earlier dreams is also an important piece in understanding his downward turn. Joseph's dream is predicated to a certain degree upon his father Jacob's dream, the dream of '...a ladder standing on the ground, its top reached up toward heaven...God's angels were going up and down on it...'. Joseph, too, dreams of the two elements in his father's dream, the earth and the heavens. His first dream is of the earth – stalks of wheat – and his second dream is of the heavens – sun, moon and stars. But there are two major differences between the dreams of father and son. Jacob's dream is one: he yearns to connect heaven and earth. Joseph has two separate dreams. In Jacob's dreams, God and the angels are at its center; in Joseph's dream he himself is at the center, with the eleven stalks of wheat and eleven stars, sun and moon bowing down to him. God is absent from Joseph's subconscious; he, Joseph, wishes dominion on earth and even in the heavenly cosmos.

But as the Joseph stories develop, a much chastened Joseph, as well as his repentant brothers, learn invaluable lessons. The brothers learn that they should have tried to teach – not tear away – their errant and supercilious brother. Joseph learns that his abilities of economic and administrative leadership must *serve* the higher power of God and Torah. Joseph's dreams are realized in Egypt – when his family must bow to him as Grand Vizier of Egypt. But in the greater dream of Israel, the vision of the Covenant between the Pieces and the ultimate goal of world peace and redemption, Joseph will serve Judah, the guardian of tradition and Torah. Jacob only gives Joseph the 'blessing' of a double portion; the 'birthright' of spiritual leadership and direction is granted to Judah [Gen. 49:8–10]. When Joseph truly understands his proper position, he is able to rise above his fall into the pit and take his place as the heir to the blessing.

Why Joseph Did Not Fax His Father

> *And Joseph knew his brethren, but they knew him not. But he behaved like a stranger and spoke harshly to them. And Joseph remembered the dreams which he dreamed of, and said unto them, You are spies, to see the nakedness of the land you have come.*
>
> GENESIS 42:8–9

In the Torah portion of *Miketz*, the drama of Joseph and his brothers takes on new dimensions. From a situation in which Joseph is the hunted and the brothers are the hunters, we move into the very opposite. Joseph becomes the hunter and the brothers the hunted, although they don't understand why! But we also realize that until now the text has been silent about Joseph's relationship to his past. This forces us to query how Joseph can spend twenty-two years of his life in a foreign country like Egypt without ever looking over his shoulder to find out how his family in Canaan is faring. When he sat in Egyptian prisons it was impossible to communicate, but what about the years when he ruled as the Grand Vizier of a great empire? Could he not have sent servants, carrier pigeons, messages on papyrus? Even if he had no desire ever to see his brothers again, should his aged father who loved him so much have been made to suffer for their sins? Nahmanides tells us that Egypt is only a six-day journey from Hebron but '... even if it was a year's journey, he should have notified him' [Gen. 42:9]. The longer Joseph is silent, the longer Jacob is deprived of his beloved son, the greater our question on Joseph's character.

Nahmanides explains that Joseph was prevented from contacting his father because he was driven by his dreams, and guided by their inevitable course. It was his intention to wait until all elements of his dream – the sun, moon and eleven stars, symbolic of his father, mother and eleven brothers bowing down to him – came together in Egypt, when and where the details could be fulfilled exactly. The dreams controlled Joseph. Emotions could not outweigh what he believed was destiny. Therefore, sending word home before the famine would force his entire family to go down to Egypt and would have negated the possibility of his dreams being fulfilled [Nahmanides on Gen. 42:9].

Abarbanel paints Joseph differently, saying that it was impossible for him to contact his father until he was convinced that his brothers had truly repented; otherwise the joyous news that Joseph was still alive would have also meant a father facing ten lying brothers who now would be forced to reveal their role in the murderous deception amidst all sorts of recriminations. From this perspective everything Joseph does while concealing his identity is intended to increase the brothers' awareness, reliving what they inflicted upon him. Since he was thrown into a pit, he puts them in a pit. Then he tells them to return home without Shimon whom he keeps in prison as a hostage until Benjamin will be brought to Egypt. This should make them realize that for the second time in their lives they are returning with a brother missing – and Shimon had been the primary instigator against Joseph. And indeed they declare,

> We deserve to be punished because of what we did to our brother. We saw him pleading with us, but we would not listen....
>
> Gen 42:21

It is only after Joseph treats Benjamin with favoritism, and then condemns him to imprisonment as a thief – and Judah offers himself and all the brothers in Benjamin's stead – that Joseph realizes the depth of his brothers' repentance. After all, Benjamin is also a son of Rachel, a favorite of Jacob – and this could have been a marvelous opportunity to be rid of him as they had gotten rid of Joseph. If the brothers are now willing to offer themselves as slaves so that their father will not have to suffer further grief at the loss of Benjamin, they apparently really have changed and repented for their sale of Joseph!

A third way to understand why Joseph didn't get in touch with his family is the simplest in terms of the plain meaning of the text. What happened to Joseph in Egypt was a natural result of remembrances of past resentments, a man who was almost murdered by his own brothers, whom he never suspected bore him such evil designs. Until he had been cast into the pit, Joseph was basically an innocent child, basking in the love of his father with no comprehension as to how much his brothers hated him. He was so beloved that he took that love for granted; he naïvely and unselfconsciously believed it was shared by everyone in his family. Only someone with absolutely no guile could have advertised his supercilious dreams of mastery over his brothers to those very same brothers. But in the harsh reflection of the fact that his brothers were willing to leave him to die in a provision-less pit, the venom of their hatred was clear. And in addition to condemning his brothers, he lays a good part of the blame upon the frail shoulders of his father, who should have realized where his unbridled favoritism would lead. The coat of beautiful colors was the first thing the brothers tore off him, eventually turning it into a blood-soaked rag. In the pit, Joseph comes to realize that the ingredients of excessive love can be transformed into a poisonous potion and that his father had totally mismanaged the family dynamic. One might even justify Joseph's uttering in the pit: 'I hate my father's house. I will never communicate with my father or my brothers again.'

Joseph's subsequent behavior in Egypt would indicate that he really tried to escape his father's house, severing all ties to the past. The Midrash teaches that there are three reasons why the Jews didn't assimilate in Egypt: 'They didn't change their names, their clothes, or their language.' If the Midrash is an indication of how to protect oneself against assimilation, Joseph, who changed all three, left himself completely open.

The first step begins after his success in interpreting Pharaoh's dreams. In reward, Joseph is appointed Grand Vizier, and the text is explicit about his change of garb; '[Pharaoh] had him dressed in the finest linen garments; and placed a gold chain around his neck...' [Gen. 41:42]. The second change is a new name which Pharaoh gives him, Tzofnat Paneach, from all textual indication, an Egyptian name. With this new name, he marries Asnat, the daughter of the priest of On, hardly a fitting match for Jacob's beloved son and Abraham's great-grandson.

When the first child of Tzofnat and Asnat is born, the name given to the boy, Menasheh, seems to hammer in the nail of farewell to Joseph's former life. 'God has allowed me to forget my troubles and my father's house' [Gen. 41:51], the verb *nasheh* meaning forgetting.

And although the Jewish slaves in Egypt may not have changed their language, Joseph obviously did. Amongst themselves, his brothers speak Hebrew; '...They knew not that Joseph understood them, for the interpreter was between them' [Gen. 42:23] testifies the biblical text. Given such changes, one may very well conclude that the Grand Vizier and Joseph, the son of Jacob, had drifted worlds away from each other.

To be sure, in his moral life, Joseph certainly remains true to the teachings of his father and grandfather. He demonstrates almost superhuman piety in rejecting the advances of Mrs. Potiphar – being unable to display faithlessness to his generous employer and still unwilling to 'sin against God' [Gen. 39:9]. And indeed, he turns to God constantly, stressing that whatever he accomplishes is actually due to the Almighty. However, the name of God the text chooses is *Elokim*, the universal presence of the universe, while the four letter personal and more nationalistic (Abrahamic) name is deliberately avoided. Joseph remains moral and may even privately have conducted himself in accordance with his childhood rituals. However, certainly from the public perspective, he willfully turned himself into a consummate Egyptian. And I would certainly maintain that he has no desire to contact the family which caused him such pain and suffering, especially his father, who must ultimately assume responsibility, albeit inadvertent, for the sibling enmity. And indeed it would seem that Joseph had succeeded in erasing his childhood years and settling in quite well in the assimilating environment of Egypt – until his brothers' arrival to purchase food.

Their arrival brings back a flood of thoughts, memories and emotions which Joseph had desperately tried to repress. First we see his anger. He treats his brothers with understandable hatred and punishes them by taking his revenge and casting them into a dungeon similar to the one they had cast him into. But that night he cannot sleep, his mind overactive with pining for his full brother Benjamin, who had been too young to join his half-brothers in their crime against Joseph. Joseph aches to see this pure and whole brother from his same mother – and so sends the brothers (sans Shimon) back with the mission to return with Benjamin.

Joseph's ruse with the silver goblet plan may very well have been to keep Benjamin at his side, thereby holding on to a part of the past he now realizes he has deeply missed, while rejecting the rest. But when Judah evokes the image of an old grieving father whose life will be reduced to a pathetic waste if word reaches him that Benjamin has become a slave in Egypt, Joseph, the Grand Vizier breaks down.

Perhaps as Judah speaks, Joseph poignantly remembers Shabbat moments inside his father's tent, whose simple beauty far eclipses the rowdy Egyptian debaucheries. Perhaps, he conjures the wisdom of Jewish teachings he heard as a child at his father's knee. The mature Joseph finally understands that although his father may have 'set up' the family dysfunction, it was not because he loved Joseph too little, but rather because he loved Joseph too much. And if Jacob's love had been the first step causing Joseph's alienation from the family, it was that same love which had given him the ego strength to always land on his feet and eventually return to his father's and brothers' embrace. In effect, according to this interpretation Joseph was our first *ba'al teshuva* (penitent). The Joseph stories – and the book of Genesis – conclude, 'And Joseph dwelled in Egypt, he and his father's house' [Gen. 50:22] – he and his father's household, he and his father's lifestyle from their common home in the land of Canaan. He even recognizes the centrality of the land of Israel, telling them with his dying breath that God will surely remember them and take them to the land He promised their fathers, adjuring them at that time 'to bring up my bones from this place [Egypt] with you' [Gen. 50:22].

From this perspective, Joseph teaches that no matter how far one wanders, one always returns in some fashion to *bet abba*, one's earliest memories and one's original traditions. This is especially true if those formative years were filled with parental love.

Vayigash

The Tears of Joseph and Benjamin

*And Joseph fell on his brother Benjamin's neck
and wept, and Benjamin wept on his [Joseph's]
neck.*

GENESIS 45:14

This poignant moment when these two brothers are reunited after a separation of twenty-two years is one of the most tender scenes in the Torah.

After a long chronicle of difficult brotherly relationships – Cain and Abel, Ishmael and Isaac, Esau and Jacob, Joseph and his other siblings – we finally come across two brothers who truly love each other. The only children of Jacob's beloved Rachel, Joseph and Benjamin shared the same womb, and when their mother died in childbirth, we can feel assured that Joseph drew Benjamin close to him, protected him, and shared with him the precious memories of the mother Benjamin never knew. Their exclusive relationship must have made their eventual separation even more painful and traumatic. After all, Benjamin was the only brother totally uninvolved in the family tension and sibling rivalry against Joseph.

But I'm left wondering: Where is the joy, the elation, the celebration? Why does the Torah only record the weeping of the brothers at this dramatic moment of their reunion?

Rashi cites and explains a midrashic interpretation which suggests that these tears relate to the future destruction of the two Temples allotted to the portion of Benjamin, and to the destruction of the sanctuary in Shilo allotted to the portion of Joseph. Rashi stresses that Joseph's tears are for Benjamin's destruction, and Benjamin's tears are for Joseph's destruction.

But why should Rashi extrapolate such terrible events in the future from the tears of the brothers? I believe that the answer lies in our being mindful of the two archetypal sins in the book of Genesis: The first is the sin of eating of the fruit of the Tree of Knowledge, which symbolizes rebellion against God, and the second is the sin of the sale of Joseph by his brothers, which epitomizes the sins of enmity between people, internecine strife.

Of the two, the *Zohar* considers the latter more severe. In the tradition of 'the events of the fathers foreshadow the history of the children,' we can see that all tragedies to befall the Jewish people have their source in the 'DNA' of the sale of Joseph as a slave. This act was the foundation of causeless hatred between Jews.

The Talmud [*Gittin* 55b], in isolating the cause of the destruction of the Second Temple, reports an almost mundane event. A wealthy man had a party and wanted to invite his friend Kamtza. Inadvertently, his avowed enemy Bar-Kamtza was invited instead. Thrown out and shamed, Bar-Kamtza took revenge. He went to the Roman authorities and lied in order to implicate the Jews in crimes against the state. The rest is history. Josephus writes that even as the Romans were destroying the Temple, Jews were still fighting amongst themselves. Down to this very day, we find the Jewish people hopelessly split in enemy camps politically and religiously, with one group cynically and sometimes even hatefully attacking the other.

Thus it is the sin of causeless hatred, the crime of the brothers against Joseph, that can be said to be our 'original sin'. Indeed, during the

Yom Kippur additional *Amida,* the author of the mournful *Eileh Ezkera* hymn of doxology, links the Temple's destruction and the tragedy of Jewish exile with the sin of the brothers' sale of Joseph.

Now Rashi's interpretation assumes profound significance. In the midst of brotherly hatred, the love between Joseph and Benjamin stands out as a shining example of the potential for unconditional love. Rashi links their tears during their meeting to the destruction of our Sanctuaries – the result of jealousy and enmity between Jew and Jew. Indeed, they each weep for the future tragedies that will befall their descendants. But although each brother will be blessed with a Sanctuary on his allotted land, the brothers weep not for themselves, but each for the other. This act of selfless weeping and unconditional love, becomes the only hope against the tragedies implicit in the sale of Joseph into slavery. The only thing which can repair that sin – and by implication the sins of all the causeless hatred between factions down the long road of Jewish history – is nothing less than a love in which the other comes first, causeless love, when one weeps for the other's tragedy rather than for his own.

Rabbi Abraham Isaac Hakohen Kook taught that if the Temples were destroyed because of causeless hatred, the Temple will only be rebuilt because of causeless love, exemplified by the tears of Joseph and Benjamin. Rashi is providing a prescient lesson for our troubled times.

A Tearful and Faithful Reunion

> *Joseph made ready his chariot, and went up to*
> *meet his father, to Goshen; and he presented*
> *himself unto him, and fell on his neck, and wept*
> *on his neck a good while.*
>
> GENESIS 46:29

Of all the figures in Genesis, Jacob's life is the most clearly depicted, his emotional experiences ranging from ecstatic heights to painful descents clearly recorded. And of all his sufferings, probably the most painful moment occurs when the brothers bring home the blood-soaked coat of many colors and ask their father if indeed it belongs to Joseph. Whatever happened until then – his running away from Esau, his discovering that he'd been hoodwinked by Laban, his burying of his beloved Rachel on the side of the road after less than a decade of married life – cannot compare to the moment when he is led to believe that his beloved son has been ripped apart by a wild beast. The text is explicit concerning Jacob's suffering; inconsolable, he mourns many days, and accepts the fact that he will even go to his grave a mourner.

In a sense Jacob's life is over, since all his hopes for the future had been bound up in his beloved Joseph. Abraham almost lost his future with the binding of Isaac, but Jacob actually did lose his future for the twenty-two years he lived thinking his favored son and heir for the birthright had been torn by a wild beast. And if his confrontation with the bloodied coat marks the greatest suffering in Jacobs's life, then the encounter between Jacob the elderly father and his living son Joseph must be the most significant moment of Jacob's life.

When father and son do meet at last, the tears flow freely. Indeed, the Torah records the very words of Jacob which reflect the feelings of a man who has achieved total peace and serenity with God:

> Now I may die, since I have seen your face, that you are yet alive.
> Gen. 46:30

If it is true that Jacob's encounter with Joseph is the central experience of his life, redeeming not only his own faith but the promises God has given to Jacob's descendants, then the meeting should illuminate basic truths not only about a father and son, but also about the nature of the Jewish people and our destiny.

What immediately strikes us is the ambiguity in the account of the tears. We don't know who fell on whose neck, or who wept. Was it Jacob or Joseph? Rashi comments that it was Joseph who wept. And then what was Jacob doing at that moment? According to the Midrash, Jacob was busy saying the Shema, 'Hear O Israel, the Lord our God the Lord is One.'

Nahmanides disagrees with Rashi, arguing that simple common sense doesn't allow for the view that the old father held back his tears while the younger Joseph gave vent to his emotions. After all, everybody understands that if you have an old father who finds his son alive after believing that he's been dead for the last twenty-two years, and a son who has reached the position of second-in-command to Pharaoh, how could we doubt that the tears must have emanated from the elder Jacob's eyes? It would certainly have been understandable for both to have wept, but since the weeping in this verse is done in the singular, it must have been Jacob who wept.

And yet Rashi's interpretation must be addressed. Why does he assign Joseph the tears and his father the Shema? What's so significant about the Shema, especially at this moment?

During the twenty-two years of mourning, Jacob's life had been hopeless. For so long he'd been living in a fog of despair, in sharp contrast to the years prior to Joseph's death when his entire life had been pregnant with meaning as he prepared his favorite son for eventual leadership of Israel, as he fashioned for him the mantle of the birthright. He had certainly reiterated the tradition of the Covenant between the Pieces, the mission of Israel to the nations, the ultimate goal of ethical monotheism to perfect the world under the kingship of God. And then arrived the black, bleak day when 'Joseph has been torn, yes, torn by a wild beast,' when the bloodstained garment was brought to him; he could hardly be blamed if he allowed himself a momentary lapse of faith. Until then, it had been so clear to him that all of the divine promises which were to befall his descendants were to be realized through Joseph, first-born of his beloved Rachel, devoted student of family lore, dreamer of lofty dreams. And now without Joseph, what is to become of the divine promises?

From this vantage point, it makes very good sense that Jacob's immediate response to his encounter with Joseph was the profound confirmation of his faith in the traditions of his father, and in the future of his people. Hence he declares the formula of Jewish faith, the acceptance of the yoke of divine kingship, *Shema Yisrael*, our belief in ultimate world acceptance of ethical monotheism. In effect, Jacob is telling Joseph that now he understands that God's covenant with Abraham will indeed be fulfilled, no matter how bleak the picture, no matter how dark the exile. Hear O Israel, the Lord who is now our God will eventually be crowned as the ruler of universe, on that day God will be one and His name will be one. Never give up on our faith, no matter what. From the perspective of my life, I now realize that the tragedy which I experienced was merely God's preparation of the Covenant between the Pieces, the survival of the family, the enslavement in and eventual exodus from Egypt, the redemption of the world.

* * *

A striking example of how we can either control our emotions, and live, or be controlled by them, and die, is to be found by comparing two biblical personalities described in the book of Samuel. Book One opens with the account of a childless woman named Hannah visiting the Sanctuary in Shilo to pray to God. She vows that if God remembers her and gives her a son, she will dedicate him to the service of God. When the high priest, Eli HaKohen, sees a woman whose lips move but no words are heard, he wrongly suspects her of being drunk. 'She speaks above her heart [*he medaberet al libah*]' [1 Sam. 1:13] is how the text describes her concentration. Hannah cannot possibly be drunk, the text is teaching us. A person who drinks to inebriation is not in control of his emotions; he is a slave to instinct and desire. Hannah 'speaks above (*al*) her heart' means that she stands over and above the emotions of the heart. After all, hasn't she dedicated the son of her prayers to divine service? She is willing to give up a mother's desires and send the child she hopes God will grant her to another home – the Sanctuary – and place him in the care of Eli HaKohen. Hannah speaks not merely to (*el*) but rather above (*al*) her heart, and is therefore in control of her emotions. No, she cannot be drunk. She is sincerely praying, and her prayer will be answered.

In contrast, the story of Nabal, which takes place one generation later, describes a rich shepherd protected by David but whose own selfish desires make him reject David in his hour of need. The young David, anointed by Samuel (who has grown up to become a judge in Israel) as the future king, is being harrassed and hunted down by Saul. David sends some of his young men to the wealthy Nabal during the shearing season with a request for provisions. The selfish scoundrel (which is the literal meaning of his name) refuses to part with even a small portion of his wealth, not even for David himself. The text describes him as '…a hard man, evil in deeds, like his heart' [I Sam. 25:3], and the verse ends with the word '*kalibi*,' which can either be taken as a description of lineage, 'from the house of Caleb,' or as a description of personality, subservient to his emotions. Angered, David plans a deadly attack on this ungrateful man. In the meantime, word reaches Nabal's wife, who plans to rescue her husband by sending David two hundred loaves, two bottles of wine, five prepared sheep, five measures of parched corn, one hundred clusters of raisins, and two hundred cakes of figs. Nabal is none the wiser since he celebrates the festival of sheep shearing with a kingly feast and, true to form, considering his character of identifying with – and not controlling – his heart, he gets drunk. Only in the morning is he told of Abigail's gift, and in an instant Nabal's '...heart died within him and he became as a stone' [I Sam. 25:37]. Apparently Nabal was so obsessed by the desires of his heart, a slave to his emotional needs and demands, that his death is described as the death of his heart. His very essence was not his mind or his God, but was rather his heart and his emotions.

Hannah and Nabal stand at opposite ends of the spectrum, Hannah speaks to her heart and makes her heart listen, while Nabal's heart ordered him to do what it wanted, and not what God would have wanted.

Jacob's recital of the Shema at this intense moment is a supreme lesson to teach Joseph the importance of God over emotions and is built into the continuation of the Shema: 'You shall love the Lord your God with all your heart, and with all your soul, and with all your might' [Deut. 6:5] – even to the point of *mesirat nefesh*, the willingness to give up your soul, your very life, for God. To have discovered that Joseph is still alive is to have endowed Jacob's life with renewed meaning and significance. Instead of losing control, he says the Shema, acknowledging that a Jew must be willing to give up his life for God, not only when he has nothing left to lose, but even now, when life has become so exquisitely precious. And remember that the Shema is recited before death and has historically been recited by our holy martyrs. 'Now I can die,' Jacob says to Joseph, which may be understood to mean that even now he's willing to die for God; this is real *mesirat nefesh*. Such is the lesson Jacob wants to impart to Joseph in his recitation of the Shema: one must be willing to give up for God even that which is most beloved and precious.

* * *

On one of my visits to America, a man whom I had always thought to be very serious about his Judaism said to me: 'You know why I'm not making *aliya*? I don't want my son to go to the Israeli army.'

As a father, I certainly understand his feelings, but as a Jew I can hardly justify them. This attitude is the very opposite of what Jacob was trying to teach Joseph. We have to be able to overcome even the deepest of our emotions in our commitment to God. We should not forget that when Jacob declares the Shema and his commitment to God, it is over-heard by his sons. And perhaps it is precisely that message which inspires Joseph to re-establish close family ties and to request that his remains be returned to the land of Israel when his descendants leave Egypt.

The True Art of Negotiation

You are to be acknowledged master by your
brothers; the sceptre of rulership shall never
depart from Judah, nor the lawgiver from between
his feet ... unto him shall be the gathering of the
nations.

GENESIS 49:8, 10

Who is really the most important of the brothers, Joseph or Judah? At the outset of the Joseph stories, it is clear that at least Jacob and Joseph believe that it is Joseph. After all, Joseph is the one who receives the coat of many colors from his father – a clear symbol of the birthright – and Joseph is the one who dreams that all the brothers, and indeed all the cosmos – will bow down to him. Yet, by the end of the sequence, at least Jacob has changed his mind. Judah is granted the birthright and not Joseph. Joseph seemingly accepts the situation. What happened and why?

The dramatic change in Judah is clearly delineated in the Bible. We first meet him in depth as a clever salesman, driven more by profit motive than sibling sensitivity when he cleverly suggests selling Joseph as a slave to a caravan of Midianite traders passing in the distance rather than leaving their hapless brother in the pit, waiting for the scorpions to unleash their poison. True, Judah thereby saved his brother from certain death (at least by starvation, if the pit was empty), yet we cannot overlook the fact that the brother who actually initiates Joseph's sale into slavery is none other than Judah. Perhaps Judah should have tried harder to rescue Joseph completely! And from the moment he is sold, Joseph's fate appears likely to be sealed; the likelihood of any of the brothers ever seeing him again is virtually nonexistent. Because of Judah, Joseph the dreamer is as good as dead, certainly to his aged father.

More than two decades later, Judah makes a selfless plea to the Grand Vizier (Joseph) that instead of imprisoning Benjamin as a slave in Egypt because the missing silver goblet was found in his food sack, he – Judah – will stand as a substitute. This reveals a total turnaround in the character of Judah. He emerges as the classic penitent, since true penitence involves correcting one's sin at its core; if in the past he was instrumental in turning Joseph into a slave, then the only possible restoration is for Judah to now make himself a slave instead of Benjamin. The nobility of spirit demonstrated by Judah's willing sacrifice of his own life – a spiritual descendant of Isaac on the *Akeda* – is enough to thrust him into a position of leadership, to cause Jacob to declare concerning Judah: 'from the "torn" [Joseph], you have arisen...' [Gen. 49:9].

But Joseph also changes, and his change involves a new-found humility which enables him to recognize Judah's superiority. But this change is more subtle, and requires our reading between the lines of the text. Joseph first appears as an arrogant youth, his dreams testifying to an exalted sense of self. He sees himself as king over his brothers, their sheaves of wheat bowing down to his, the sun, the moon and the planets all genuflecting before him. And as long as he dreamt dreams of agriculture in Egypt, universal power and domination, far removed from the family shepherding in the land of Israel, Joseph understood that he had constructed an internal grammar alien to his family, a language his brothers and ancestors didn't speak. Joseph seemed a mutation, an alien revolutionary independent of the family traditions. He was apparently gifted, but he dare not be accepted by his brothers. They were not ready to take him for what he was, a man of many colors, of manifold visions and cosmopolitan dreams. And so when his brothers sold him into slavery, they dealt with him more as a stranger than as a brother, an outsider having more in common with Esau than with Jacob. And Joseph accepted his brothers' judgement. He was truly different, a seeker after the novel and dynamic Egyptian occupation of agriculture, a citizen of the world, rather than a lover of Zion. When in Egypt, he easily accepts the Egyptian tongue, answers to an Egyptian name (*Tzafenat-Pane'ah*), and wears Egyptian garb. He has graduated from the family; not only are they not interested in him, he is not really interested in them!

It is only in the Torah portion of *Vayigash* that Joseph pulls away the mask and stands revealed before his brothers and sends for his aged father. But to understand why it takes place right now, we first have to understand why our portion *Vayigash* begins in the midst of one of the most tension-filled encounters in the entire Torah. Is the Torah merely interested in the dramatic effect, presenting the life and death struggle of Benjamin as a cliff-hanger, keeping us in suspense by ending the preceding portion right when it seems that there is no hope left for the wrongly accused Benjamin, whose sack of food turned out to be the hiding place of the Grand Vizier's missing silver goblet?

Judah's defense speech keeps returning to the theme of an old father waiting at home for his youngest son. The word 'father' appears thirteen times (Jacob is a father to thirteen children), an extraordinary emphasis if directed to a stranger with no knowledge of the family. Would it not have been more logical for Judah to have based his defense on the circumstantial nature of the evidence against Benjamin? Indeed, since their payment for all food purchases keeps turning up in each of the brothers' sacks, there is a clear indication that a foreign hand has taken the freedom to open their bags. Once a strange hand is moving about freely within the brothers' property, that same hand could have easily planted the evidence in Benjamin's sack. But instead of this defense, Judah sticks to one tale, the story of their family and the sufferings of their aged father. If Benjamin is a thief, why should the age or mental condition of Benjamin's father matter to the Egyptian Grand Vizier? A thief must be punished; Benjamin should have been concerned for his aged father and not have perpetrated a crime against the Grand Vizier.

Why should one expect the Grand Vizier to be concerned about the thief's ancient father?

Admittedly, the situation is extremely tense. After having nearly brought their father to his death with their sale of Joseph, the brothers dare not now contemplate returning home to Israel bereft of Rachel's second son. Judah, who promised his father that he would be responsible for his father's youngest, initially steps forward and speaks up at the end of *Parashat Miketz*:

> ...What shall we say unto my lord? What shall we speak? Or how shall we justify ourselves? God has found out the iniquity of your servants. Behold we shall be my lord's servants, also us, and also the one in whose hand the goblet was found.
>
> Gen. 44:16

Judah recognizes the 'iniquity' of the brothers, a continuation of a theme first expressed when the Grand Vizier originally confronted them with the charge that they were spies:

> And they said, one to another, 'We are verily guilty concerning our brother, in that we saw the distress of his soul, when he implored us, and we would not hear; therefore is this distress come upon us.'
>
> Gen. 42:21

These words of Judah to the Grand Vizier are the culmination of this theme. Why are the brothers being mistreated to such an extent by this Grand Vizier? It is an act of God, think the brothers, obviously punishing them for their mistreatment of Joseph – measure for measure. The brothers behaved ignominiously toward Joseph, and now they must pay the price. Judah's offer that the brothers become slaves to the Grand Vizier because 'God has found out the iniquity of your servants' is a clear expression of Judah's conviction that they must all now be punished together – all but Benjamin who had nothing to do with the sale of Joseph. They must accept the will of God.

But the Grand Vizier shifts the tables on Judah. He rejects the offer of all the brothers becoming servants. He wants only Benjamin:

Only the man in whose hand the goblet is found, he shall be my
servant. And as for you, go up in peace unto your father.

Gen. 44:17

This is when Judah grows confused. According to his calculations, God
was punishing the brothers as a result of the evil they had perpetrated
against their brother. That is how he understood the mishaps which had
befallen the family ever since they met this Grand Vizier. The way Judah
surmised it, since the brothers had sinned as a collective unit, they must
now suffer as a collective unit. But Joseph's singling out of Benjamin as
the only brother who would be enslaved challenged Judah's perception.
After all, Benjamin had never been part of the conspiracy against Joseph.
He was too young; if any of the brothers were innocent, Benjamin was
innocent. Why should he be the only one punished?

Now we can understand why the portion of *Miketz* ends precisely
when it does. It has little to do with the desire to create suspense, and
largely to do with Judah's new-found awareness as to the identity of the
Grand Vizier. Because if it wasn't God who had planned their experiences
in Egypt, it could only have been the Grand Vizier. And why would the
Grand Vizier have it in for them, unless…

The portion of *Vayigash* opens with the words,

Then Judah stepped near unto him [Joseph], and said, 'Oh my
Lord, let your servant, I pray thee, speak a word in my lord's
ears….'

Gen. 44:18

Until this point, Judah had believed that the Kafkaesque nightmare they
were experiencing was the result of God's punishment. Judah now realizes that this cannot be the case. He now begins to perceive the unfold-
ing of a trail of evidence that casts new light upon the Grand Vizier's
true identity. He recalls that Shimon, the brother who instigated casting Joseph into the pit, was singled out to sit in prison as a hostage after
their first sojourn to Egypt for food. He now remembers how, upon their
second visit, the Grand Vizier arranged their seats according to their
ages when he invited them for a celebratory repast [Gen. 43:33]. Only

283

two people aside from the family who were present could have known the proper ages of the brothers: father Jacob and brother Joseph. And Jacob was in Israel!

Yes, an Egyptian, a Grand Vizier couldn't care less about an old father – unless it was *his* old father as well. Every word of Judah's is now calculated – and successfully earns him a bull's eye. Joseph also now recognizes Judah's profound wisdom and the ability of Judah to have pierced through his veil of deception and revealed his true identity. Judah has now emerged as the *tikkun*, i.e., repair – and thereby the most proper heir – of Jacob. Jacob's tragedy was his sin of deception, perversely continued by Joseph's pose as Egyptian Grand Vizier; Judah's mastery is his gift of cutting through the deception, and in so doing becomes worthy of the Abrahamic birthright.

The moment of Judah's understanding is also the moment of Joseph's understanding – as well as Joseph's repentance. He now sees the master plan, the divine guidance in all that has transpired. The brothers must come to Egypt not to serve him – Joseph – but rather to fulfill the vision of Abraham at the Covenant between the Pieces. The family of Abraham must live to spread the message of ethical monotheism throughout the world, but they will first return to the land of Israel which will always be the familial and national homeland. Joseph is ready now to recognize Judah's superiority, and to subjugate his gifts of technology, administration and politics to Judah's Torah and tradition. Joseph is now able to surrender his dream of kingship over the brothers and request that his remains be eventually brought to Israel. Joseph is now ready to reunite the family under the majesty of Judah. And such is the case in Jacob's blessing.

But Jacob does not express forcefully enough the vision of unity, the initial dream of Rebecca when she merged the Esau-like skins with the hands and voice of Jacob.* The aged patriarch merely creates a split between the double material portion of land which goes to Joseph, and the spiritual leadership, which goes to Judah [Gen. 49:8–10, 22–26], an understandable replay of the same split his father Isaac had effectuated a generation earlier; apparently we most often do repeat the mistakes of

---

* See also 'Rebecca's Choice', pp. 167–171.

our parents, especially if we feel guilty toward them and seek their forgiveness. Hence, in First Temple history, Judah-Jerusalem will separate from Ephraim-Northern Israel, and the seeds of a difficult exile were planted, whose bitter fruits would last for close to 2,000 years. And if Ephraim represented material prosperity, technological and admnistrative know-how, scientific and philosophical expertise, then Judah – bereft and isolated, exiled and violated – could hardly be expected to stand up to a holocaust!

However, the prophet Ezekiel, in this portion's prophetic reading (*haftorah*), provides an ultimate rapprochement – nay, unity – between all of the tribes; 'Now you, son of man, take yourself one wooden tablet and write upon it, "for Judah and the children of Israel, his companions," and take another wooden tablet and write upon it, "for Joseph, the wooden tablet of Ephraim, and all the children of Israel, his companions." And bring close to yourself one to the other, for you as one tablet, and they shall become one' [Ezekiel 37:16, 17]. Rabbi Abraham Isaac Hakohen Kook, the first Chief Rabbi of Israel, felt the footsteps of the Messiah and the nearness of redemption. He saw in Theodor Herzl, architect of the administrative and political characteristics of the Jewish State, the Messiah from the House of Joseph-Ephraim (he eulogized Herzl as such upon his death, in his famous encomium from Jerusalem); he anxiously awaited the coming of the Messiah from the House of David-Judah, who would give spiritual meaning and universal redemptive significance to the hands of Esau which so successfully waged wars and forged an advanced nation-state phoenix-like, from the ashes of the Holocaust. Hopefully, the vision of Rebecca will soon be realized...

Why Do We Weep?

And he lifted his voice in weeping, and the
Egyptians heard, and the house of Pharaoh heard.

GENESIS 45:2

Joseph, the hero of the last portions of the book of Genesis, has a number of appellations; Joseph the Dreamer, Joseph the Grand Vizier, Joseph the Righteous One. However, it seems to me that the appellation Joseph the Weeper also fits the second most powerful man in Egypt because he – unique among all the personalities of the Bible – is pictured four times in the Bible and a fifth time in the Midrash as one who weeps. Joseph is hardly a weak personality who melts into tears at any crisis; much the opposite, he demonstrates an iron will, obdurate and optimistic despite setbacks of near-homicide, exile and imprisonment. Moreover, he doesn't weep during the difficult periods; rather it is during moments of revelation and reunion when his tears cannot be held back, which may be described as times of desperate joy.

In order to understand the meaning of Joseph's weeping – and perhaps to gain an insight into the phenomenon of tears in general – let us examine the biblical scenes which portray a weeping Joseph. The first time Joseph's tears are mentioned in the Bible is when his brothers, who do not recognize him, come to the Egyptian palace to purchase food and he charges them with espionage. When they speak in Hebrew among themselves – obviously assuming that the Grand Vizier does not understand their language – they blame themselves for having sinned against their brother, accepting their punishment as a natural consequence of their heartless cruelty at the pit two decades before. It is at this point that the text records: 'And he [Joseph] turned aside from them and wept' [Gen. 42:24].

Subsequently, at the very beginning of *Vayigash* and immediately following Judah's stirring speech for clemency, we read:

> And Joseph could not restrain himself before all who were standing near him; …and no man stood with him when Joseph revealed himself to his brothers. And he lifted his voice in weeping….
>
> Gen. 45:1, 2

Joseph continues to weep as he kisses each of brothers [Gen. 45:14, 15] – he weeps and they do not.

Finally, after the description of Jacob's death and burial, Joseph's brothers seeing '…that their father died,' and fearing that Joseph would now punish them, informed the Grand Vizier that before his death, their father commanded them to tell Joseph to forgive the brothers. 'And Joseph wept when they spoke with him' [Gen. 50:15–17]. Why does Joseph cry so much – and especially at moments of rapprochement with his family?

Rabbi Joseph B. Soloveitchik makes the very telling point that tears well up from the deepest and frankest recesses of human emotion, expressing genuine feelings that the individual himself is sometimes unaware that he possesses. The Psalmist announces Rosh Hashana, the New Year Festival of repentance, with the charge:

> Trumpet the shofar on the [first of the] month, when the day of our festival is hidden.

Ps. 81:4

The reference to 'hiddenness' (*bakeseh*) relates not only to the hidden-ness of the moon, since Rosh Hashana falls out on the first of the month when the moon is barely visible, but also to the hidden recesses of the human heart, from which the truest feelings of repentance must emanate. Therefore the symbol of Rosh Hashana is the shofar, which expresses sounds of *shevarim* and *truah*, sighs and sobs, weeping and wailing. These cries convey concealed, but very genuine feelings of remorse and angst.*

King David, sweet psalmist of Israel, is a deeply religious poet, a unifier of the twelve tribes of Israel, a fearless warrior on behalf of God, and a sensitive human being who refuses an opportunity to slay King Saul although the madly jealous ruler of Israel is dedicated to David's destruction. At the same time he has an adulterous relationship with Bathsheba, sending her husband Uriah to his death in the first lines of battle. Is King David worthy of our veneration as the forerunner of the Messiah? Is he a just and good man who had a single, uncharacteristic, tragic mishap, or is he a wicked hedonist who occasionally expresses religious feelings? Will the real King David stand up!

Nathan the prophet stands before the King and presents him with an allegory of a rich farmer snatching the only ewe owned and loved by his poor neighbor, concluding with the charge: 'You are that [wicked] man.' King David cries out: 'I have sinned before the Lord.' And in all masoretic versions of the Bible, there is an empty space fol-lowing King David's confession [II Sam., Chap. 15]. The great Gaon of Vilna comments:

> It was at that point that King David wept; the empty space sym-bolizes his tears, the emotions which are deeper than words.

King David's tears testified as to who the real King David was, and as to the ideals to which the real King David dedicated his life.

Joseph had spent twenty-two years in Egypt, and certainly dur-ing the last period when he was Grand Vizier and second-in-command

---

* Joseph B. Soloveitchik, *Days of Remembrance*, pp. 221–224.

only to Pharaoh, he endeavored to forget his jealousy-inflamed home, his brothers' hatred, his father's unwise and dangerous favoritism. He wears Egyptian garb, assumes an Egyptian name, speaks the Egyptian tongue, marries the daughter of a Priest of On, and names his eldest son Menashe '…for God has enabled me to forget all of my toil and the entire household of my father' [Gen. 41:51].

Assuming that Joseph had his wife 'convert' and maintained whatever ethical and ritual traditions he had absorbed in his youth – he certainly harbored a great deal of resentment against his brothers and even against his father, who could not escape responsibility for the dysfunction of the family vis-a-vis Joseph. Indeed, he had deeply buried all familial feeling and only wished to punish his brothers for their insensitive cruelty.

Eventually, he meets his brothers after some two decades, face to face. When they confess their guilt to each other, he weeps. His weeping teaches him that despite his legitimate resentments, one can never really escape one's family, one's parental dwelling, one's earliest influences. First he is filled with longing for the innocent Benjamin, and then for his father, whose mistake, after all, was not that he loved too little but that he loved too much. Ultimately he realizes that he also contributed to his brothers' hatred by his arrogance and insensitivity towards them. Even after his father's death, he understands that, in the final analysis, to deny them forgiveness would be denying his own deepest feelings, shutting off the most genuine wellsprings of the most profound part of his heart and soul.

In the end, Joseph understands that to deny his family would be to deny himself. He learns this from his tears, for our tears teach all of us what we really feel and who we really are.

Of Wagons and Heifers, Trains and Planes, Guilt and Forgiveness, Fathers and Sons

And they told him all the words of Joseph which he had said unto them. And when he saw the wagons which Joseph had sent to transport him, the spirit of Jacob revived.

GENESIS 46:27

One of the most poignant moments in the Bible is the meeting between the old father Jacob and his beloved son Joseph, from whom he had been estranged for twenty-two years. Jacob-Israel leaves the land of his heritage and sets out for the strange, unfamiliar and gentile Egypt in order to reunite with his long-lost child. The Bible tells us that when Jacob 'saw the wagons which Joseph had sent to transport him, his spirit was revived' [Gen. 45:27]. What is there about the wagons which revives Jacob's spirit? Was the cost of travel so prohibitive for the patriarch that just because his son was willing to provide transportation he was ready to make such a difficult journey?

Rashi comments that the 'wagons' are a subtle allusion to a particular section in the Torah, the account of the *egla arufa* (the heifer whose neck is broken by the elders as atonement for a murder whose perpetrator is unknown), which was the very Torah portion father and son had been engaged in studying immediately prior to Joseph's disappearance. Perhaps Rashi's citation of the Midrash is not merely to expose word play on *egla* and *agalah*, a reminder of their last study session together. Remember that it is the elders of the city who have to go out to a stream and bring the sacrifice of the heifer as an atonement for the unidentified murderer. The elders must declare 'Our hands have not shed this blood and our eyes have not seen' [Deut. 21:7]. Does anyone actually believe that the elders are directly responsible for the crime? But the Jerusalem Talmud maintains that they do have ministerial responsibility for a murder in their town; apparently the perpetrator was in need of money or drugs or was mentally deranged, and there were no adequate social services in place to prevent such a crime from happening. The elders must seek atonement for their lack of foresight, and the heifer (*egla*) is the symbol of their forgiveness.

Similarly, Jacob, the elder of the family, was not directly responsible for the sale of Joseph, but he certainly lacked proper foresight in 'sibling management.' If he ever suspected what really happened – a suspicion he dared not utter or he would have had to banish all the sons except Benjamin – he must have been consumed by guilt for having sent the hapless Joseph to seek after his brothers' welfare. Perhaps the *agalah-egla* is Joseph's message to his father that he accepts his expiation of twenty-two years of aggrieved mourning, and he completely forgives him.

Additionally, I heard a completely different interpretation of the verse,* a commentary which strikes a particularly human chord of truth. To what may this be compared in modern times? A rather precocious and cosmopolitan son leaves his traditional father's house to pursue his studies or to practice his career on far off shores. After a long hiatus in the relationship, the son lets the father know that he is ready for a reunion. The father, however, is filled with agonizing fear and uncertainty.

---

*   This was told to me by Rabbi Isaac Bernstein, in the name of Dayan Golditch of London.

Is the son still true to the traditions of his people? How far has he wandered spiritually and emotionally from his ancestral home? If the son then visits the father for a Sabbath or a festival, the father's questions remain unanswered. After all, his son could always 'play religious' for a short period of time. But if the father then receives from his son a train or plane ticket with the request that the meeting take place in the son's home and environment, the father is very relieved and understands that he has nothing to fear. After all, if the son's lifestyle had become so very different from his father's values, the son would not invite his father into his home. Inviting Jacob to Egypt meant that Joseph was certain that his father would not be mortified at his beloved son's life style even in the alien environment of Egypt. Therefore, when Jacob saw the wagons sent by Joseph to transport him to Egypt, his spirit was revived...

Does Distance Make the Heart Grow Fonder – Or Distant?

> *And they told him all the words of Joseph which he had said to them. He then saw the wagons which Joseph had sent to transport him, and the spirit of Jacob their father was revived.*
>
> GENESIS 45:27

Joseph sends wagons to transport his father to Egypt 'and the spirit of Jacob is revived' [Gen. 45:27]. But how close does Joseph really want his father and brothers to be to him? After all, Joseph's invitation is not to Egypt proper, the capital city and seat of power where Joseph rules second-in-command to Pharaoh, but rather to the more remote area of Goshen: 'And you shall dwell in the land of Goshen, and you shall be near me, you and your children's children ...' [Gen. 45:10]. 'Near me,' but not next door to me. Why this degree of distance? Why settle your family in a different city?

We can approach Joseph's choice of Goshen from two very

different perspectives. On the one hand it reflects the wisest move Joseph could have made for the sake of protecting the moral and religious identity of his family. He understands how crucial it is for Jacob's family to live in a Jewish area, dedicated to sustaining its own value system. In fact, when Jacob sends Judah on ahead 'to direct [or prepare the area] before [the patriarch will arrive] in Goshen' [Gen. 46:28], the word for 'to prepare' is *lehorot*, which generally means to teach or to give religious-legal direction. The Midrash [Gen. Raba 95:3] teaches that Jacob sent Judah ahead to establish a house of study, a yeshiva, which is a necessary central institution for a Jewish religious community. In other words, in order for Israel's children and grandchildren to survive as a Jewish community in the Diaspora, Joseph and Jacob agree that the community must provide the necessary Torah teaching and religious atmosphere which will nurture Jewish consciousness and continuity.

Our Sages convey this message in a very fascinating way. In the standing, silent *Amida* prayer, Jews all over the world begin praising God as the disperser of rain (*mashiv ha-ru-ah u-morid ha-geshem*) on Shmini Atzeret, the beginning of the rainy season in Israel, the universal Jewish homeland. However, all Diaspora Jews, no matter where they live outside Israel, begin requesting the Almighty to send rain (*ten tal u-matar*) at the end of the first week in December, the beginning of the rainy season in Babylon [*Ta'anit* 10a]. Why must Diaspora communities in Brooklyn or Belgium follow the rainy season in Babylon, and not the rainy season specific to their own locations? And if they are to follow another land's rainy season, why should not the obvious choice point in the direction of Israel, the universal Jewish homeland?

I would suggest that Jewish prayer ritual is teaching that in order for a Diaspora community to survive, it can only do so by following the model of the Diaspora of Babylon, which in its golden age effectively created a Jewish state within a state: a Jewish Exilarch, a Jewish educational system and a Jewish legal structure. Indeed, the Boro Parks, Monseys, Teanecks, Stamford Hills and Hendons did not spring up from nowhere; they all keep alive the tradition of the Babylonian Diaspora, which itself goes back to the days of Goshen.

But there is also another way to consider the choice of Goshen. Joseph may have been a bit nervous about there being close contact between royal Pharaoh and his committed Jewish father, Jacob-Israel. This may have been partially due to self-consciousness on his part about his Jewish background. After all, Pharaoh must have looked upon Joseph as a 'born-again Egyptian,' and the Grand Vizier played this role, at least externally. Undoubtedly, Pharaoh feared lest Jacob lead Joseph back to a more intensive Abrahamic life style.

And indeed, according to the Midrash, Jacob was in the traditional mold of his grandfather, Abraham, who understood his mission in life was to bring the message of the One God to the whole world [Gen. Raba 84:4]. The opening verse of *Vayeshev* reads as follows: 'And Jacob dwelt in the land of his father's sojournings, [*megurai*], in the land of Canaan' [Gen. 37:1]. By reading the word '*megurai*' (sojourns) as '*megiyurai*' (conversions), the Midrash suggests that Jacob returned to Israel in order to create 'converts' to the monotheistic faith. Jacob was very much a Jew in the tradition of Abraham.

I would like to suggest that, given the proud and feisty nature of Jacob, a careful reading of the text gives credence to Joseph's fears.

We read towards the conclusion of this Torah portion how

> ...Joseph brought in Jacob his father, and set him before Pharaoh. And Jacob blessed Pharaoh. And Pharaoh said unto Jacob 'How many are the days of the years of your life?' And Jacob said unto Pharaoh: 'The days of the years of my sojournings are a hundred and thirty years, few and evil have been the days of the years of my life, and they have not attained unto the days of the years of the life of my fathers in the days of their sojournings.' And Jacob blessed Pharaoh and he went away from the presence of Pharaoh.
>
> Gen. 47:7–10

Taken at face value, the exchange between Pharaoh and the patriarch hardly makes sense. Since when does any commoner (albeit the father of an important member of the cabinet) dare to bless a Pharaoh, the very apex of human civilization who considers himself to be a god? Then, when Jacob answers Pharaoh's question, he seemingly compounds confusion by adding further irrelevancies, giving information regarding the difficulties of his own life which Pharaoh had never asked him about.

This entire conversation hardly seems worthy of being recorded in our eternal Bible.

Clearly before this meeting Joseph had to prepare his father. If before meeting the royalty of England a visitor must be adequately prepared, this was certainly true of a meeting with the 'holy and royal' Pharaoh of Egypt. Undoubtedly, Pharaoh was a disperser of blessings, the first one to speak, the leader of the interview. Joseph certainly communicated this protocol to his father. But Jacob saw himself as royalty with a greater majestic splendor than Pharaoh. After all, he was a descendant of Abraham and Isaac; he was the one who was bringing people to faith in the One God, and it would be absurd for him to receive a blessing from an idolater. Hence, Jacob enters, and the patriarch immediately bestows a blessing upon the ruler of Egypt. No one had ever before dared speak first to Pharaoh, no less given him a blessing. That is why Pharaoh asks Jacob for his age. Perhaps this elderly man is senile, thinks Pharaoh, a condition which might excuse his unseemly behavior. Jacob understands the meaning behind Pharaoh's words, so he wants to reassure Pharaoh that he does not suffer from senility; he looks a lot older than he actually is as a result of a difficult life. His forefathers lived to a far greater age, and he too should live to their age. And to leave no room for doubt, Jacob then again blesses Pharaoh, and leaves his presence. Clearly Jacob and not Pharaoh is in control of the encounter.

Joseph welcomes his family to Egypt – but understands for both these reasons that they had best keep a respectable distance from the Pharaonic, idolatrous capital city. Such an arrangement was best for Joseph as well as for Israel's children and grandchildren.

The Evil Eye Cannot Control You

> *Be a fruitful vine, a fruitful vine by a fountain*
> *[alei ayin].*
>
> GENESIS 49:22

And how old is your grandchild now?' 'Three, *kinenahora*.' It took years before I realized the most common word I'd heard at weddings and other family celebrations wasn't the name of some long-lost Irish relative, a Conan O'Hara I had never met, but was rather the traditional Jewish way of protecting loved ones against the 'evil eye.' After centuries of usage, the Hebrew *ke-neged ayin ha-ra* (against the evil eye) has jelled into a multi-syllabic Yiddish utterance, *kinenahora*. Once you've uttered this formulaic phrase, you've deflected all possible envy in the Evil One who might just overhear that Mrs. Steinberg has five children, *kinenahora*.

Jewish folklore is rich with customs, tales and preventive measures against the powers of the evil eye. Those who are illustrious, charming, smart, beautiful or rich fear the most from the gaze of a jealous neighbor, co-worker or employee who can throw crippling darts of hate from the silent rage of his eyes. Have you ever noticed the number of doorways in Safed painted blue, or the red threads given away at Rachel's Tomb to guard against the evil eye? But what is this power of the eye? Does it really exist? How seriously are we supposed to take it?

The first rabbinic midrashic source I know dealing with the evil eye relates to the biblical Joseph [Gen. Raba 91:6]. Among all the biblical figures, no one is more enviable than Joseph. Born with a silver spoon in his mouth, placed there by his doting father, he grows to be handsome, perceptive, wise and moral. Moreover, he is also possessor of a dream vocabulary that arouses unmitigated jealousy in his brothers. They recognize that the messages of Joseph's dreams are not exaggerations, but are rather confirmations of his superiority expressed in symbolic terms.

People who think their own lives have been ruined by an evil eye could easily explain the tragedies of Joseph's life from the moment he is cast in a pit as a result of his being the victim of the evil eye or twenty evil eyes arrayed against him (Benjamin is exempt).

One day, Joseph is on top of the world; the next day, he's at the bottom of a pit literally staring into the eye of a scorpion. If he doesn't die from fright, surely thirst and hunger will kill him. Sold by Midianites to Egyptians, he ends up living the life of a slave. But instead of being rewarded by his master, Potiphar, for his moral integrity in resisting sexual temptations, Joseph is thrown into jail like a rapist caught in the act. Who knows where he will end up? Undoubtedly for those who believe in it, were there someone nearby who could cast off evil eyes, this might be the right moment to invoke some help for Joseph.

However, as his story unfolds, it is clear that the consummately successful Joseph is hardly a victim of the evil eye. On the contrary, the Sages of the Talmud speak of Joseph as having overcome the evil eye. They interpret Jacob's blessing of Joseph: 'Be a fruitful vine, a fruitful vine above a fountain [*alei ayin*, literally, above the eye, *ayin*, meaning both eye and spring],' to mean 'Be a fruitful vine, a fruitful vine that is higher than the [evil] eye,' that overcomes and conquers the evil eye. And Rabbi Yosi, son of Rabbi Hanina, cites a second verse, also dealing with Jacob's blessing, but this time the blessing of his grandchildren Efraim and Menashe: '[May the angel who has redeemed me from all evil, bless the lads] and let them grow into a multitude in the midst of the earth' [Gen. 48:16]. The verb *ve-yidgu* (grow into a multitude) comes from the word *dag* (fish), and Rabbi Yosi concludes: 'for just as fish in the sea are covered by water and the evil eye does not rule over them, so too shall the seed of Joseph not be ruled by the evil eye' [*Berakhot* 20a].

Rabbi Joseph B. Soloveitchik once explained that the evil eye refers to the individual who watches how others look at him and then acts in a manner that will please them. This is negative and destructive, teaches Rabbi Soloveitchik, because playing to the eyes of others means not dancing to the tune of God. Joseph was always his own person; that way, he was able to conquer the evil eye.

How does a person begin to feel the evil eye? I would add one more dimension to the issue. An evil eye is an eye of jealousy and envy. Many individuals of talent and beauty are quick to believe that their failures are a result of other people's envy and the damning eyes of jealous onlookers. After all, it is much easier to blame others – and not ourselves – for our life's failures. Certainly, Joseph had every reason to blame his misfortunes on his brothers' evil, envious eyes; indeed, they were truly responsible for his sale into Egypt, and so – by extension – for his imprisonment. Had he not been sold into Egypt, he would never have come into contact with Potiphar's wife!

But did Joseph blame his brothers' envy for the bad events of his life? Much the opposite, he attributes all that has happened to him – meeting a man in Shekhem who directs him to Dotan, being sold by Midianites to Egyptians, and his interpreting dreams of deposed ministers in jail – as originating in heaven. This is not a midrashic nicety, but Joseph's own words to his brothers when he reveals his true identity:

> Don't be angry with yourselves, for God sent me before you to preserve life.
>
> Gen. 45:5

Again, several verses later,

> And God sent me before you to give you a remnant of the earth, and to save you alive for a great deliverance. It was not you who sent me here, but God, and He made me a father to Pharaoh.
>
> Gen. 45:7–8

In contrast with those who see their failures as a direct result of another's jealous hatred, of an evil eye, Joseph learns to read events that evoke God in a new and powerful way. Until this point, God's contact with the patriarchs has been direct. His will is close to their hearts, and never further away than an accommodating angel. But we never read of Joseph having direct one-on-one contact with God, or of his being visited by angels. What Joseph opens up is a revolutionary step in our understanding of God. His presence in the world does not hit us on the head with a symphonic vision, but we can discern Him and His divine message in all the daily events of our own lives, and even in our failures. God provides us with manifold opportunities. We must take proper advantage of them to bring the world closer to redemption. When this happens, *we* help to bring about God's design – and that is ultimately the greatest expression of the divine will. A wise Hassidic sage once said that *mazal* (usually translated as luck) is the contraction of three Hebrew words: *makom* (place), *zman* (time) and *limmud* (knowledge) – being at the right place at the right time, and knowing how to take proper advantage of the opportunity for the sake of heaven. We must help make our own *mazal* by overcoming 'the evil eye' just as Joseph did.

The believer in an evil eye is himself being blind to human responsibility and ability. He is ignoring the divine master plan that directs the world, contending that his failures result not from his own actions or inactions, but rather from evil people's jealousies and enmities. He denies God's power to extract sweet results from bitter experiences, to turn lemons into lemonade. 'One who works to purify is helped from on High' [Berakhot 20a]. Joseph is the biblical archetype of the person who has learned not to place value on the evil eye of others; his descendants will hopefully never consider themselves victims of a certain Conan O'Hara.

*   *   *

Neither the Jerusalem Talmud nor Maimonides make any reference whatsoever to the 'evil eye'. It was reportedly taught by the Kotzker Rebbe that Maimonides was so great that he succeeded in vanquishing the evil eye. When we remember the Islamic Almohad persecutions he suffered, and the paltry, pygmy-brained abuse he suffered from within the Jewish community, some of whom actually burnt his books, and when we consider his enormous accomplishments in Torah and great stature in medicine despite this – it is clear that he, like Joseph, indeed destroyed the evil eye!

Vayeḥi

The Beginning of the End

> And Jacob lived in the land of Egypt for seventeen
> years, so the whole age of Jacob was one hundred
> and forty-seven years. And the days of Jacob drew
> near to die...
>
> GENESIS 47:28, 29

The final verse of the last portion of *Vayigash* summarizes the astonishing achievement of the Israelites in Egypt: 'And Israel dwelt in the land of Egypt in the country of Goshen and they took possession of it, and were fruitful and multiplied exceedingly' [Gen. 47:27]. Could anything be a clearer testament to the resilience of Jacob's descendants who, in a relatively short period of time, managed to grow rich in real estate, to be fruitful and to multiply?

Yet according to Rashi, this very next verse, the opening of *Vayehi*, sends us in the exact opposite direction, a 180-degree turn for the worse, informing us that the Egyptian bondage was then beginning! Interestingly, Rashi's interpretation is not based on the words of the verse itself [Gen. 47:28], but rather on the almost hidden or interior meaning of the

Torah embedded in the white space – or lack of white space – between the final verse of *Vayigash* and the opening verse of *Vayeḥi*. The portion of *Vayeḥi* opens without a parchment hint that a new chapter is beginning, or that a new story is being told.

There are no paragraphs or indications of chapters in the text of the Torah scrolls. Rather, a white space – anywhere from a minimum of nine letters wide to the end of the entire line – is the Torah's way of indicating that a pause or separation of some kind exists between the previous verse and the following section.

What is unique about *Vayeḥi* is that it is the only portion in the Torah with no white space preceding it, as the last verse in *Vayigash* flows right into the opening verse of *Vayeḥi*. This lack of a division leads Rashi to comment that the reason why our portion is *setumah* (closed) is because '…with the death of Jacob the hearts and eyes of Israel become closed because of the misery of the bondage with which they [Egyptians] had begun to enslave them' [Rashi ad loc.].

For Rashi, the achievement of *Vayigash* lasts no longer than the blink of an eye, or the amount of time it takes to finish one verse and begin another. In one verse the Israelites may be on top of the world, but Rashi wants us to understand that the message of the lack of white space is that we are now witnessing the beginning of the end.

But the truth is that the slavery does not come until a generation – and a biblical book – later, when we are told of the emergence of a new king over Egypt, 'who did not know Joseph' [Ex. 1:8]. In the meantime we are still in the book of Genesis; Joseph, with the keys to the treasury in his pocket, is the Grand Vizier of Egypt, second only to Pharaoh, and his kinsmen are doing astonishingly well on the Egyptian Stock Exchange. So why does Rashi's commentary appear to be 'jumping the gun'?

Rabbi David Pardo explains in his commnetary *Maskil l'David* that the first intimations of Jewish slavery are indeed to be found in the portion of *Vayeḥi*, but in a later verse describing an apparently uncomfortable situation in the wake of Jacob's demise:

> And when the days of mourning for Jacob were over, Joseph spoke to the house of Pharaoh saying, 'If now I have found favor

in your eyes, speak, I pray you, in the ears of Pharaoh, saying, my father made me swear, and he declared: I am dying. In my grave which I have dug for myself in the land of Canaan, there shall you bury me ...'

Gen. 50:4–5

Does this request sound like the words spoken by the Grand Vizier of Egypt? Does the number two figure at a Fortune 500 company, who undoubtedly confers with the president on a daily basis, need an appointment to see him, forced to go through the usual hierarchy of secretaries that junior staff have to go through? Why not a simple knock on the door on the part of Joseph? Why does the Torah even go to the trouble of reporting the process by which Joseph presents a petition – through intermediaries – to have his father buried? And Joseph doesn't even go through a secretary; he begs ('if I have found favor in your eyes') the 'house of Pharaoh', which generally refers to the household staff, the servants of Pharaoh. The Grand Vizier asks a maid or butler to whisper his need to bury his father in Pharaoh's ear. Is this the level to which a second-in-command must stoop in order to get time off for a parent's funeral?

Seforno explains that in this particular instance, court etiquette prevented Joseph from making his request personally of Pharaoh because he was dressed in mourning clothes (and was presumably in need of a haircut and shave). However, Jewish law dictates that whatever one has to do in order to properly bury one's dead is permissible. Joseph certainly could have made himself presentable had his external appearance been the major problem. *Maskil L'David* maintains that a careful reading of the verse indicates a change in Joseph's status. His sudden loss of 'access' could well be a warning of new palace tremors which would eventually erupt into the enslavement of his descendants. Joseph had been demoted in position.

I would suggest another explanation. Perhaps the almost obsequious manner in which Joseph must arrange to have his request brought before Pharaoh indicates not so much a general change in Joseph's political position, as the delicacy of this particular petition. Therefore, it serves as a moment of truth for Joseph as well as for the readers of his story.

Joseph may have reached the top of the social ladder in Egypt.

He speaks Egyptian, dresses as an Egyptian, has become renamed Egyptian (Tzafenat-Pane'ah), and is married to a native Egyptian (perhaps even to his previous master's daughter). From slave to Prime Minister, Joseph has certainly lived out the great Egyptian dream. Now, however, he is forced to face the precariousness and vulnerability of his position.

Ordinarily a person wants to be buried in his own homeland where his body will become part of the earth to which he feels most deeply connected. Indeed, in the ancient world the most critical right of citizenship was the right of burial. The wise Jacob understands that Pharaoh expected Joseph to completely identify with Egypt, to bring up generations of faithful and committed Egyptians after all that his adopted country has given to him. But this was impossible for Jacob – and the patriarch hoped that it would also be impossible for his children and grandchildren as well. They were *in* Egypt but not *of* Egypt. They might contribute to Egyptian society and economy, but they could never become Egyptians. Jacob understood that his burial in Canaan would be the greatest test of Joseph's career, and would define the character of his descendants forever. Hence he makes his beloved son solemnly swear not to bury him in Egypt.

Joseph, too, understood that Pharaoh would be shocked at the request, a petition expressing the Hebrew rejection of the most powerful and civilized nation on earth. Indeed, it is such a difficult and sensitive matter that Joseph cannot face his patron Pharaoh directly with it. At that moment Joseph understands an even deeper truth: were he, his brothers, his children and grandchildren to make the choice to live as Egyptians and to die as Egyptians, the chances are that they would be totally accepted into the mainstream of the land and life in that country. However, were they to choose to live as Jews, with their own concepts of life and death, they would never be accepted and would probably be persecuted. It is this realization in the aftermath of Jacob's death which Rashi correctly sees as the beginning of the slavery of the Israelites. In Egypt, Joseph's kinsmen may have everything: Goshen Heights and Goshen Green, progeny and patrimony. But as long as they are determined to remain Jews, servitude and persecution are inevitable. They may rejoice in their preferred Egyptian status, where 'they took possession of it and were fruitful and multiplied exceedingly,' but they cannot ever pause to enjoy this good fortune. The realization upon Jacob's death of the transient and illusory nature of their good fortune comes upon them inexorably and imperceptibly, as in the blink of an eye, as in a following sentence without a change of paragraph.

And so this portion is closed just as Egypt will soon be closed to their children. Such is the ultimate fate of the children of Israel in every exile.

To Whom Do You Belong?

> *And Israel saw the children of Joseph, and he said,*
> *Who are these?*
>
> GENESIS 48:8

Jacob's death, which occurs towards the end of the book of Genesis, brings the era of the patriarchs to an end. He will be the last person to be buried in Ma'arat Ha Makhpela in Hebron. He will be the forefather whose name, Israel, given to him after defeating the angel in an all-night wrestling bout, is the same name the Jewish people will carry forever. He will be the one patriarch whose twelve sons are transformed into the chiefs of their respective tribes, paving the way for a disparate family to emerge as a nation.

In the lead-up to his death, *Vayeḥi* opens with Jacob in his old age asking Joseph not to leave his dead body in Egypt, but to transport his bones back to the burial-place of his fathers. When he takes sick, Joseph arrives with his two sons, Ephraim and Menashe. At the deathbed scene, Jacob narrates his whole history: how he was blessed by God in Luz that he would be fruitful, that his descendants would inherit the land, and that there would eventually be an ingathering of all nations to the land and faith of Israel (the Messianic promise).

But don't we know this already? And if this story is so important, why doesn't he repeat it to all the brothers who will soon be arriving for their blessings, instead of keeping this moment as a private encounter between himself and Joseph and his sons?

Stranger still, in his very next breath the aged patriarch tells Joseph that he wants Ephraim and Menashe to be considered his and not Joseph's '…just as Reuven and Shimon are mine.' (Although Jacob does allow for any sons that Joseph may have afterwards to be regarded as his own.) Jacob then concludes his own history, recounting the sudden death and burial of Rachel. And suddenly, almost as an afterthought, he turns to Ephraim and Menashe asking, 'Who are these?'

Given that Jacob has just been talking about Menashe and Ephraim, his question doesn't make sense. Doesn't he know who they are? After all, they are the focus of the scene. It sounds as if words spoken one moment are forgotten only moments later, a state of mind that could be seen as bordering on senility. Is Jacob losing his wits?

On the contrary! Of all the profound questions that Genesis raises, I think that these two words – '*Mi eleh?*' (Who are these?) – contain a library of existential philosophy constricted into one line of dialogue. It is a question that could have implications not only for Genesis, but for the entire destiny of the Jewish people. It could well be the question that Grandfather Israel (Jacob) is asking each and every one of us, his descendants.

Jacob knows that his death is the bridge into the next stage of Jewish history. We have reached the point in the evolution of his family where the seventy souls who came down to Egypt are going to become a fully fledged nation. They are about to embark on a 210-year period of expansion that will see them emerge from slavery into nationhood. Many of them will suffer, many will assimilate, and some will wander across a desert under the leadership of Moses and ultimately return, as Israelites, to the very place where the family had its origins.

Dying, Jacob clearly understands how the pattern of his life will mirror the subsequent experience of the Jewish people throughout their history. Born in Israel, Jacob goes into exile for twenty years, and returns to the land of his forefathers in an attempt to live out his remaining years in peace. But circumstances don't allow the peace to prevail. Through the mitigating circumstance of hunger, he is forced to leave Canaan for Egypt, where ironically the family of Israel will emerge into a nation. What happens to them among the Egyptians – seventy pioneering souls increasing and multiplying and thriving – is the essential experience of Jews scattered across the Diaspora from Casablanca to Cracow, from Toledo to Texas. They arrive few in number and thrive until either the Pharaohs of each community rise in protest and expel them, or until assimilation takes over. While the majority of the Jewish community will dissolve in the great melting pot, there will still be a chosen minority who will endure as children of Israel, who will survive as committed Jews.

At this point in time, Jacob stands at the midpoint of five generations. Gazing back, he sees his grandfather Abraham; gazing ahead, he sees his grandchildren Ephraim and Menashe. Each generation is characterized by a unique relationship with the land of Israel. Abraham, born in another land, reveals the One God to the world, and arrives in the land towards which God has directed him, the land of Israel. His son, Isaac is the first native son, a true citizen in that he never leaves the land in which he is born. Jacob, in contrast, becomes a modern Jew because his exile and wanderings parallel the exile and wanderings of the Jews in Diaspora. Joseph, born in Israel, will leave, never to return while he is alive – the experience of many Jews who find their success in business ventures and opportunities across the major capitals of the globe. And finally we have Menashe and Ephraim, the sons of Joseph, for whom the land of Israel is only a legend. They weren't born there, and they will not die there. Their entire lives are spent in the exile of Egypt.

These sons of Joseph represent the longest period of our history, where for 2,000 years – until the early part of the twentieth century – Israel was also only a legend. Until 1948, most Jews in the world could identify with Ephraim and Menashe because for them, Israel was also unattainable. How did we survive? How did the dream and vision of Abraham cling to generation after generation of Jews who never lived in the land, and whose great-great-grandchildren would not live there? Would they retain the dream of their great-grandfather Israel, or would they disappear into the rainbow of nations?

When Jacob asks Joseph to give him his sons, his true intention can be deduced from the very fact that Jacob asks for them in the midst of recounting his own history, the blessings that God gave him at Luz and the promise that his descendants will inherit the land. Jacob sees a successful Joseph, acculturating within the Egyptian milieu. He places a claim on Menashe and Ephraim. He wants them to be his, and not Joseph's; he wants their first allegiance to be to the Abrahamic culture and not to the Egyptian culture; he wants them to at least yearn to live in Israel, not to be content with remaining in Egypt.

Hence Jacob insists on his question, the question that must plague every single Jew in every generation: 'Who are these?' Do these sons belong to Joseph, Grand Vizier of Egypt, or do they belong to Jacob, the old bearded Jew? Do they belong to the civilization of the pyramids or do they identify with the 'Covenant between the Pieces'? Are they content in Egypt or do they long for Israel?

The answer is clear. Not only does Joseph receive a double blessing, but his sons become tribal heads, equal to Reuven and Shimon, Jacob's eldest sons. Later in the portion Jacob will inform Joseph that all future generations will use Ephraim and Menashe as a paradigmatic blessing: They will say, 'May God make you like Ephraim and Menashe,' which is how parents bless their sons on Friday night. Menashe and Ephraim were children of Egypt who were nevertheless claimed by and chose to adopt Jacob-Israel as their true father. It is only those children who make a similar choice who remain part of the eternal Jewish people.

Why We Bless Our Sons Like 'Ephraim and Menashe'

> *And he blessed them on that day, saying, Through you shall Israel be blessed, saying, May God make you like Ephraim and Menashe and he placed Ephraim before Menashe.*
>
> GENESIS 48:20

For many parents, the highlight of the Friday evening home celebration and meal, indeed the highlight of the entire week, is the moment when they bless their children. However, even this could be tension producing if your son suddenly wants to know why his sister is blessed to grow up like Sarah, Rebecca, Rachel and Leah, while he has to settle for Ephraim and Menashe, Joseph's Egyptian born sons, instead of the patriarchs. Is it possible that boys are finally getting the short end of the blessing?

I believe the reason can be found if we study the book of Genesis from the perspective of family psychology. Sibling rivalry constantly surfaces as a powerful motif indicating love-hate relationships that end up more bitter than sweet. Right from the opening pages in the Bible, Cain is jealous of Abel whose offering to God was found more pleasing than his own. Before we know it Abel is dead, killed by his own brother – the Torah's first recorded murder.

Of course this takes place in the early stages of recorded time, but how much has really changed by the time we get to Abraham? His two sons, Ishmael and Isaac, cannot live under the same roof. Sent into the desert with his mother Hagar, who watches helplessly as he nearly dies from thirst and hunger, Ishmael's fate is doomed if not for the *deus ex machina* appearance of the angel. True, Isaac cannot be legally charged with Ishmael's suffering, but Ishmael and his mother are driven away only because of Sarah's concern that Ishmael will have a negative influence on Isaac, destined carrier of the torch of Israel.

In the next generation, things get worse. Jacob spends twenty-two years away from home because he's afraid Esau wants to kill him. Upon returning from his long exile, richer, wiser, head of a large household, he makes all kinds of preparations to appease his brother, and if that should fail, he devises a defense strategy should Esau's army of four hundred men attack. All of this hatred came about as a result of Jacob's having deceived his father, at the behest of his mother, in order to wrest the birthright and blessings away from his less deserving brother.

Jacob's own sons live through aspects of their father's sibling experiences; since Jacob felt unloved by his father, he lavished excessive favoritism upon his beloved son Joseph. As a result of the bitter jealousy the brothers harbor toward Joseph, they take the radical step of slow but inevitable death by casting their defenseless brother into a dangerous pit. Had Judah's last-minute advice to sell the boy to a caravan of Ishmaelites been ignored, Joseph would have been torn to death by some wild animal, or at the very least – died in the pit from starvation.

When the Torah commands '…do not hate your brother in your heart' [Lev. 19:17], it could have easily used the word 'friend' or 'neighbor.' The word 'brother' is deliberate; the people we are most likely to hate are the ones closest to us. If the natural affection between brothers backfires, the very same potential for closeness turns into the potential for distance. No silence is more piercing than brothers who refuse to speak to each other because of a dispute over an inheritance. Unlike a feud between strangers, family members do not bury the past – they live with it, and all too often, continue to fight over it. There is even a custom, retained by some old Jerusalem families, that children should not attend their parent's funeral. The esoteric reason which is given by the more mystical commentaries is that the illegitimate children of the parents – the spirits born of the father's seminal emissions – will fight with the legitimate biological children over the inheritance. All too often we find the legitimate children fighting over the inheritance at the grave site.

There is one remarkable exception to the pervasive theme of sibling hatred in Genesis. In contrast to their ancestors, Joseph's sons, Ephraim and Menashe, do not fight when Jacob favors the younger brother, Ephraim, with the birthright blessing. Joseph even tries to stop Jacob. 'That's not the way it should be done, Father…the other one is the firstborn. Place your right hand on his head' [Gen. 48:18]. But Jacob knows exactly what he is doing. 'The older one will also become a nation…but his younger brother will become even greater…' [Gen. 48:19].

As a result of this seeming favoritism of the younger Ephraim, one might expect a furious reaction from Menashe, lashing out like Cain. But Menashe overcomes personal feelings. Unlike his forebears, there is no biblical hint of sibling rivalry between these two sons of Joseph, despite what could well be seen as unfair favoritism. Since we each want our children to be there for each other no matter what – and indeed, this is chiefly what my wife prays for as she lights the Sabbath candles each week – every parent blesses his sons that they have as harmonious a relationship as Ephraim and Menashe.

There still remains, however, a nagging question. Why did Jacob bestow the birthright upon the younger Ephraim? What lies substantively behind the words – and order – of this particular blessing?

As usual, the Midrash fills in the missing pieces. When the brothers first meet the Grand Vizier in their attempt to purchase food, the Bible tells us that the Egyptian provider appeared not to understand Hebrew, 'there was an interpreter between them' [Gen. 42:23]. The Midrash identifies this interpreter as Menashe, apparently a PhD in languages and diplomacy from the University of the Nile. Menashe seems to have been his father's trusted aide in all important affairs of state. Ephraim, on the other hand, was studious, devoting his time to learning Torah with his old and other-worldly grandfather Jacob. In fact, when we read in our Torah portion of how Joseph is brought news of his father's illness, the text does not reveal the messenger's name but the Midrash identifies him as Ephraim returning from Goshen where he had been studying with his grandfather.

Perhaps Menashe, the symbol of secular wisdom, does not object when his younger brother – expert in and dedicated to the wisdom of family tradition – receives the greater honor. From this perspective Jacob is expressing in his blessing the deepest value of Judaism: secular and worldly wisdom is significant and represents a giant achievement, but Torah must take preference and emerge as the highest priority. From the prism of the Midrash, we bless our children to excel in worldly knowledge, wisdom and Torah together, but with Torah receiving the greater accolade.

The capacity to submerge one's abilities and gifts to those of another, especially to a sibling who is younger, shows true commitment to the direction of the divine, an overriding concern for the welfare of the nation as a whole, and a profound maturity. This is precisely the character displayed by Joseph when he gratefully accepted his double portion (blessing), but conceded the true sovereign, international and ultimately, redemptive leadership to his brother Judah (as expressed in Jacob's final blessings, [Genesis 49:8–10, 22–26]).

In a much later period (eighth century BCE), Jeroboam of the tribe of Ephraim, whom King Solomon had appointed over the taxation of both tribes of Ephraim and Menasheh, waged a revolution on behalf of the ten Northern Tribes against the tribe of Judah, against Rehoboam, the son of King Solomon and grandson of King David, and against the Holy Temple in Jerusalem. Our Talmudic Sages, who respected Jeroboam's administrative abilities and cultural accomplishments, predicate the following conversation in the name of Raba:

> The Holy One Blessed Be He grabbed the garment of Jeroboam and told him, 'Repent, and I and you and the son of Jesse [David, King of Israel and progenitor of the Messiah] will join together,

for our travels in Paradise.' Said [Jeroboam], 'Who will take the lead?' Said [the Almighty] 'the son of Jesse.' [Said Jeroboam] 'If that is the case, I am not interested.'

Sanhedrin 102a

Apparently, the descendants of Joseph were not gifted with the largesse of their ancestor – and herein lies the tragedy of the split between Jerusalem-Judea and Ephraim-Northern Israel as well as between Torah study and secular wisdom.

Thankfully, our Ephraim and Menashe were different. And the importance of this filial ability to overlook favoritism and remain together takes on added significance when we come to the book of Exodus, the saga of the birth of our nation. Before the nation of Israel could be molded, a family had to emerge in which a profound harmony reigned. The heroic relationship between Menashe and Ephraim paved the way for a similar harmony between Aaron and Moses, where the younger brother served as the great leader, while the elder remained his loyal spokesman and interpreter to the people. These represent a crucial beacon of possibility, especially since our nation still in formation – from the rebellion of Korah to the Knesset inter- and intra-party eruptions – has constantly been plagued by sibling strife.

When parents bless their daughters to be like Sarah, Rebecca, Rachel and Leah, what is being evoked is the very bedrock of Jewish existence, our matriarchs. When they bless their sons to be like Menashe and Ephraim, the blessing evokes the long slow process of Genesis which finally bears fruit with the sons of Joseph, the only brothers who overcome sibling rivalry and achieve an incredible unity, with wordly wisdom merging with Torah traditions to bring the promise of redemption to a strife-torn world.

The Millennium and Normative Messianism

> *Judah is a young lion, from the prey my son you*
> *have risen. He stooped down, but couched as a*
> *lion, and as a lioness who shall dare rouse him?*
>
> GENESIS 49:9

A new millennium has dawned, and with it, the whispers of Armageddon and 'Second Coming' which emanated from many sectors of the Christian world. I once participated in a forum on Messianism with Professor David Flusser, of blessed memory – the eminent authority on early Christianity – who maintained that were the Messiah to appear tomorrow morning almost no one would really be interested in changing their life styles or beliefs and opinions because of his advent. The exceptions would be Jewish and Christian theologians, who would rush up to him with the question: Is this your first or your second coming?

In any event, the year 2000 had a certain symmetry and powerful attraction for those waiting for a Second Coming. They were certainly disappointed by the year's end in a 'no show.' But since the Jews are still waiting for a First Coming, any year is desirable and the year 2000 was no better –nor worse – than the year 1999 or 2001. If 5764 does not reveal the 'anointed ruler of Israel' and bring about universal redemption, we will wait for 5765. In the meantime life goes on, because the major rabbinical commandment is that we 'await [and prepare for] the advent of the Messiah.' Thomas Cahill, in his best selling book, *Gifts of the Jews*, points out that it was the people of Israel who bequeathed to the world the idea of the progress of history, the ideal of the ultimate perfection of humanity and human society, the goal of a messianic age of peace. Greco-Roman civilization saw the world and history in cyclical terms, iterating and reiterating much like the myth of Sisyphus, never truly reaching any kind of end-game:

> Tomorrow and tomorrow and tomorrow beats on this petty pace until the last syllable of recorded time. Life is a tale told by an idiot, full of sound and fury, signifying nothing.

It was Judaism which provided a lineal imagery, insisting that there is purpose and significance to world history and human life. What is important for us is that we constantly strive to be worthy of the period of perfection, understanding that with each passing year that the Messiah is not revealed, yet another opportunity has passed us by. Indeed, the Hatam Sofer teaches that in every generation there is an individual worthy of being King-Ruler-Messiah – but the generation has got to be worthy as well.

Interestingly enough, the first biblical reference to the Messiah appears in *Vayeḥi*, when Jacob blesses each of his twelve sons. The major issue for each of the patriarchs is which child will receive the gift of the birthright. They must decide who will carry the mantle of the Abrahamic blessing for all the families of the earth, bringing the ultimate ingathering of the nations when a universal acceptance of ethical monotheism will usher the world into a period of tranquility.

Jacob establishes the character of Judah by comparing him to a lion, and bestows upon him the gift and responsibility of the birthright:

The scepter shall not depart from Judah, nor the judicial inter-preter's staff from between his feet, until Shilo shall come and unto him shall be the ingathering of nations.

Gen. 49:10

The meanings of the first parts of the verse and the last part of the verse are relatively clear. The scepter is a symbol of kingship, the judicial interpreter refers to the Princes of the Sanhedrin (great court). As the two concepts merge together in one individual they create the power-ful image of a Philosopher-King, Scholar-Sovereign. At the end of the verse, the Hebrew '*yikhat amim*' probably means a gathering of nations as in the word *kehillah*, congregation, or *kohelet*, collection. The real lin-guistic difficulty of this verse is found right in the middle of the blessing, where we come up against the etymological mystery of the word Shilo. It appears only this once in the Bible (except as a name of a city in Israel which housed the Sanctuary, precursor to the Holy Temple during the period of the Judges).

Onkelos renders the word as '*meshicha*', the Messiah, anointed king, leader of Israel during the period of world peace. Similarly the Talmud [*Sanhedrin* 98b] states that Shilo is a proper noun, the name of the Messiah!

Rashi also speaks of the word "*shilo*" in its messianic implication, quoting first from Targum Onkelos, and then adding that the etymol-ogy is derived either from the Hebrew pronoun of possession ('until the coming of the one to whom [the kingdom] is his – *shelo*') or a con-traction of 'the gift [or prize] is his' (*shai lo*). Ba'al Haturim discovers a striking *gematriya* (arithmetical equivalency) between the phrase '*yavo* (13) *shilo* (345) [shilo comes]' and the word *mashiach* (messiah, which likewise adds up to 358). Seforno takes the word *shilo* as being synony-mous with *shalom* or peace, and writes that it refers to the ultimate peace at the time of redemption.

All these comments make it clear that our Sages understood that the initial reference to the emergence of a messianic line in Judaism is to be found in the blessing to Judah, who is the progenitor of Boaz, Yishai and David, model and ancestor of the long awaited Messiah.

An even more interesting nuance appears in the commentary of Ibn Ezra, where he explains *shilo* as being related to the word *shelya*, which means womb.*

In making this etymological connection, Ibn Ezra is insisting that the ultimate Messiah ruler will be naturally born to woman, the product of a naturally male-fertilized ovum, a fetus formed by mother and father. In so interpreting, he is clearly denying the Christological notion of a Messiah born by immaculate conception, which means without male sexual fertilization.

Furthermore, just as the Messiah must be a natural child of a mother and father, so will he bring about the millennium of peace in natural and normative ways – at least according to twelfth century Maimonides, probably the greatest Jewish theologian-halakhist of all time. Maimonides turns to the historical occurrence of Bar Kokhba, a courageous, devout Israeli warrior whom Rabbi Akiva and the majority of second-century Talmudic sages considered to be the Messiah. After all, Bar Kokhba was a very human being who used politics and warfare as legitimate means to facilitate Jewish sovereignty and to exercise world leadership. 'Do not think that the King Messiah must perform signs and miracles, and create new things in the world, or resurrect the dead,' insists Maimonides [Laws of Kings 11:3]. The natural way of things will continue even into the messianic age, during which time the Holy Temple will be built, Israel's enemies will be vanquished, and the Israelites, as well as the entire world, will live in peace, harmony and tranquility under God. 'Nation will not lift up sword against nation, and humanity will not have war anymore. There will be no evil or destruction throughout thy holy mountain. The knowledge of the Lord will cover the earth as the waters fill the seas' [Is. 2:11].

Maimonides insists upon 'normative messianism,' an age of peace brought about in a natural and human process of evolution. Anyone who dies before having fulfilled the messianic goals of redemption and salvation cannot possibly have been the real Messiah. Maimonides' proof text is Jewish history: 'Once Bar Kokhba was killed, he could not have possibly have been the Messiah.' So insists Maimonides. If that is the

---

* See Deuteronomy 28:57.

case, although the founder of Christianity may well have been a God-fearing and even charismatic rabbinical figure, once he was crucified by the Romans he forfeited all claims to the title of Messiah. Normative Judaism knows of no first and second coming.* And Rabbi Menachem Mendel Schneerson, the seventh Rebbe of Chabad Hassidut, may have been a fascinating candidate for King-Messiah when he was alive, but with his death no traditional believing Jew can rightfully consider him to be the Messiah.

In Jewish theology, the drama of turning to certain specific years which are especially potent, like the recent millennium, is a gratuitous gesture, and has no real significance for us. We must continue to prepare ourselves in repentance and good deeds, especially in the realm of interpersonal relationships, in order for the Messiah to come; he will arrive only when we are worthy of welcoming him.

A bookseller in Mea Shearim once told me that the Messiah was in Jerusalem. Despite my rationalistic bent, I found myself praying at the Western Wall, searching devout faces in the hope of identifying the savior. At last in despair I returned to my bookseller in frustration and perplexity. 'But didn't you tell me the Messiah was in Jerusalem?' I accusingly asked. 'Rabbi Riskin, you have it all wrong,' he replied. 'You think that we are waiting for the Messiah. In reality, the Messiah is waiting for us!'

---

*   *Mishneh Torah*, Laws of Kings, 11:12–13.

Biblical Commentators Cited in this Volume

9–10th Century

Sa'adia Gaon (Egypt & Babylonia c. 1000). Head of Babylonian Academy towards the end of the Geonic period. Translated the Torah into Arabic.

11th Century

Yitzhaki, Shlomo. RASHI (France, 1049–1105). Our foremost commentator on the Torah and the Talmud.

12th Century

Avraham ben David. RA'AVAD (Provence, 1120–1197). Author of many talmudic commentaries, including his critical glosses to Maimonides' Mishneh Torah.

Halevi, Yehuda (Spain, 1075–1141). Noted Torah scholar and poet. Author of the *Kuzari*.

Ibn Ezra, Abraham (Spain, 1089–1164). Noted poet and grammarian. Author of commentary to the Bible.

Kimhi, David. RADAK (Provence, 1160–1235). Author of commentary to the Bible, and also noted grammarian.

Maimonides, Moshe ben Maimon. RAMBAM (Spain & Egypt, 1135–1204). Author of *Mishneh Torah*, a comprehensive halakhic code of Jewish law; and of the famous philosophical treatise *Guide to the Perplexed*.

Shemuel ben Meir. RASHBAM (France, 1080–1158). Grandson of Rashi, one of the Ba'alei Tosafot. Author of commentary to the Torah.

Yehudah the Pious (Germany, 1150–1217). Author of *Sefer HaHasidim*.

13ᵗʰ *Century*

Nahmanides, Moshe ben Nachman. RAMBAN (Spain, 1194–1270). Famous biblical commentator and Talmudist. His biblical commentary will often quote the commentaries of Rashi and Ibn Ezra.

14ᵗʰ *Century*

Ba'al Haturim, Jacob ben Asher (Germany & Spain, 1275–1340). Son of the famous Talmud commentator known as the 'Rosh,' the Ba'al Haturim composed the four volume halakhic work known as the 'Tur.' He also wrote a commentary to the Torah, making extensive use of *gematria*.

Ibn Kaspi, Joseph (Provence & Spain, 1279–1340). Biblical commentator, philosopher, and grammarian.

15ᵗʰ *Century*

Abarbanel, Don Isaac (Spain & Italy, 1437–1508). Noted statesman

and minister for Kings of Spain, Portugal and Italy. Author of commentaries to the Bible, the Pesaḥ Haggada and *Pirkei Avot.*
Arama, Yitzhak. (Spain, 1420–1494) Author of *Akedat Yitzḥak.*

16–17ᵗʰ Century

Horowitz, Isaiah. Shelah HaKadosh (Prague & Israel, 1565–1630). Noted Kabbalist. Author of *Shnei Luḥot Habrit.*
Seforno, Ovadiah (Italy, 1470–1550). Author of commentary to the Bible.

18ᵗʰ Century

Attar, Chaim ibn (Morocco, 1696–1743). Author of *Ohr Haḥayim* commentary on the Bible.
Ba'al Shem Tov, Israel. BESHT (1700–1760). Founder of the Hassidic movement.
Gaon, Eliyahu ben Shlomo Zalman. GRA (Vilna, 1720–1797). Noted Talmudist and biblical scholar. Fierce opponent of Hassidism.
Joseph, Jacob (Polnoy d. 1785) Student of the Ba'al Shem Tov. Author of *Toledot Yaakov Yosef,* which contains many direct quotes from the teachings of the *Besht.*
Nachman of Breslav (1772–1811). Author of 'Likutei Moharan.'
Pardo, David (Italy, 1719–1792). Author of *Maskil Ledavid,* a commentary on Rashi.
Sofer, Moshe. ḤATAM SOFER (Pressburg 1762–1838). Rabbi of Pressburg. Fierce opponent of the Reform movement. Author of many halakhic works.

19ᵗʰ Century

Alter, Yehuda Arye Leib. SEFAT EMET (Poland, 1847–1905). Head of the Gur Hassidic sect. Noted biblical and Talmudic scholar.

Berlin, Naftali Tzvi Yehuda. NETZIV (Russia, 1817–1893). Head of famous Yeshiva of Volozhin. Author of commentary to the Torah called *Ha'amek Davar*.

Hirsch, Samson Rafael (Germany, 1808–1888). Author of six-volume commentary to the Bible.

Kotzk, Menachem Mendel (1787–1859). Noted scholar and disciple of Rav Simcha Bunim of Pesishcha.

Levush, Meir Yehuda. MALBIM (Russia, 1809–1878). Author of extensive commentary to the Bible.

Meckelnburg, Ya'akov (Germany, 1785–1865). Served as Chief Rabbi of Koenigsberg. Author of famous biblical commentary *Haktav v'Hakabbala*.

Sofer, Avraham (Pressburg, 1815–1872). Son of the Hatam Sofer, author of the biblical commentary *Ketav Sofer*.

20th Century

Besdin, Moshe (New York, 1913–1982). Director of James Striar School, Yeshiva University.

Halevi, Haim David (Tel Aviv, 1924–1988). Served as Sephardi Chief Rabbi of Tel Aviv. Author of numerous halakhic works, including the eight-volume series *Ase Lecha Rav*.

Kaminetzky, Yaakov (Toronto & New York, 1891–1986). Head of Torah VaDaas Yeshiva. Author of *Emet Le-Yaakov*.

Kook, Abraham Isaac Hakohen (Jaffa & Jerusalem, 1865–1935). Founder of the Israel Chief Rabbinate. Author of many philosophical works and a commentary to the prayer book called *Olat Re'iyah*.

Leibowitz, Nechama (Jerusalem 1905–1997). Noted biblical scholar and teacher. Author of thousands of 'stenciled' sheets prepared as 'guides' to assist in the study of the weekly portion.

Schneerson, Menachem Mendel (New York, 1902–1994). Seventh Rebbe of Chabad Hassidut. Noted Torah scholar and author of *Likutei Sichos*, insights into the weekly portion with emphasis on Rashi's commentary.

Soloveitchik, Aaron (Chicago, 1917–2001). Noted Talmudic scholar and halakhic authority. Head of Yeshivas Brisk in Chicago. Younger brother of Rabbi J.B. Soloveitchik.

Soloveitchik, Joseph B. (Boston, 1903–1993). Master Talmud teacher, Yeshiva University. Author of numerous philosophical and halakhic works including *Ish Hahalakha* and *The Lonely Man of Faith*. Famed worldwide for his lectures in Talmud and biblical exegesis, and credited with being a major interpreter of Modern Orthodoxy.

Index of Biblical & Talmudic Sources

The fonts used in this book are from the Arno family

Other works by Shlomo Riskin
available from Maggid

Shemot: Defining a Nation

Vayikra: Sacrifice, Sanctity & Silence

A Gift for My Grandchildren
God Messages: Just Listen

Yad L'Isha

Si'aḥ Shulḥan

Maggid Books
Contemporary Jewish Thought
from
Koren Publishers Jerusalem